THE ENGLISH SENTENCING SYSTEM

By

SIR RUPERT CROSS, D.C.L., F.B.A.

*Solicitor; Vinerian Professor of English
Law in the University of Oxford and
Fellow of All Souls College, Oxford*

AND

ANDREW ASHWORTH, LL.B., B.C.L., Ph.D.

Fellow of Worcester College, Oxford

THIRD EDITION

LONDON
BUTTERWORTHS
1981

ENGLAND:	BUTTERWORTH & CO. (PUBLISHERS) LTD. LONDON: 88 Kingsway, WC2B 6AB
AUSTRALIA:	BUTTERWORTHS PTY. LTD. SYDNEY: 271–273 Lane Cove Road, North Ryde, NSW 2113 Also at Melbourne, Brisbane Adelaide and Perth
CANADA:	BUTTERWORTH & CO. (CANADA) LTD. TORONTO: 2265 Midland Avenue, Scarborough M1P 4S1
NEW ZEALAND:	BUTTERWORTHS OF NEW ZEALAND LTD. WELLINGTON: 33–35 Cumberland Place
SOUTH AFRICA:	BUTTERWORTH & CO. (SOUTH AFRICA) (PTY.) LTD. DURBAN: 152–154 Gale Street
U.S.A.	BUTTERWORTH & CO. (PUBLISHERS) INC. BOSTON: 10 Tower Office Park, Woburn, Mass. 01801

First Edition .... *June 1971*
Second Edition .... *March 1975*
Reprinted .... *August 1976*
Third Edition .... *July 1981*

© Butterworth & Co. (Publishers) Ltd.
1981

ISBN — Casebound: 0 406 57014 0
         Limp: 0 406 57015 9

Reproduced from copy supplied
printed and bound in Great Britain
by Billing and Sons Limited
Guildford, London, Oxford, Worcester

PREFACE TO THIRD EDITION

It is with deep sadness that I find myself writing this Preface alone. By the time of Sir Rupert's death in September 1980, we had completed the revision of Chapter III and part of Chapter I. My hope is that the remainder of the revision succeeds in reflecting the tremendous benefit (and pleasure) which I derived from working beside one of the most accomplished lawyers and textwriters of our time. We had discussed in broad terms the changes which were to be made to these other parts of the book. I have attempted to effect those changes.

The six years since the appearance of the Second Edition have seen a wide range of developments. Although the legislature has not, apart from the Criminal Law Act 1977, been particularly active on sentencing matters, the activities of the Court of Appeal (Criminal Division) have more than compensated for this. The tide of appellate decisions on sentencing rises each year, and there have been three noteworthy landmarks in the form of the publication of the second edition of David Thomas's *Principles of Sentencing* in 1979, the introduction of a new series of law reports devoted exclusively to sentencing cases (the Criminal Appeal Reports (Sentencing)), and the judgments of Lord LANE, C.J., in *Upton* and in *Bibi*. The reform bodies have also been active in this sphere: recent reports of the Law Commission and of the Criminal Law Revision Committee have sentencing implications, and two reports of the now defunct Advisory Council on the Penal System, on The Length of Prison Sentences and Sentences of Imprisonment: a Review of Maximum Penalties, have made significant and provocative contributions to debate about the sentencing system.

Both the structure of the book and its aims remain essentially the same as for previous editions. The main task has been one of bringing the text up to date, and it is hoped that the book reflects the sentencing system at 1st October 1980. The form of Chapters I, II and IV has been little altered in the process of up-dating; the opening section of Chapter III remains unchanged, but there has been considerable re-writing in the remainder of Chapter III and in Chapter V.

ANDREW ASHWORTH

Worcester College,
  Oxford,
March, 1981

PREFACE TO FIRST EDITION

This book is based on lectures given in the University of Oxford and primarily designed for candidates for a law degree who had opted, or were thinking of opting, for a paper on criminal law and penology; but it is hoped that the book may appeal to all those concerned with the penal system and indeed to all who are interested in the problems of punishment and sentencing. For this reason I have been deliberately "elementary" at certain points in my account of the law. The book is not a textbook, although the first two chapters contain about as much information concerning the law of sentencing as most students are likely to require; my aim has been to provoke thought and further reading. This accounts for the note on further reading in the appendices. I have deliberately made it brief and it has accordingly been necessary to be highly selective.

I lay no claim to originality of thought or research. So far as the thought is concerned, all that I have done which others have not done in works of a similar nature is to link the theories of punishment with sentencing practice, and to say something of the whys and wherefores of the latter. So far as research is concerned, the only out of the ordinary information on which the book is based is the response of a number of Queen's Bench Judges, Recorders, Chairmen of Sessions and Magistrates to a variety of oral and written questions. I wish to express my deep gratitude for this cooperation so willingly given by such busy men.

RUPERT CROSS

All Souls College
   Oxford,
March, 1971.

CONTENTS

TABLE OF CASES

INTRODUCTION

The aim of the first two chapters of this book is to give a reasonably comprehensive account of the law and practice of sentencing in England and Wales with the exception of the practice followed by the Courts in fixing the length of a prison sentence. This is considered in Chapter IV after the different theories of punishment which influence it have been examined in Chapter III. In Chapter V we discuss some recent proposals for reform of the sentencing system.

At the beginning of Chapter V we raise the question, "Is the present English sentencing system too retributive?" The answer must of course be largely dependent on the meaning to be attached to the word "retributive"; but the question has a special contemporary relevance on account of the recent return to forms of retributivism, following widespread disillusionment with reformation and rehabilitation as aims of sentencing. Such research as has taken place has produced little evidence that sentences intended as reformative or rehabilitative are more effective in preventing reconvictions than other kinds of sentence. It is in this sense that some contemporary penologists refer to the decline of the rehabilitative ideal. There has also been a general decline in confidence in the ability of research to provide satisfactory evidence of the effectiveness of sentences, as awareness of the difficulties which beset thorough research has grown. Both sources of penological pessimism result partly from the building of artificially high hopes. For years we have all been too ready to say that the answer to some problem will be provided by research and all that we need to do is to contrive some short-term makeshift. It is essential to realise that there are sentencing problems which will probably never be solved by research, that in the case of others the research will be very long term, and that there are matters with regard to which it is difficult even to see how a satisfactory beginning to research can be made.

These changes in prevailing penal philosophy have led to some changes in the law and practice of sentencing—not great changes,

1

since the English sentencing system never abandoned retributivism and proportionality as leading principles and bears relatively few marks of the emphasis on rehabilitation and "effectiveness" which characterised penological debate in the 1960s and early 1970s. But some changes have taken place. In the 1960s short prison sentences were anathema to the advanced penologist because they contaminate the offender without reforming him; but now there is scepticism about the reformative and, as regards the individual offender, the greater deterrent effects, of longer sentences. The late 1970s saw many exhortations to sentencers to pass shorter prison sentences, and in 1980 the Lord Chief Justice added his authority to this movement. In the 1960s it was the unquestioned penological doctrine that, although it might be right for the judge to have the power of determining the maximum period for which an offender should be in custody or otherwise subject to state control, the executive should decide when the offender should be released from custody. This doctrine led to the introduction of parole, and it remained influential with the Advisory Council on the Penal System in 1974 when they recommended changes in the sentencing of young adult offenders (aged 17 to 21). But there is now widespread scepticism about the greater ability of those, such as prison governors, psychiatrists and social workers, to decide upon the optimum moment for release, not to mention reservations about the propriety of leaving such questions to be determined by them. In the 1960s there was optimism about the rehabilitative potential of the probation order; in the 1970s the use of probation declined substantially, and the ethos of "treatment" is now increasingly questioned. The arrival of the community service order may be said to be consistent with the philosophies of both the 1960s and the 1980s, since it contains variable elements of reform and retribution. The interaction of the different and changing views in this paragraph is reflected at various points in this book.

For the benefit of the occasional reader who is neither a lawyer nor a law student a few words may be added about the criminal courts and some of the other matters about which a rudimentary knowledge is assumed in the following pages.

The lower courts are Magistrates' Courts, which try summary offences and offences "triable either way". A summary offence is one which can generally only be tried by a Magistrates' Court; an offence "triable either way" is an indictable offence which may be tried either in a Magistrates' Court or in the Crown Court with a jury. According to the procedure introduced by the Criminal Law Act 1977, where a person appears before a Magistrates' Court charged with an offence triable either way, the Magistrates may decide that the charge is so serious that it should be tried in the Crown Court; if they do not so decide, then the accused is asked whether he consents to be tried summarily or wishes to be tried by a jury, so that his wishes then determine mode of trial. The powers of Magistrates' Courts are now consolidated in the Magistrates' Courts Act 1980: the sentencing powers of Magistrates are in general limited to six months' imprisonment, but they may commit someone convicted of an indictable offence to the Crown Court if they think that the sentence which they can impose would be inadequate. A glance at Table I, in Appendix I, should suffice to show that the vast majority of crime in this country is tried by the Magistrates. The table is confined to offenders of 21 and over. When it is recalled that a great deal of crime is committed by persons under that age and that practically all offenders under seventeen are tried in Magistrates' Courts, it should not come as a shock for anyone to discover that nearly 98% of the offenders brought to trial each year are tried by Magistrates' Courts. The Crown Court tries indictable offences with a jury. Its judges are High Court judges, Circuit judges and Recorders, of whom the latter are almost all practising barristers or solicitors serving as judges on a part-time basis. The Crown Court, sitting without a jury, hears appeals from the decisions of Magistrates' Courts. It sits at various places on the six circuits into which the country is divided and, since the beginning of 1972, it has taken the place of Assizes and Quarter Sessions. Indictable offences were formerly tried by Quarter Sessions with a jury and appeals from Magistrates' Courts were heard by Quarter Sessions.

Appeals against convictions after trial with a jury in the Crown Court are heard by the Criminal Division of the Court of Appeal, since 1966 the successor of the Court of Criminal Appeal which used to hear appeals from convictions at Quarter Sessions and Assizes. Subject to the fulfilment of the necessary conditions, there is an appeal by the prosecution or the defendant from the Court of Appeal to the House of Lords.

Throughout this book the word "judge" should generally be taken to mean High Court judge, Circuit judge, Recorder or Magistrate.

The sources of the law relating to sentencing are, like the sources of the general criminal law, statutes and judicial decisions. The principal statute is the Powers of Criminal Courts Act 1973, although some provisions of the Criminal Justice Acts of 1948, 1967 and 1972 remain in force. In order to understand the law and practice of sentencing it is necessary, in addition to consulting text-books and periodicals, to refer to reports of Royal Commissions, Departmental and Interdepartmental committees, and white papers. A selection of documents of this nature is to be found in Appendix II.

The minister responsible for the penal system is the Home Secretary. He was until 1978 assisted by the Advisory Council on the Penal System (formerly the Advisory Council on the Treatment of Offenders) and its recommendations are contained in reports, some of which are also mentioned in Appendix II. The Advisory Council has now been abolished, and there exists no standing body to review and make recommendations upon matters of penal policy and sentencing policy.

This book is exclusively concerned with the law and practice in England and Wales, but reference is made at various points to the provisions relating to sentencing in the American Law Institute's Model Penal Code, the final draft of which was published in 1962 after some ten years' deliberation. It has not been fully adopted anywhere in the United States, but its provisions have had a considerable influence on some of the modern codes in that country. The reader should bear in mind, when considering the provisions of the Model Code, that the distinction between felonies and misdemeanours, abolished in England by the Criminal Law Act 1967, is still recognised in the United States.

The reader should consult the statistical tables in Appendix I at the points at which reference is made to them in the text. The tables are mainly based on the annually published volumes of criminal statistics. Table I should be consulted by anyone who wishes to have an overall picture of the sentencing problem. He will see that, in addition to allowing for disposals by the courts, allowance must be made for a good deal of formal police cautioning. When, in addition, the reader realises that the sentences and cautions mentioned in Table I related to a mere fraction of offences known to the police in any year, he will appreciate that sentencing is but one aspect of the penal system. In 1978 the grand total of indictable offences known to the police was 2,395,757; the corresponding figure for 1969 was 1,498,703 and for 1973 was 1,657,699, although changes in the recording procedure mean that these figures cannot quite be taken at face value. Tables I, II and III enable some comparisons to be made of sentencing in 1969, 1973 and 1978. It is important for the student to have some idea of trends in relation to the sentencing policy of the courts and these are most conveniently shown in statistical tables. Some of the other tables in Appendix I should be studied with the trend in mind.

I

THE ENGLISH
SENTENCING SYSTEM

A sane adult of twenty-one or over has been convicted of an offence punishable with imprisonment. What can the Court do? The object of the first three sections of this chapter is to answer that question; section 4 is concerned with mentally disordered offenders, section 5 with offenders under twenty-one.

There will no doubt be those who will say that the first sentence of this chapter begs a very large question by taking it for granted that an adult who has been convicted of an offence, and may therefore be presumed to have committed it, can be sane. The "crime is a disease" dogma is treated with varying degrees of seriousness by very different people. Few would contend that all those who commit any offence, including a motoring offence, are mentally sick; but quite a number of people maintain that all serious crime is a manifestation of some kind of mental illness. It is not the purpose of this book to join issue with those who are of that persuasion; even if it were, the proper place to do so would be in Chapter V where certain criticisms of the present English sentencing system are considered. In this chapter we are concerned with the powers of the Courts in the matter of sentencing, and those powers are certainly both conferred and exercised on the assumption that the overwhelming majority of offenders is perfectly sane.

In order to allow for the discussion of the different types of prison sentence in section 2, the question with which this chapter begins posits an offence punishable with imprisonment. A very large number of summary offences cannot, in any circumstances, be so punished; for those who commit one of them the worst that can happen is a fine. Even when an offence is punishable with imprisonment, there are many cases in which it is virtually certain that the offender will not be sent to prison. This is because the most significant feature of the English sentencing system is the breadth of the judge's discretion in the selection of penal or corrective measures to be applied to a particular offender. It is only where there has been a conviction for treason or murder that the judge's hands are tied, in the case of treason to the death sentence and in the case of murder to sentence of life imprisonment. In all other cases, the first question that the judge will ask himself is whether he can avoid sending the offender to prison.[1] Occasionally that question does not call for much deliberation because the gravity of the offence plainly necessitates a negative answer, but the lack of any need for judicial deliberation is accounted for more frequently by the fact that no one would seriously contemplate imprisonment for the offence under consideration. It should not be forgotten that the question with which we are primarily concerned is "What *can* the Court do?" not "What *will* the Court do?" although it is to be hoped that the references to be made to the use by the Courts of the different measures will improve the reader's capacity to answer the second question.

Section 1.—**Non-custodial measures other than suspended imprisonment**

The seven possible non-custodial measures are an absolute discharge, a conditional discharge, binding over, probation, a fine, a community service order and deferment of sentence. The Court may resort to any one of them in the case of any offence punishable with imprisonment except murder and they may be imposed by any Court, Magistrates' Courts as well as the Crown Court, with the unimportant exception that one method of binding the defendant over ("the common law bind-over") can only be employed by the Crown Court.

The word "measure" is employed advisedly because it has a wider meaning than punishment. "Punishment", as used in this book, means the infliction of pain by the State on someone who has been convicted of an offence. Of the non-custodial measures to be discussed, only the fine and community service orders rank as punishment. There is, as we shall see, room for argument on this point, but it is clearly not the view of the law that either form of discharge, binding over or probation, is a punishment. Lest the use of the word "pain" in the above definition of punishment should be liable to conjure up pictures of the direct infliction of physical injury, it should be stressed that the word is employed primarily to describe financial loss and loss of liberty.

---

[1] In effect the judge is under a statutory obligation to ask himself this question in the case of those who have not been previously sentenced to imprisonment. (Powers of Criminal Courts Act 1973, s. 20(1); *ibid.*, s. 19(2)).

A. ABSOLUTE DISCHARGE

Section 7 of the Powers of Criminal Courts Act 1973 deals with both absolute and conditional discharges. S. 7(1) reads as follows:

"Where a court by or before which a person is convicted of an offence (not being an offence the sentence for which is fixed by law) is of opinion, having regard to the circumstances including the nature of the offence and the character of the offender, that it is inexpedient to inflict punishment and that a probation order is not appropriate, the court may make an order discharging him absolutely, or, if the court thinks fit, discharging him subject to the condition that he commits no offence during such period, not exceeding three years from the date of the order, as may be specified therein."[1]

Effect. If he is granted an absolute discharge the offender is completely free of any future liability in respect of the offence of which he has been convicted, however badly he may behave in the future. Section 13 of the 1973 Act deals with some of the other effects of a conviction followed by an absolute discharge. It does not count as a conviction for any purposes other than those of the proceedings in which the discharge was ordered. For example, the conviction does not count for the purpose of determining, in subsequent proceedings, whether the accused is a persistent offender and therefore liable to an extended sentence under the provisions of s. 28 of the Act discussed in section 2 of this chapter. It is expressly provided that the conviction must be disregarded for the purposes of any statute, such as a statute relating to pensions, which imposes any disqualification on a convicted person. The offender's rights to appeal against his conviction and to plead *autrefois convict* in the unlikely event of his being charged again with the same or substantially the same offence, are expressly preserved.

The powers of the court which directs an absolute discharge to order the offender to pay costs or compensation are expressly preserved by s. 12(4) of the Act. Nowhere in the statute is there anything in the nature of an express prohibition on the accompaniment of an absolute discharge by an order under s. 43 for the deprivation of property used or intended to be used for the purpose of committing, or facilitating the commission of, any offence, or an order under s. 44 disqualifying the offender from driving on the ground that a motor vehicle was used for these purposes. Nevertheless, such orders are, unlike an absolute discharge, punitive. For that reason the Court of Appeal has held that an absolute discharge ought not to be accompanied by an order under s. 43.[2] The principle

---

[1] The period of three years may be varied by the Home Secretary under s. 7(5), added by s. 57(2) of the Criminal Law Act 1977.
[2] *Hunt*, [1978] Crim. L.R. 697.

of the decision appears to apply to orders under s. 44 as well as to conditional discharges and probation orders. The effect of s. 102 of the Road Traffic Act 1972 is to permit the accompaniment of an absolute discharge by endorsements of, or the disqualification from holding, a driving licence under the Act.

Conditions precedent. It follows from the wording of s. 7(1) of the Powers of Criminal Courts Act 1973 that three conditions must be fulfilled before the Court can grant an absolute discharge. The punishment for the offence of which the accused has been convicted must not be fixed by law, the Court must be of opinion that it is inexpedient to inflict punishment, and the Court must also be of opinion that a probation order is not appropriate. The first condition simply means that there may not be an absolute discharge on a conviction for treason or murder, and it is unnecessary to enlarge upon the third condition. The reference to expediency in relation to the second condition should be of interest to penal philosophers.

The idea that punishment for an offence may be withheld on the ground of expediency would have been anathema to the eighteenth-century German philosopher Immanuel Kant for whom the failure to punish someone guilty of an offence on the ground of expediency was no less unjust than the punishment of the innocent; in fact he regarded the two cases as equivalent.

> "The law concerning punishment is a categorical imperative, and woe to him who rummages around in the winding paths of a theory of happiness looking for some advantage to be gained by releasing the criminal from punishment or by reducing the amount of it—in keeping with the Pharisaic motto: 'It is better that one man should die than that the whole people should perish.' If legal justice perishes, then it is no longer worth while for men to remain alive on this earth."[1]

It is doubtful whether anyone holds quite such extreme views today, and it is as well to recognise at the outset that although, as we shall see in Chapters III and IV, the English sentencing system is profoundly influenced by theories of punishment, not least by the retributive theory with which the name of Kant will always be associated, there is much in the system which can only be explained on the basis of expediency. "Expediency" is, generally speaking, a pejorative term, but few would be prepared to maintain that there is anything bad in a court's concluding that it is inexpedient to punish an offender who is unlikely to repeat an offence which was, in any event, committed in circumstances that render it a comparatively

---

[1] *The Metaphysical Elements of Justice*, translated by John Ladd (Bobbs-Merrill U.S.A.) p. 100.

venial one. This is what usually happens when an offender is granted an absolute discharge.

Use. Absolute discharges are granted relatively rarely. It will be seen from Table I that the number of occasions on which defendants over twenty-one were absolutely discharged by the Crown Court in 1978 was statistically insignificant (91 in all), while they were only granted in 1 per cent of each type of case tried by a Magistrates' Court.

It is said in *The Sentence of the Court*, a handbook on the treatment of offenders prepared for the use of the courts by the Home Office, that an absolute discharge "may reflect the triviality of the offence, the circumstances in which it came to be prosecuted, or factors relating to the offender."[1]

An illustration of the first two points is provided by the facts of *Smedleys Ltd.* v. *Breed*.[2] The question was whether Smedleys were guilty of an offence under the Food and Drugs Act 1955 as manufacturers of a tin of peas containing a dead caterpillar. The insect had escaped detection by a mechanical screening device because it was of the same weight and diameter as a pea, and it had not been observed by sorters employed to check the peas on the conveyor belt because its colour was that of a pea, but it had been pressure cooked for twenty-two minutes in the course of the canning process with the result that it was perfectly harmless. The House of Lords held that, as a matter of construction, the special defence provided by s. 3(3) of the Act was not available, but three of their Lordships considered that the public interest had not been served by the prosecution, and that the case was an appropriate one for an absolute discharge. The possibility of such a discharge is sometimes urged in defence of the imposition of strict liability, but this is a doubtful argument if only because a conviction involves social stigma which is not likely to be affected by the fact that it is followed by a non-punitive measure.

The circumstances in which the offence came to be prosecuted may also be reflected by an absolute discharge in cases in which a considerable time has elapsed between the prosecution and the incident which gave rise to it. In *The Decision to Prosecute* A. F. Wilcox mentions a case in which a chauffeur of twenty-two was prosecuted at the Middlesex Sessions in 1969 for breaking into a house in 1961 and stealing a radio. When giving an absolute discharge the Deputy Chairman said: "It is utterly monstrous that a man who has pulled himself together, having committed offences when he was a boy, is dragged back into court for an offence which

---

[1] Para. 24.
[2] [1974] 2 All E.R. 21.

was eight years old."[1] But in some instances it is no doubt right that "stale offences" should be prosecuted. An incident may have caused considerable public concern and a judicial investigation may be desirable even at some distance of time, or the accused may have cunningly concealed his crime. But there seems to be a common belief that stale offences should generally either not be prosecuted at all, or else be punished less severely on account of the delay in prosecuting them.

The cause of the common belief probably varies from case to case. Sometimes it is the feeling that the offender ought to be rewarded for having "pulled himself together"; on other occasions it may be the fact that he has suffered a great deal from anxiety brought about by the delay in prosecuting, and the matter may sometimes be looked upon as one of personal identity. The offender who comes up for sentence may be thought to be a different person from the one who committed the crime many years ago. Whatever the cause of the common feeling about stale offences may be, the exhortation to "let bygones be bygones" expresses a popular sentiment which should generally be recognised in legal practice.

Any number of factors relating to the offender may justify an absolute discharge. Examples are provided by an ambulance driver charged with a driving offence while answering an emergency call,[2] or any case in which the judge considers that the offence was not a serious one and a mere isolated instance, calling for no action by the court save one aimed at minimising the stigma of a conviction.

B. CONDITIONAL DISCHARGE

Effect. The only respect in which the effect of a conditional discharge differs from that of an absolute discharge is that, if the defendant is convicted of another offence during the period specified by the Court, he is liable to be sentenced for the original as well as the subsequent offence. It does not follow that he will be sentenced for the original offence because the Court dealing with the breach of the conditional discharge may make no order and the order of conditional discharge would remain in force; this could well happen when the subsequent offence was of a different nature from that for which the discharge was granted, as where someone conditionally discharged for stealing commits a motoring offence. If the defendant is sentenced for the original offence, the order of conditional discharge is at an end, and the original conviction will count as a conviction for all purposes, not merely for the limited number of

---

[1] P. 67.
[2] *O'Toole* (1971), 55 Cr. App. Rep. 206.

purposes for which it counted during the currency of the order. These latter purposes are the same as those mentioned on p. 7 with regard to the effect of an absolute discharge.

Why should a Court ever make the period of conditional discharge anything less than the permitted maximum of three years? Conditional discharges are quite often granted for lesser periods, but it is exceedingly difficult to find an entirely convincing reason. One answer to the question is that some judges and magistrates seek to relate the period of a conditional discharge to the gravity of the offence for which it was imposed. They would contend that a period below the maximum is appropriate when the offence was not a particularly serious one. The gravity of the offence plays a large part in the penal philosophy of the English judge and the subject is discussed *in extenso* in Chapter IV; but it is closely associated with retributive and deterrent theories of punishment. Many people may think that it is carrying these theories too far to apply them to the period for which an offender whose punishment is regarded as inexpedient should be liable to be brought back and sentenced for his offence. Some people may, however, be impressed by an argument based on fairness. If the offender had been sent to prison for three months instead of being conditionally discharged, he would have been entirely quit of the crime after two months (assuming that he earned full remission). It may be right that, in return for not being sent to prison, he should have a sword of Damocles hanging over him for a longer period, but it is not right that the period should invariably be three years.

It is sometimes said that when the defendant is an "old lag" and it is none the less thought proper to grant him a conditional discharge, his sense of justice would be affronted if he were punished for the original offence as much as two years and eleven months after being found guilty of it and what might be a very considerably longer time after its commission.

The old lag's capacity for sensing an injustice may well be more highly developed than that of most other people; perhaps there is no harm in pandering to it to the limited extent of a period of conditional discharge of less than three years. The principal thesis of this book is that the object of our sentencing system is not merely to make people obey the criminal law but also to make them want to do so. We shall see that, in furtherance of this object, the Courts are prepared to go to considerable lengths to avoid grounds for a sense of injustice on the part of convicted criminals.

Conditions precedent. The same three conditions must be fulfilled before an order of conditional discharge can be made as in the case of an absolute discharge. The requirements that the punishment for the offence should not be fixed by law and that the Court should be of opinion that a probation order is inappropriate do not call for comment, but a further word may be added concerning the requirement that the Court should also be of opinion that it is inexpedient to inflict punishment. One consequence of this requirement is that a person cannot be conditionally discharged and fined for the same offence because a fine is certainly punishment; a Court cannot be of opinion that punishment for the same crime both is and is not expedient.[1] In some cases it might be thought desirable to impose a fine when granting a conditional discharge in order to add sting to what might otherwise be thought to be a "let off", but it is in relation to probation orders that the inability to fine for the same offence has aroused most criticism.

A fourth condition is that the Court should explain to the offender in ordinary language that, if he commits another offence during the period of discharge, he will be liable to be sentenced for the original offence.

Use. It will be seen from Table I that conditional discharges are used much more extensively than absolute discharges. They were granted after 4 per cent of the convictions of offenders over 21 in the Crown Court in 1978; it was only in relation to motoring offences that the use of conditional discharges was statistically insignificant in 1978. The way in which the Court treats a convicted motorist is supposed to have some effect on the conduct of other motorists. For this purpose fines are thought to be superior to discharges. A conditional discharge cannot be expected to have much deterrent effect on potential offenders; it should be imposed where supervision of the accused by a probation officer is thought to be unnecessary, but it is none the less thought right that he should be subject to the pressure of the possibility of punishment for his former offence should he commit a later one.

The measure is employed in a great variety of cases, some of which are comparatively serious. A typical instance is the case of an elderly person in regular humble employment who has been convicted of shoplifting. There is not much point in adding his case to the probation officer's load, and a fine might cause great hardship for what might after all be a first offence. In some such cases the offender is warned that it could be prison for him or her next time.

Conditional discharges are also granted in cases where mitigating circumstances render the case one in which punishment would be inappropriate. In *Jagger*,[2] for example, the accused was convicted of

---

[1] *McClelland*, [1951] 1 All E.R. 557.
[2] [1967] 3 All E.R. 545, n.; 51 Cr. App. Rep. 473.

being in possession of amphetamine tablets. He would have had a good defence to the charge if his possession had been pursuant to a doctor's prescription. He had purchased the tablets in Italy and, on informing his English doctor of this fact, had been told that it would be all right for him to take one in an emergency when tired as a result of his activities as a pop singer. The trial judge held that the doctor's oral statement did not amount in law to a prescription and sentenced the accused to three months imprisonment. The Court of Appeal upheld the judge's view of the law but granted a conditional discharge on account of mitigating circumstances.

Conditional discharges sometimes have to be ordered *faute de mieux*. The fact that an offender is unable to pay a fine is not a ground for imposing a prison sentence, immediate or suspended, instead. In such a case it may well be that the only realistic thing the court can do is to order a conditional discharge.[1]

There is no appeal against such an order, but the Court of Appeal has jurisdiction to deal with the contention that the order is a nullity. Now that it has been decided that this is not the result of the judge's delegation to the offender's counsel of the duty of explaining the effect of a conditional discharge,[2] it is difficult to think of arguments by which such a contention could be supported.

C. BINDING OVER

When a person is bound over, he enters into recognizances, with or without sureties (guarantors). A recognizance is an undertaking and various forms of undertaking may be required by Courts under various powers.

i. *Binding over to come up for judgment.* The Crown Court may, in lieu of passing sentence, in any case other than murder require the offender to enter into a recognizance to come up for judgment if called upon to do so. This is usually accompanied by further recognizances to keep the peace and be of good behaviour. The effect is substantially similar to that of a conditional discharge and, as the procedure is more elaborate, the discharge is generally preferred. The binding over to come up for judgment and the accompanying recognizances may, however, be for a longer period than three years, and the recognizances may be broken by conduct falling short of a further offence. This procedure is often spoken of as "common law bind-over" because it is carried out pursuant to the common law powers of the Court preserved by s. 6(4) of the Courts Act 1971. The remaining types of bind-over may be

---

[1] *McGowan*, [1975] Crim. L.R. 113.
[2] *Wehner*, [1977] 3 All E.R. 553.

employed by any Court and are based on an amalgam of powers some of which are traceable to the Justice of the Peace Act 1361.

ii. *Binding over in a fixed sum.* In all the other types of bind-over the offender enters into a recognizance to forfeit a specified sum in the event of his failing to keep the peace or be of good behaviour. The effect is that of a suspended fine.

The whole subject of binding over is in need of clarification. It is of some constitutional importance because it is possible for people who have not been proved to have committed any offence to be made to enter into recognizances but, owing to the comparative rarity with which recognizances are employed as part of sentencing procedure, it is unnecessary to consider the matter any further. Charges of assault occasionally result in both parties being bound over to keep the peace and be of good behaviour, and to forfeit a specified sum in the event of the recognizances being broken. Conditions are sometimes inserted in the undertaking to forfeit a fixed sum on failure to be of good behaviour or to keep the peace, such as a condition that someone convicted of some type of assault at a football match should not attend a particular ground on Saturday afternoons, but the legality of such conditions is not clear and the prospects of enforcing them are negligible. None the less, it is probably cases of this nature which account for a substantial proportion of the 1 per cent of recognizances following convictions for offences, other than motoring offences, recorded in Magistrates' Courts in 1978.

D. PROBATION

Section 2(1) of the Powers of Criminal Courts Act 1973 provides:-

"Where a court by or before which a person of or over seventeen years of age is convicted of an offence (not being an offence the sentence for which is fixed by law) is of opinion that having regard to the circumstances including the nature of the offence and the character of the offender, it is expedient to do so, the court may, instead of sentencing him, make a probation order, that is to say, an order requiring him to be under the supervision of a probation officer for a period to be specified in the order of not less than six months[1] nor more than three years."

Under s. 2(3) a probation order may, subject to the restrictions mentioned below,

"require the offender to comply during the whole or any part of the probation period with such requirements as the court, having regard to the circumstances of the case, considers necessary for securing the good conduct of the offender or for preventing a repetition by him of the same offence or the commission of other offences."

---

[1] Changed from one year by S.I. 1978 No. 478 under powers conferred by s. 2(9), inserted by the Criminal Law Act 1977, s. 57(1).

Common requirements are that the probationer should be of good behaviour and keep the peace, keep in touch with his probation officer, and notify him of any change of address; more venturesome conditions are sometimes inserted, but probation officers tend to frown upon them.

Section 2(4) prohibits the inclusion of requirements of payments by way of damages for injury or compensation for loss. Orders with regard to these matters may be made concurrently with a probation order, but that order may not include conditions requiring the offender, on pain of a breach of probation, to pay damages or compensation.

Three requirements specially mentioned in the Act are those relating to the residence of the offender, his undergoing mental treatment and his attendance at a day training centre.

Under s. 2(5) the court must, before making a requirement relating to the residence of the offender, consider his home surroundings, and, if the requirement relates to residence in an approved probation hostel or any other institution, the requisite period of residence must be specified. Probation hostels are run by the probation service or by voluntary organisations approved by the Home Secretary. According to *The Sentence of the Court* they "provide a stable supportive environment in which groups of between fifteen and twenty-five offenders may learn how to get on with their contemporaries and other people, including those in authority, and may be helped to develop regular work habits and to achieve satisfaction in work and at leisure."[1] Probationers go out to daily employment or training from some hostels and contribute to their board and lodging. Other hostels cater for less adequate offenders who initially receive full-time training on the premises, but commonly go out to employment during the later part of their stay.

Section 3 of the Act governs probation orders containing a requirement that the offender should undergo mental treatment, and they are mentioned in section 4 of this chapter.

Section 4 of the Act empowers the court to include a requirement that the offender shall attend a day training centre specified in the order. Although provision for them was first made by the Criminal Justice Act 1972, day training centres are still very much at the experimental stage and at present only exist in Glamorgan, Inner London, Liverpool and Sheffield. Accordingly the first restriction on the insertion of a requirement of attendance is the necessity of the court's having been notified of the availability of a centre in the appropriate area for persons of the offender's "class or description".

---

[1] Para. 60. See further, Home Office Research Study No. 52, *Hostels for Offenders*.

The court must also be satisfied that arrangements can be made for the offender's attendance at the centre, and the requirement of attendance may not be included in a probation order containing a condition that the offender should undergo mental treatment. The effect of a requirement of attendance at a day training centre is that the offender must attend in accordance with the instructions of his probation officer concerning attendance for not more than sixty days and, while at the centre, he must obey the instructions of the person in charge. Under s. 51(2) of the Act the Home Secretary has power, with the approval of the Treasury, to provide for the maintenance of persons attending day training centres and of their dependants.

The Home Office guide for the courts relating to the Criminal Justice Act 1972 says that the centres "will provide full time non-residential training for offenders with the aim of equipping them to cope more adequately with the normal demands of modern life." The scheme has been framed with a particular view to the inadequate recidivists for whom short prison sentences have proved to be of no avail. These offenders tend to lack the basic social skills such as the ability to use the telephone or to apply for, let alone retain, a job, and they are frequently illiterate. While at the centre, they will receive remedial formal education, simple work training, matrimonial counselling and advice about home economics.

The Home Office guide was quoted with approval by LAWTON, L.J., when delivering the judgment of the Court of Appeal in *Cardwell*.[1] Cardwell, described by the Court of Appeal as a "socially inadequate pest", had been convicted in the Crown Court at Sheffield of stealing from purses and wallets at a college of education. He had a bad work record and a number of previous convictions of theft for some of which he had received short prison sentences. The Recorder sentenced him to eighteen months imprisonment, but the Court of Appeal substituted a probation order with a requirement of attendance at a day training centre. The court stressed the point that the centres are intended for a very limited class of offender and ought not to be used for those whose offences would, in the ordinary way, carry longish sentences of imprisonment; still less should a requirement be regarded as something to be tacked on to a probation order.

> "Experience has shown for many, many years that, if new penal measures for the treatment of offenders are used in inappropriate cases, they often fail to obtain the support of the judiciary and the public which they would have deserved had they been properly used, and then fall into disuse."[2]

---

[1] (1973), 58 Cr. App. Rep. 241.
[2] LAWTON, L.J., at pp. 246–7

Of the 26,313 probation orders made in 1978 only 182 contained a condition of attendance at a day training centre.[1]

The experimental nature of day training centres, involving as it does their use in specially selected neighbourhoods, poses ethical problems. Had Cardwell not had the good fortune to live in the vicinity of Sheffield, the Court of Appeal might well have allowed his prison sentence to stand. Have the "socially inadequate pests" of Leeds who might have been made the subjects of day training centre probation orders in and after 1973 but were sent to prison because no such centre was available a ground of complaint on the score of injustice? A negative answer to this question is sometimes supported by reference to what has been termed the principle of "less severity".[2] The "socially inadequate pests" of Leeds have not been treated more severely in consequence of the experiment, Cardwell was simply treated less severely than would otherwise have been the case. But, if justice requires that like cases should be treated alike, it must be conceded that experimentation of the kind under consideration does involve injustice. The case is one of many in which justice has to be tempered with expediency, if we are ever to have any new penal measures. Adherence to the principle of less severity simply makes the injustice more palatable by insuring that no one shall receive harsher penal treatment than would previously have been the case in consequence of the experiment.

Effect. A probation order resembles a conditional discharge in that the conviction on which it was made only counts as such for the purposes specified on p. 7 and, under s. 8 of the Powers of Criminal Courts Act 1973, the offender is liable to be sentenced for the offence in respect of which the order was made if he is convicted of a further offence during the currency of the order. The effect of a probation order differs from that of a conditional discharge because of the conditions inserted in the order and, under s. 6 of the Act, the offender is liable to be brought before the court for breach of any condition. If the breach is established, the offender may be fined up to £50, or, (when the relevant provisions of s. 6 are brought into force) a community service order may be made against him, or the court may deal with him in any manner in which it could have dealt with him if he had just been convicted of the offence.[3] If either of the

---

[1] For an account of day training centres see *Chance to Change* by Elizabeth Burney (Howard League).

[2] Norval Morris 'Impediments to Penal Reform', 33 Chicago L. Rev. 627 at p. 648.

[3] If the offender is under 21, a Magistrates' Court may make an attendance centre order in accordance with the provisions of s. 19 of the Criminal Justice Act 1948.

first two of the above courses is adopted, the probation order remains in force, but, if the offender is sentenced for his original offence, the probation order ceases to have effect.[1]

Conditions precedent. The conditions precedent to the making of a probation order mentioned in s. 2(1) of the Powers of Criminal Courts Act 1973 are that the sentence for the offence should not be fixed by law, and that the court should be of opinion that it is expedient to make the order, having regard to the circumstances, including the nature of the offence and the character of the offender. These provisions do not call for comment, but a further condition precedent emerges from s. 2(6) of the Act. After requiring the court to explain the effect of the order to the offender, the subsection goes on to provide that the court shall not make the order unless he expresses his willingness to comply with its requirements. This emphasises the theoretically non-punitive nature of probation for it is at least doubtful whether any pain to the infliction of which upon himself a person can consent should be described as punishment in anything other than an extended or metaphorical sense. The point is, however, rather a theoretical one because the offender often knows perfectly well that, if he does not consent to probation he will be sent to prison.

Nonetheless, it is essential to the validity of a probation order that the offender should have been given a fair opportunity to make his choice. In *Marquis*[2] a girl of 19 had been put on probation for handling stolen goods after she had said that she did not want probation and only consented to it because she believed that she was being offered the alternative of a custodial sentence. On the facts, such a sentence would have been no more than a remote possibility, and the Court of Appeal took the view that no legally effective probation order had been made with the result that they felt justified in making an order for a conditional discharge although there is no appeal against a probation order because the conviction on which it was made only counts for the purposes of an appeal against conviction as opposed to an appeal against sentence.[3]

Although s. 2 of the 1973 Act, unlike s. 7 which deals with conditional discharges, contains no express requirement that the Court should consider punishment inexpedient, it does say that a

---

[1] Powers of Criminal Courts Act 1973, s. 5(2).
[2] [1974] 2 ALL E.R. 1216.
[3] See p. 7 *supra*, and *Tucker*, [1974] 2 All E.R. 639. The rather odd result of the statutory provisions as they were construed by the Court of Appeal in this case is that, although a person put on probation has been "sentenced" within the meaning of the Criminal Appeal Act 1968 (see s. 50), he has not been "convicted" because of what is now s. 13 of the Powers of Criminal Courts Act 1973.

probation order may be made "instead of sentencing" the accused
and it has been held that these words mean "instead of punishment"
with the result that a person cannot be both fined and put on
probation for the same offence.[1] Many judges regret this and some
even say that many an accused would have been spared imprisonment but for their inability to combine probation with a fine. Some
probation officers consider that the probationer who had been fined
for the same offence would have a grievance and thus be a bad
starter for probation; but it must not be forgotten that, where a
person has been convicted of two offences, he may be fined for one of
them and put on probation for the other.[2] Allowance must also be
made for the fact that, under s. 71 of the Magistrates' Courts Act
1952, a Magistrates' Court may, when imposing or enforcing payment of a fine, make a money payment supervision order placing the
offender under the supervision of a specified person. That person
may be a member of Probation and After-Care Service. When this
is so the offender is, as long as the fine is unpaid, subject both to a
fine and to supervision which resembles probation in some respects.

Probation is said to be regarded as a "let-off" by some offenders.
This was the principal reason why the report of the Advisory Council on the Penal System on Non-Custodial and Semi-Custodial
Penalties, published in 1970, recommended that the law should be
changed so as to make it possible for an offender to be fined and put
on probation for the same offence.[3] The report recognised that two
of the present provisions with regard to probation would have to go
in such a case. These are the requirement that the offender must
consent to the order and the power of the court before which he is
brought in the event of breach of the order to deal with him as if he
had just been convicted of the original offence. If the fine came first,
the consent to probation might be withheld, or, if the probation
order preceded the fine, the consent might be withdrawn. If the fine
were paid before the order was broken, further punishment for the
original offence would mean that the offender had been sentenced
for it on two separate occasions. The Council therefore proposed
that there should be a penalty for the breach of the probation order
and nothing more. Its recommendation has not been accepted. It
would have involved a fine, plus compulsory supervision without
one of the principal sanctions of a probation order, but its supporters
might pray in aid the current law under which a fine may be coupled
with a sentence of immediate imprisonment.

---

[1] *Parry*, [1951] 1 K.B. 590. The effect of this decision is expressly recognised by
s. 30(1) of the Powers of Criminal Courts Act 1973.
[2] *Bainbridge* (1979), 1 Cr. App. Rep. (S) 36.
[3] Paras. 173–92.

Use. A glance at Tables I–III shows that the use of probation declined over the decade 1968–78. In 1968 nine per cent of the sentences for indictable offences in the Crown Court were probation orders; the percentage had declined to five by 1978. The corresponding percentages for Magistrates' Courts were eight and six. The tables are confined to offenders over twenty-one. The decline was even more striking in the case of offenders aged seventeen and under twenty-one. The percentages of probation orders made by all courts with respect to offenders in this age group in 1968 were fourteen in the case of males and thirty-four in the case of females; the 1978 percentages were six and eighteen respectively.[1]

Three reasons may be given for this decline in the use of probation. First, there is the introduction of suspended prison sentences and community service orders by the Criminal Justice Acts of 1967 and 1972 respectively. They were intended for offenders who would formerly have been sent to prison, but there is no doubt that a significant number of these new sentences have been passed on those who would formerly have been put on probation. Secondly, though this is a more speculative matter, the stress on the superior efficacy of fines in the first two editions of *The Sentence of the Court*, published in 1964 and 1969 respectively, may have induced courts to resort to them in cases in which probation would have been employed in the past. Finally, it seems that probation officers tend to recommend probation less frequently than they did, and their recommendations for and against different types of sentence are probably accepted by the courts more frequently than was formerly the case.

The figures for probation orders made in respect of offenders over twenty-one suffice to show that it would be a mistake to regard probation as a measure used primarily in the case of the very young. It is frequently employed in the case of the elderly and middle-aged who are felt to be in need of support. Another mistake would be to suppose that probation is intended for the first offender, or even for someone who has not, in any serious sense of the word, embarked upon a criminal career, although it is of course employed in these cases. There are quite a few cases in which the Criminal Division of the Court of Appeal, or its predecessor the Court of Criminal Appeal, has made a probation order in lieu of an extended prison sentence, or of the predecessor of such a sentence, a sentence of preventive detention, and these sentences can only be passed on persistent offenders. Occasionally there is evidence of a reasonable

---

[1] *Statistics of the Criminal Justice System England and Wales 1968–78* (H.M.S.O.) Table 4.4.

chance that a hardened criminal may be reclaimed by a particular individual and residence with that individual will be made a condition of the probation order. Again, there are cases in which, although the accused has been subjected to every other measure known to our penal system, probation has never been tried before. Even when probation has been tried at some stage and it has failed, it is sometimes tried again as the accused's last chance before a protracted period of imprisonment. These well-intentioned probation orders sometimes succeed in the sense that the accused is not convicted again for a reasonable period after their making, if at all; but it is probably true to say that, in this sense, they fail more often than not. Nevertheless, even if they mean that crimes are committed which might not have been committed had the protracted period of imprisonment imposed for the next offence not been preceded by a probation order made on the "now or never" principle, it is submitted that a system in which such attempts at reclamation are made is vastly preferable to one in which they are not made. It must be conceded, however, that much depends on the type of offence for which the accused has been convicted and is given to committing. Most people would surely agree that greater risks can be taken in the case of non-violent than in that of violent offences, although the agreement might be more readily forthcoming if there were either a compulsory contributory insurance scheme in the case of crimes causing proprietary loss, or a scheme for *ex gratia* payments such as that administered by the Criminal Injuries Compensation Board in the case of personal injury.

According to the Report of the Interdepartmental Committee on the Probation Service, published in 1962, there is an *a priori* case for putting a convicted person on probation when four conditions are fulfilled. The conditions are

(a) The circumstances of the offence and the offender's record are not such as to demand, in the interests of society, that some more severe method be adopted in dealing with him;

(b) the risk, if any, to society through setting the offender at liberty is outweighed by the moral, social and economic arguments for not depriving him of it;

(c) the offender needs continuing attention (otherwise, if condition (b) is satisfied, fine or discharge will suffice);

(d) the offender is capable of responding to this attention while at liberty.

A matter on which views appear to be somewhat divided is whether conditions like these should be set out in a statute as a guide to the judicial exercise of discretion in the matter of sentencing.

This course is adopted in the American Law Institute's Model Penal Code. Article 7.01 is headed "Criteria for Withholding Sentence of Imprisonment and for Placing Defendant on Probation" and reads in part as follows:

"(1) The Court shall deal with a person who has been convicted of a crime without imposing sentence of imprisonment unless, having regard to the nature and circumstances of the crime and the history, character and condition of the defendant, it is of the opinion that his imprisonment is necessary for protection of the public because:

(*a*) there is undue risk that during the period of a suspended sentence or probation the defendant will commit another crime; or

(*b*) the defendant is in need of correctional treatment that can be provided most effectively by his commitment to an institution; or

(*c*) a lesser sentence will depreciate the seriousness of the defendant's crime.

"(3) When a person who has been convicted of a crime is not sentenced to imprisonment, the Court shall place him on probation if he is in need of the supervision, guidance, assistance or direction that the probation service can provide."

For the purposes of the Code a "crime" is any offence which may be punished with death or imprisonment. A crime may be a felony, misdemeanour or petty misdemeanour. The other class of offence is a violation for which a court may either suspend the imposition of sentence or sentence to a fine. Subject to special provisions concerning murder, the scheme of the Code with regard to the disposition of those convicted of a crime is that a court may suspend the imposition of sentence for a prescribed period (a procedure roughly equivalent to our deferment of sentence but without its restrictive provisions), or, in the case of misdemeanours and the less serious felonies ("felonies of the third degree"), order the civil commitment of an offender who is a chronic alcoholic, narcotics addict, prostitute or mentally abnormal person. If it does not adopt one of these courses, the court may sentence the offender to pay a fine, to be placed on probation or to imprisonment for a variety of specified terms. Probation or imprisonment may be combined with a fine, but they cannot be combined with each other, except that a sentence of not more than thirty days imprisonment may be imposed for a felony or misdemeanour as a condition of probation. The exception is roughly equivalent to our partially suspended sentence for which provision is made in the Criminal Law Act 1977. The permission to combine probation or imprisonment with a fine is subject to important qualifications contained in article 7.02.(2). It is set out on p. 27 and there are those who think that it should represent English law.

Article 7.01.(2) lists no less than eleven grounds to be accorded weight in favour of withholding a sentence of imprisonment. They include items relating to the culpability of the offender, such as the existence of provocation, and to his previous good character. One of the major problems with regard to guidelines of this sort is the extent to which they should go into detail.[1]

E. FINES

All Courts have power to fine a sane offender over twenty-one except when obliged to sentence him to imprisonment for life (murder), or to death (treason). At common law there was no limitation on the amount unless the principle that fines must not be excessive can be said to have been part of the common law before it was enunciated in the Bill of Rights. There is now no limit on the amount of a fine which may be imposed by the Crown Court.[2] Magistrates' Courts are limited to a maximum of a thousand pounds in the case of most offences triable either way;[3] and there is a variety of limited maxima for other such offences as well as for those triable summarily.

General principles. We shall see in Chapter IV that, when fixing the length of a prison sentence, the Courts operate a rough tariff system based on the gravity of the offence; the graver the offence, the longer is the sentence likely to be. Generally speaking a similar system appears to prevail with regard to fines, but the need to have regard to the offender's means has produced important ancillary principles.[4] Furthermore, no Court can be expected to disregard the profit derived from an offence when fixing the amount of the fine to be imposed on its perpetrator. In *Lewis*[5] the Court of Criminal Appeal said:

> "The first consideration in a matter of this sort is whether the accused person should go to prison or whether he can be properly dealt with by way of fine. Once the Court has decided that a fine is proper then there are obviously in each case many factors which may follow, but amongst the factors which the Court must consider one can mention first the amount involved in the fraud, which in this instance was enormous, secondly the amount obtained out of it by the accused if known . . . ; thirdly his capacity to pay. It is in the view of this Court wrong in principle to impose such a fine as may be utterly beyond the accused's means and will only result in the prison sentence which is mentioned at the time of the trial as the sanction for failure to pay."

---

[1] See discussion in Ch. 5, p. 207, *infra*.
[2] Criminal Law Act 1977, s. 32(3).
[3] *Ibid.*, s. 28(4).
[4] The requirement depends on case law so far as the Crown Court is concerned, but s. 31(1) of the Magistrates' Courts Act 1952 requires a Magistrates' Court to take the offender's means into consideration so far as they are known or appear to the Court.
[5] [1965] Crim. L.R. 121. The extract from the judgement of the Court of Criminal Appeal is taken from D. A. Thomas's *Principles of Sentencing* (1st Edn., 1970) p. 221, n. 1.

If the first ancillary principle in the application of the tariff to fining is that the amount of the fine imposed must never exceed the defendant's ability to pay, a second and equally important principle is that a heavy fine must not be imposed upon a wealthy person in a case in which a man of lesser means would have been sent to prison. Our Courts are certainly fully conscious of the Kantian principle that "legal justice ceases to be justice if it can be bought for a price". A vivid illustration of the principle is provided by *Markwick*.[1] Markwick, a member of a golf club, appealed against a fine of £500 for stealing 2s. 6d. from the pocket of a pair of trousers left by another member in the changing-room. Speaking for the Court of Criminal Appeal, Lord GODDARD, C.J. said that the sentence was about as wrong in principle as any sentence could be. He deplored the use of fines to give persons of means an opportunity of buying themselves out of being sent to prison, and said that:

> "The gravamen of the offence was not only its essential meanness, but also the aura of suspicion which must have been thrown over the servants and other members of the club."

Acting under powers which have since been curtailed, the Court substituted a sentence of two months imprisonment for the fine. It is possible that imprisonment would be eschewed in such a case today in favour of a fine more proportionate to the gravity of the offence; but, as recently as 1972, the Court of Appeal considered that the smallness of the amount stolen was not conclusive against immediate imprisonment.[2]

The decision in *Reeves*[3] is the converse of that in *Markwick*. When passing sentence of nine months immediate imprisonment for obtaining property by deception the trial judge said:

> "You are in no position to pay a financial penalty. If you were a man of means I should make a heavy fine on you, but it is no good doing that in your present position."

The Court of Appeal held that this was completely wrong, and, although they considered that the offences in fact merited the sentence, they varied it to one of nine months suspended imprisonment on account of the grievance which Reeves might entertain in consequence of the judge's remarks.

What is the position when a wealthy man is convicted of an offence for which there could be no serious question of sending the offender to prison whatever his means might be? The orthodox

---

[1] (1953), 37 Cr. App. Rep. 125
[2] *Bowler* (1972), 57 Cr. App. Rep. 275.
[3] (1972), 56 Cr. App. Rep. 366; *cf. McGowan*, [1975] Crim. L.R. 113, p. 13, *supra*.

answer seems to be in terms of a third ancillary principle, namely, that the ability of the offender to pay is relevant only as a mitigating factor, reducing the amount which might be fixed by reference to the gravity of the offence alone.

If this view is correct, a Metropolitan Magistrate fell into serious error when he fined a senior civil servant £75 for stealing a tube of tooth-paste from a chemist's shop; but the opposite view was stated with great force in para. 18 of the Advisory Council's Report on Non-custodial and Semi-custodial Penalties:

> "In our view, it is right that penalties for similar offences should as far as possible be designed to make an equal impact on offenders, and that the well-to-do should pay more than the less affluent. The fine will be equitable only if it is assessed in this way and constitutes something more than payment for a licence to commit the particular offence."

Moreover, at least in the case of acquisitive offences, it is surely arguable that the wealth of the offender aggravates the crime just as his poverty mitigates it. A heavier fine would be justified on tariff principles because the offence is graver.[1] From time to time there are cases in which very heavy fines are upheld, but they are not strictly relevant to the question of the correctness of the orthodox view because the offenders had profited greatly from their crimes and very substantial fines were justified provided the offenders had the wherewithal to meet them.

The Swedish day fine. The Advisory Council's report characterises the Swedish "day fine" system as "a sophisticated method of ensuring that a fine is related to the offender's means".[2] Put very briefly the scheme is that the offender should be ordered to pay a sum arrived at by multiplying a day fine of from 200–500 Kroner, representing a thousandth of his gross annual income, by a figure varying from 1–120 based on the gravity of the offence.[3] Deductions to allow for expenses and liabilities are permissible and the day fine may be increased if the offender's capital exceeds a specified amount. The system only applies to the more serious offences, minor ones being dealt with by a fine of up to 500 Kroner.

The Council concluded that it would not be practicable to incorporate the Swedish scheme into our system, principally because it could not be fitted in with the variety of maxima fines which may

---

[1] *Cargill*, [1913] 2 K.B. 271; 8 Cr. App Rep. 224, a decision on the length of a prison sentence.

[2] Para. 1.9. For a fuller account than that in the text see paras. 20 *et seq.* and Appendix B of the report, together with H. Thornstedt, "The Day Fine System in Sweden" [1975] Crim. L.R. 307. There are similar systems in force in Denmark and Finland.

[3] A maximum of 180 day fines is permitted for a multiplicity of offences. The figures in the text are those given in Thornstedt's article.

at present be imposed by Magistrates' Courts and on account of the difficulties which would be encountered in ascertaining the offender's means.[1] This latter matter does not appear to cause trouble in Sweden where reliable information on people's incomes is said to be more readily available than in this country. The Council was, however, of opinion that sentencers should be encouraged to adopt the general principle of the day fine by addressing their minds separately to the two issues of the gravity of the offence and ability of the offender to pay.

Combination with imprisonment. We have seen that a fine cannot be combined with a conditional discharge,[2] or a probation order[3] for the same offence. Section 14(1) of the Powers of Criminal Courts Act 1973 empowers the court to make a community service order "instead of dealing with [the offender] in any other way". These words have been held to preclude the combination of such an order with a fine for the same offence.[4] The effect of s. 30(1) of the 1973 Act, read together with s. 32(3) of the Criminal Law Act 1977, is that the Crown Court can combine a sentence of imprisonment, subject to the statutory maximum, with a fine which is not subject to any such maximum. Magistrates' Courts are empowered to combine a fine with imprisonment by a large number of statutes specifying maxima for both.

In practice it seems that a fine is only combined with a sentence of immediate imprisonment where the offender has made a profit out of his offence.[5] Thomas refers, without approval, to a possible exception in cases in which a shorter prison sentence is imposed than that which the offender would otherwise have received because it is accompanied by a fine for the same offence. For example, in *Savundranayagan*,[6] a case of very extensive fraud, the defendant was sentenced to eight years imprisonment and a fine of £50,000 or two further years imprisonment in default of payment. The judge appears to have thought that ten years imprisonment would have been a proper sentence, but discounted it by two years because of the imposition of the fine, and the Court of Appeal appears to have approved of his reasoning. Savundranayagan had made an enormous profit out of his crimes and, although much of it may have

---

[1] This reasoning was recently repeated in the White Paper on *The Reduction of Pressure on the Prison System* (Cmnd. 7948, 1980), para. 15.
[2] P. 12, *supra.*
[3] P. 19, *supra.*
[4] *Carnwell* (1978), 68 Cr. App. Rep. 58.
[5] E.g. *Forsythe*, [1980] Crim L.R. 313.
[6] [1968] 3 All E.R. 439. The reasoning in this case was applied in *Lott-Carter* (1978), 67 Cr. App. Rep. 404 (fines totalling £2,000 combined with a year's imprisonment for profitable thefts). See on the whole subject D. A. Thomas, *Principles of Sentencing* (2nd Edn.), pp. 323 *et seq.*

been dissipated by the time he was sentenced, it was possible that some of it had been "salted away" abroad. On this basis the decision is unobjectionable, but, in cases where no profit has been made, the practice of discounting a prison sentence could have the effect of allowing an offender with means to buy himself out of a portion of his sentence. This is exactly what would have happened if A, without means, were sentenced to six months imprisonment for an affray while B, who had some means, were sentenced to three months imprisonment plus a fine of £200 for his equally guilty part in the same affray.

The Court of Appeal has held that there is no rule restricting the imposition of a suspended prison sentence in combination with a fine to cases in which the offender has made a profit.[1] Different considerations may be applicable because the defendant is able to earn money with which to pay the fine, and it has been said that a fine may be imposed to "add a sting to the suspended sentence". Even so, there is a risk that the fine will come to be regarded as the price with which an offender with means may buy a suspension of sentence. Further reference is made in section 2 of this chapter to problems created by the suspended sentence. At this stage it is sufficient to draw attention to the merits of article 7.02(2) of the American Law Institute's Model Penal Code. It is arguable that it should be adopted in this country with the addition of a reference to suspended imprisonment. At the moment there is no statutory declaration of the principles on which fines may be combined with prison sentences, suspended or otherwise, and little help is to be derived from the case-law. The other clauses of article 7.02 may cause some to wonder whether guidelines of this nature are desirable if they can do no more than provide the courts with glimpses of the obvious.

Article 7.02 of the American Law Institute's Model Penal Code is entitled "Criteria for Imposing Fines". It reads as follows:

"(1) The Court shall not sentence a defendant only to pay a fine, when any other disposition is authorised by law, unless having regard to the nature and circumstances of the crime and to the history and character of the defendant, it is of the opinion that the fine alone suffices for protection of the public.

(2) The Court shall not sentence a defendant to pay a fine in addition to a sentence of imprisonment or probation unless:

(a) the defendant has derived a pecuniary gain from the crime; or

(b) the Court is of opinion that a fine is specially adapted to deterence of the crime involved or to the correction of the offender.

(3) The Court shall not sentence a defendant to pay a fine unless:

(a) the defendant is or will be able to pay the fine; and

---

[1] *Genese* (1976), 63 Cr. App. Rep. 152.

(*b*) the fine will not prevent the defendant from making restitution or reparation to the victim of the crime.

(4) In determining the amount and method of payment of a fine, the Court shall take into account the financial resources of the defendant and the nature of the burden that its payment will impose."

Enforcement. The ultimate sanction for failure to pay a fine is imprisonment; but the tendency of modern legislation is to render this sanction very much a last resort. On imposing a fine the Crown Court may allow time for payment or direct payment by instalments, and it must fix the term of imprisonment (not exceeding twelve months) to be served in default of payment.[1] A Magistrates' Court may likewise allow time for payment or direct payment by instalments of any fine it imposes;[2] but it can only fix a term of imprisonment (for a period with various restrictions) to be served in default of payment when imposing the fine if the offence is punishable with imprisonment, and the offender appears to have means to pay, or it appears that he is unlikely to remain at a place of abode in the United Kingdom for a sufficient time to enable payment to be enforced by other methods, or he is sentenced to imprisonment or a detention centre for the offence or some other offence, or is already serving such a sentence.[3] In the cases which have just been mentioned, either court can commit to prison forthwith for non-payment. Any period of imprisonment fixed for default in payment may be made consecutive to any sentence which the offender is serving or directed to serve. After committal to prison, the defaulter may obtain his instant release by payment, and *pro rata* reduction of the term of imprisonment by part payment. Where there is no committal in the first instance, the defaulter has ample opportunity of insuring that his means at the time of default are investigated before he is sent to prison.

Use. A glance at Tables I–III will show that a fine is far and away the most common sentence in Magistrates' Courts, while its use in the Crown Court is by no means insignificant. It is the appropriate sentence for most non-indictable offences, and its overall use for indictable offences is considerable. Fifty per cent of the total of 213,436 such offences, committed by offenders of all ages, dealt with by all courts in 1978 resulted in fines.[4]

According to the third edition of *The Sentence of the Court*,[5] the

---

[1] Powers of Criminal Courts Act 1973, s. 31.
[2] Magistrates' Courts Act 1952, s. 63.
[3] Criminal Justice Act 1967, s. 44(3).
[4] *Statistics of the Criminal Justice System England and Wales 1968–78*, Table. 4.1.
[5] P. 87. The first edition (1964) and the second (1969), unlike the third, contain a full account of the research and its conclusions.

research carried out for the 1964 edition is unique in having compared the effectiveness of fines, discharge, probation and imprisonment, with results which supported the first two alternatives in preference to the second two. Scepticism was expressed in some quarters,[1] and the third edition concedes that the research was rather crude. The findings reported in the first two editions may have accounted for some fines being imposed rather than probation, or even a short term of imprisonment, but the major cause of the popularity of the fine is no doubt the lack of anything more suitable for the majority of offences which come before the courts.

F. COMMUNITY SERVICE ORDERS[2]

Community service orders were recommended in the Advisory Council's report of 1970 on non-custodial and semi-custodial penalties. Provision was made for them in the Criminal Justice Act 1972 and the Powers of Criminal Courts Act 1973. After a period of experimentation in selected districts it was decided in 1975 that community service should gradually be introduced throughout the country with the result that, since March 1979, it has been possible for all criminal courts in England and Wales to make community service orders.

Section 14(1) of the Powers of Criminal Courts Act 1973 provides,

"Where a person of or over seventeen years of age is convicted of an offence punishable with imprisonment, the court by or before which he is convicted may, instead of dealing with him in any other way (but subject to subsection (2) below) make an order (in this Act referred to as a "community service order") requiring him to perform unpaid work in accordance with the subsequent provisions of this Act for such number of hours (being in the aggregate not less than forty nor more than two hundred and forty) as may be specified in the order."

Section 14(2) sets out the four conditions precedent. They are that the offender should consent to the order, that the court should have been notified that arrangements exist in the district in which the offender resides, or will reside, for the performance of work under such an order, that the court should be satisfied, after considering a report by a probation officer, that the offender is a suitable person to perform the work, and that the court is satisfied that provision can be made for him to do so. The requirement of consent to an order which is largely punitive in intent may seem odd, but it was thought to have been necessitated by international conventions about forced

---

[1] A. E. Bottoms, "The Efficacy of the Fine: a Case for Scepticism" [1973] Crim. L.R. 534.
[2] *Community Service Orders* by Warren Young (Heinemann, 1979.)

labour.[1] Presumably the second condition is otiose now that it is possible for all courts to make community service orders. The point of the third and fourth conditions is obvious enough. It is no use making a community service order unless the right type of work is available for the right type of offender.

Effect. Sections 15 and 16 deal with the effect of a community service order. The offender must report to the relevant officer and perform for the number of hours specified in the order such work at such times as the officer may direct. The officer will normally be a probation officer, although the offender is not on probation. The hours of work must be spread over a period not exceeding twelve months beginning at the date of the order but, unless revoked, the order remains in force until the number of hours specified in it have been served.[2] It is assumed that the offender will generally be employed or undergoing further education or training, the essence of the punishment being deprivation of leisure. Accordingly, s. 15(3) expressly provides that the instructions given by the officer shall be such as to avoid, so far as reasonably practicable, interference with the times at which the offender works or attends an educational establishment.

If he is in breach of the requirements of s. 15, the offender may, under s. 16, be brought before the court which may fine him up to £50 with the result that the order remains in force, or revoke the order and deal with him in any way in which he could have been dealt with for the offence. The commission of a further offence during the currency of the order is not as such a breach of the requirements of s. 15, a further indication of the difference between a community service order and a probation order.

Under s. 17 of the Act the courts have wide powers, in the light of subsequent events, of simply revoking an order, or revoking it and dealing with the offender in any way in which he could have been dealt with for the offence, or varying the order. These powers may be exercised on the application of the relevant officer or the offender.

All work done under a community service order is unpaid and of a kind normally undertaken by volunteers. According to *The Sentence of the Court* it falls into two broad categories—tasks of a practical nature not involving personal relationships with individuals, and those involving some contact with the beneficiaries. Examples of the first category are decorating houses and flats for the elderly and

---

[1] Notwithstanding the requirement of consent, there seems to be a right of appeal against sentence as well as conviction because s. 13 of the Powers of Criminal Courts Act 1973 does not apply (*cf.* n. 3, p. 18, *supra*).

[2] S. 15(2) as amended by the Criminal Law Act 1977.

handicapped, repairing toys for children in need and site clearance work. The personal tasks include swimming coaching for handicapped children and helping the elderly.[1] The orders are punitive in that they involve a relatively serious interference with the offender's leisure, but it is hoped that the nature of the work will have some rehabilitative effect.

Use. It is early days for an assessment of the use made by our courts of community service orders, but there are signs that it may increase over the years. The orders are more suitable for indictable than for non-indictable offences, a fact which is reflected in Table I. They may also prove to be more popular for the 17–21 age group than in the case of offenders over 21. In 1978 6 per cent of the 98,043 sentences passed by all courts on male members of the younger age group for indictable offences were community service orders.[2]

The legislation which made these orders possible was passed against the background of the increasing prison population. In this respect they resemble the suspended prison sentence introduced by the Criminal Justice Act 1967, but community service orders have not been subjected to anything like the amount of criticism which has been made of the suspended sentence. There is, however, still some uncertainty about their place in the hierarchy of penal measures. Are they intended exclusively for the offender who would, before their introduction, have received a short prison sentence, immediate or suspended, or may they also be used as an alternative to other non-custodial measures? The first possibility was emphatically supported by WALLER, L.J., speaking for the Court of Appeal in 1976: "[C]ommunity service orders are intended to take the place of imprisonment and should only be made where imprisonment would be appropiate in the first place."[3] There is, however, no statutory provision to this effect,[4] and *The Sentence of the Court* simply tells us that "The Community Service Order was introduced with the *primary* purpose of providing a constructive alternative for those offenders who would otherwise have received a short custodial sentence."[5] In the circumstances it is likely that probation officers, whose duty it is to make recommendations which they consider best for the individual offender, will continue to suggest community service in cases in which the court would have

---

[1] Para. 70.

[2] *Statistics of the Criminal Justice System England and Wales 1968–78*, Table 4.4 Two per cent of the sentences in 1978 on 12,711 females were community service orders.

[3] *Mulcahy* (unreported), cited in Warren Young, *Community Service Orders*, p. 29.

[4] *Cf.* Powers of Criminal Courts Act 1973, s. 22(2), p. 56, *infra*.

[5] Para. 67, emphasis supplied.

passed a non-custodial sentence in any event and their suggestions will continue to be accepted in such cases from time to time.

This seems to be a matter in which the practice, at any rate of Magistrates' Courts, varies with the result that orders for community service of from 40–100 hours are made against those found guilty of offences thought by one court to be sufficiently serious for imprisonment, while similar orders are made against others guilty of offences considered by a second court to be less serious. This is a type of sentencing disparity which causes great concern in some quarters,[1] but others may consider it a comparatively trivial gnat in a system which has swallowed the camel of the inbuilt inequity of community service orders. If we apply purely retributive considerations based on desert, it is the acme of injustice that an offender who, through no fault of his own, is reported by a probation officer to be unsuitable for community service, should be sent to prison, while those thought suitable for it are ordered to perform such service. The awkward truth is that any attempt to individualise a punishment is bound to militate against its retributive justice, but this does not mean that the attempt should be abandoned, especially when it may contribute to the public good, including that of the inmates, by reducing the prison population.

Provided the overall maximum of 240 hours is not exceeded, concurrent or consecutive community service orders may be made against an offender convicted of several offences,[2] and, subject in practice to the same proviso, a community service order may be consecutive to one made on a previous occasion.[3] Section 14(8) of the Powers of Criminal Courts Act 1973 expressly allows for the making of ancillary orders such as those discussed in section 3 of this chapter, in combination with a community service order. Such an order cannot, as a matter of law, be combined with a discharge, probation, fine or imprisonment for the same offence. As a matter of sentencing practice it ought not to be combined with imprisonment, immediate or suspended,[4] for a different offence. It may, however, be held to be permissible to make a community service order in the case of an offender who is already subject to a suspended prison sentence passed on a former occasion, or even to pass a suspended sentence on someone already performing a community service order.[5]

---

[1] See "*Community Service and the Tariff*" by K. Pease in [1978] Crim. L.R. 269 and the comments on this article in [1978] Crim. L.R. 540 *et seq.*
[2] Powers of Criminal Courts Act 1973, s. 14(3).
[3] *Evans*, [1977] 1 All E.R. 228.
[4] *Starie* (1979), 69 Cr. App. Rep. 239.
[5] See the comment on *Starie* (*supra*) in [1979] Crim. L.R. 731.

G. DEFERMENT OF SENTENCE

Section 1(1) of the Powers of Criminal Courts Act 1973 provides that,

". . . the Crown Court or a Magistrates' Court may defer passing sentence on an offender for the purpose of enabling the court to have regard in determining his sentence, to his conduct after conviction (including, where appropriate, the making by him of reparation for his offence) or to any change in his circumstances."

The offender must consent to the deferment, it can only be for one period (not exceeding six months), and, if the offender commits another offence during the period of deferment, he may be brought back to court and sentenced for his original offence; or he may be sentenced for it by the court convicting him of the subsequent offence, except that a Magistrates' Court cannot sentence for the original offence when sentence for it was deferred by the Crown Court.[1]

On an appeal against the sentence ultimately made after deferment the appellate court should consider first whether it was excessive in any event, and then whether adequate allowance was made for any progress of the offender during the deferment.[2] The Criminal Statistics of 1978 show that some 5,831 sentences were passed after deferment in that year.

The object of the section of the Criminal Justice Act 1972 which first conferred this power upon the courts was to enable them to assess the effect of some impending change in the condition of the offender such as altered accommodation, fresh employment or a marriage, before passing sentence.[3] Up to a point, similar results could have been achieved in the Crown Court by a common law bind over, and, in a Magistrates' Court, by successive remands; but, in the case of a bind over it would not be contemplated that an offender would be called upon to come up for judgment after the change in his condition had taken place so long as he behaved himself and remands are simply intended to enable the court to get more information by way of social inquiry or medical reports about the condition of the offender at the time of conviction. All other powers of deferment are expressly preserved by the 1973 Act.

The mention of reparation in s. 1(1) of the 1973 Act is of particular interest because, in the past, the Court of Criminal Appeal and Court Appeal (Criminal Division) have deplored deferment of sentence in order to see whether reparation was made. The objection

---

[1] Powers of Criminal Courts Act 1973, s. 1(4) and 1(4A) inserted by the Criminal Law Act 1977.

[2] *Smith* (1976), 64 Cr. App. Rep. 116.

[3] *Crosby and Hayes* (1974), 60 Cr. App. Rep. 234; *cf.* pp. 237–8, *per* LAWTON, L.J.

was founded either on the ground that: "It is highly objectionable to postpone sentence and at the same time turn the courts into a money collecting agency",[1] or else on the ground that: "It is undesirable that an implicit bargain of that sort should be made with the accused".[2] Such views are of course in accordance with the Kantian principle that "legal justice ceases to be justice if it can be bought for a price"; but should this principle never be tempered with expediency? Criminals may be deterred from offending again, and potential criminals from offending at all, by the knowledge that they will be pressurised into making reparation. We shall see that the fact that the offender made reparation tells in his favour when the length of a prison sentence comes to be assessed. It would be unrealistic to pretend that, in most cases, the reparation did not flow from the hope of a reduced sentence rather than a change of heart. Does it matter so greatly that the pressure to produce such a highly desirable result should come before rather than after conviction?

Section 2.—Types of prison sentence

Imprisonment is now the only custodial penal measure for mentally normal offenders over 21 known to our law. Before the Criminal Justice Act 1948 came into force it was necessary to distinguish between imprisonment and penal servitude. Penal servitude was the successor of transportation; it lasted longer than imprisonment in the sense that people were commonly sentenced to penal servitude for periods of three, five, seven or fourteen years, whereas, in the second half of the nineteenth century and the first half of the twentieth century, offenders were rarely sent to prison for more than two years. On the other hand, imprisonment was originally the more rigorous of the two regimes with its Victorian concomitants of the treadmill and the crank-shaft. For some time before the Act of 1948 abolished penal servitude, the distinction between it and imprisonment had come to be one in name only.

Before the Criminal Justice Act 1967 came into force, it was necessary to distinguish between preventive detention, corrective training and imprisonment. Preventive detention had been a possible sentence for persistent offenders falling within the appropriate definition since 1908. It was intended for the protection of the public and, although sentences to preventive detention were lengthy, they were served under somewhat better conditions than sentences of imprisonment. Corrective training was introduced by the

---

[1] LORD PARKER, C.J., in *West* (1959), 43 Cr. App. Rep 109.
[2] SALMON, L.J., in *Collins* (1969), 53 Cr. App. Rep. 385.

Criminal Justice Act 1948 and was, as its name implied, a sentence with training as its principal object. It was intended for offenders between twenty-one and thirty whose records were such as to suggest that they were in danger of becoming recidivists. The training element in the sentence was thought to justify a longer period of incarceration than that which might have been permissible on ordinary sentencing principles. Corrective training was abolished by the Criminal Justice Act 1967 because it had come to bear little, if any, difference from ordinary imprisonment owing to the development of training facilities throughout the prison system generally. Preventive detention was abolished because it was felt that the wrong type of offender tended to be sentenced, the inadequates rather than the menaces. Fewer and fewer people came to be sentenced to preventive detention and this was partly due to the fact that five years was its minimum and eight years its normal duration. No judge liked imposing such a sentence when the period of incarceration it entailed was vastly in excess of that merited by the offence for which the accused was convicted. Although the motive was the protection of the public, it was too much like punishing a man for his past offences. The difference between the conditions under which sentences of preventive detention were served and those of ordinary imprisonment were never sufficiently pronounced to put any sentencer at his ease on the ground that he was employing a protective measure rather than inflicting punishment.

This section is primarily concerned with five types of prison sentence, the ordinary fixed-term sentence of immediate imprisonment, the life sentence, the extended sentence, the suspended sentence and the partially suspended sentence. First, however, the relevance of remission and parole must be explained.

Remission and parole. Under the Prison Rules 1964 all fixed-term sentences of more than one month are subject to remission of a third for industry and good conduct. Someone sentenced to imprisonment for three years on the first of January 1981 may thus be sure from the outset of his sentence that he will be released not later than the thirty-first of December 1982, provided he works properly and behaves himself. Loss of remission may be awarded as a punishment for breach of prison discipline, and some such system is essential to the maintenance of order in prison.

All fixed-term sentences of immediate imprisonment of more than eighteen months are subject to the possibility of release on licence (i.e. "parole") after a third of the period has been served. This is the effect of s. 60(1) of the Criminal Justice Act 1967 which provides that the Home Secretary may, if recommended to do so by the Parole Board, release on licence a person serving a sentence of imprisonment, other than imprisonment for life, after he has served not less than a third of his sentence or twelve months, whichever is the longer. Someone sentenced to eighteen months precisely would not benefit from this provision because, if he had behaved himself in prison, he would be entitled to be released without licence after a year. It is true that, had he forfeited the whole or part of his remission, he would be eligible for parole, but he would hardly be a strong candidate. Someone sentenced to twenty-one months imprisonment would benefit from the parole provision as he would be eligible for release on licence after a year although, if he had earned the maximum remission, he would not be entitled to release without licence until fourteen months of his sentence had been served. The licence under s. 60 terminates when the prisoner would have become entitled to release without licence; during the currency of the licence, the parolee is liable to recall if he breaks one of its conditions. The procedure is for local review committees to consider each case in which a prisoner becomes eligible for parole and to make recommendations to the Home Office by which the case must be referred to the Parole Board. Cases in which parole is refused must be reconsidered annually. Under s. 35 of the Criminal Justice Act 1972, the Home Secretary is empowered, after consultation with the Parole Board, to determine classes of case in which he is not obliged to refer recommendations for release to the Board, but may act directly on the recommendations of the local review committees. At present the Home Secretary is acting on the unanimous recommendations of these committees where the sentence is less than three years, except when the offence was one of violence, sex, arson or drug trafficking.[1] Local review committees are attached to each prison, and the Parole Board consists of judges, former prison governors, psychiatrists, penologists and others appointed by the Home Secretary.[2]

The parole system began cautiously, but by 1975 some 40 per cent of prisoners eligible for parole were receiving it. In that year the Home Secretary made a policy statement designed to increase the use of parole, by increasing the number of prisoners to whom parole is granted and by releasing parolees earlier so that they spend longer periods on licence.[3] The Board's report for 1979 shows that some 61 per cent of all prisoners released in 1979 from sentences which qualified for parole consideration had been granted parole. The average length of parole licence for those released in 1979 was eight

---

[1] Report of the Parole Board for 1973, para. 34.

[2] Criminal Justice Act 1967, s. 59 and Sch. 2.

[3] Details may be found in the Report of the Parole Board for 1975, para. 4 and Appendix 4.

months, and the number of parolees recalled whilst on licence represented about 9 per cent of those released during the year.[1] In consequence of the introduction of parole into the English penal system in 1968, there is an element of indeterminacy in fixed term sentences of more than eighteen months. The offender knows when, subject to good conduct, he must be released; but he also knows that there is a chance that he will be released earlier. The merits of indeterminacy in sentencing have produced much discussion in the past, and no doubt they will continue to do so. There is great *prima facie* attraction in the view that, although it may be right that the judge should fix the maximum period of incarceration, prison affects different people differently and, in the case of sentences of any length, those in daily contact with the offender and their advisers will know what is the optimum moment for release; however, as Dr. Hood points out, "no evidence exists either that the length of time a man spends in custody is related to the probability of his reconviction, or that review bodies can spot a man's readiness for release on the basis of knowledge gained through observing his behaviour in custody".[2]

Then there is the objection to indeterminacy based on the sense of injustice that will inevitably be produced in the minds of those who are not released. Suppose that parole is granted to A but refused to B whose record and performance in prison appear to himself and others to be as good as A's, it is hard to believe that B will not have a grievance, and his grievance will not be diminished by the facts that, under the present practice, he will not have been represented at the deliberations of the local review committee (although he will usually have been interviewed by a member) or before the Parole Board, and he will not have been given the reasons for the refusal of parole.[3]

Although the paroling rate has risen to around 60 per cent, the tide of criticisms has not been stemmed. The psychological effects on prisoners of indeterminacy and of parole refusals, the taking of decisions about sentence length behind closed doors and without published reasons, and the absence of evidence that reports on the offender's behaviour in prison enable the paroling body to release him at the point of optimum effectiveness — these and other factors have led to the search for other methods of releasing prisoners at an earlier stage of their sentence (which, at least, the parole system has shown to be possible without social catastrophe). Dr. Hood has

---

[1] Report of the Parole Board for 1979, paras. 35, 36 and 38.
[2] [1975] Crim. L.R. 545 at p. 547.
[3] The Parole Board's view on the giving of reasons for the refusal of parole is set out in Appendix 5 of the Report of the Parole Board 1979.

proposed that prisoners serving sentences of up to three (or four) years should, subject to forfeiture of the right for a further period on account of breach of prison discipline, be entitled to release on licence after serving one-third of the sentence. In the case of longer sentences the prisoner should also generally be entitled to release on licence after serving one-third of his sentence; but with these longer sentences the court would have the discretion to order that the prisoner would not be released automatically but subject to review by the Parole Board. That discretion would be available for a limited category of "dangerous" offenders, as defined by statute. There would also be a power to impose a restricted release order in cases of longer sentences aimed at general deterrence, the effect being that the judge could ensure a minimum period of incarceration longer than one-third of the sentence. The Parole Board would under this scheme deal with only the most serious of cases, it would be reconstituted as a judicial body, and it would be obliged to give reasons for a refusal to grant parole. The licence on which all prisoners were released would endure until the end of the sentence.[1]

In Northern Ireland a system of "conditional release" was introduced in 1976. In essence, a prisoner serving a sentence of over 12 months is entitled to be released conditionally after one-half of his sentence: if he is convicted of an imprisonable offence during the remitted period of the sentence, he is liable to be returned to prison for all or for part of the balance of his sentence (in addition to any sentence imposed for the new offence). The May Committee suggested that a modified system of conditional release might be considered for England, the principal modification being that the court should "be given power to stipulate that it should not apply in respect of those on whom long sentences are passed principally for the protection of the public".[2] This modification indicates a procedure for dealing with serious and dangerous offenders similar to that proposed by Dr. Hood, whilst the bulk of offenders now dealt with by the Parole Board would be released without the elaborate, expensive, time-consuming and anxiety-generating machinery of the present parole system.[3]

---

[1] "Some fundamental dilemmas of the English parole system and a suggestion for an alternative structure" in D. A. Thomas (ed.), *Parole, its Implications for the Criminal Justice and Penal Systems*. The argument is repeated by Dr. Hood at [1975] Crim. L.R. 545, in reply to criticisms from Professor Walker at [1975] Crim. L.R. 540. Dr. Hood's proposals must be seen in the context of broader changes in sentencing policy advocated in *Tolerance and the Tariff* (NACRO papers, Reprint No. 11, 1974).
[2] Committee of Inquiry into the United Kingdom Prison Services (Cmnd. 7673, 1979), para. 3.58.
[3] The question of dealing with serious and dangerous offenders is discussed in Ch. 5, *infra*.

A. ORDINARY FIXED TERM SENTENCES OF IMPRISONMENT

Subject to restrictions mentioned in the next chapter, the judge has a discretion with regard to the length of a prison sentence provided he keeps within the maximum prescribed for the offence. The maximum is usually fixed by statute.

i. *Statutory maxima.* Many statues provide maxima for very many offences. Each maximum tends to represent the attitude towards the offence prevailing when the statute was passed; the result is a number of anomalies.[1] If a girl between sixteen and eighteen is abducted for the purposes of unlawful intercourse, the maximum possible period of imprisonment is two years; if her fortune happens to be the object of the abduction, the maximum is imprisonment for fourteen years.[2] Indecent assault upon a woman is punishable with a maximum of two years, but indecent assault upon a man is subject to a maximum of ten years.[3]

There has recently been a good deal of rationalisation of the statutory maxima. Before the Criminal Damage Act 1971 came into force, the law, mainly contained in the Malicious Damage Act 1861, was excessively fragmented. There was a large number of separate offences according to the nature of the property damaged, and, according to modern standards, the maximum punishment for some of these offences varied capriciously. In many cases malicious damage to property was punishable with a maximum of two years, but, as a relic of the days when beer was a more important commodity in English life than it is now, the maximum for damage to hop binds was fourteen years. Under the Act of 1971 there is the one offence of intentionally or recklessly damaging or destroying property with a ten years maximum, unless it is aggravated as arson, or because it is accompanied by the intentional or reckless endangering of life, in which case the maximum is imprisonment for life. The punishment for theft was likewise subject to capricious variations, but it has been rationalised by the Theft Act 1968 which prescribes a maximum punishment of ten years for theft of all kinds and for obtaining property by deception.

The Advisory Council on the Penal System was charged, *inter alia*, with the task of reviewing "the general structure and level of maximum sentences of imprisonment available to the courts". Its 1978 report, despite being entitled Sentences of Imprisonment: a Review of Maximum Penalties, contains no such review. The Advisory Council declined to reconsider the various maxima and to attempt

---

[1] For a fascinating account of the evolution of the penalty structure in English law, see D. A. Thomas, *The Penal Equation* (1978).
[2] Sexual Offences Act 1956, ss. 19 and 17.
[3] *Ibid.*, ss. 14 and 15.

to produce a new framework of statutory maxima. Their argument was essentially that the maxima rarely impinge upon sentencing practice, that the present system of sentencing commands public support, and that it would therefore be preferable to bring the legal framework closer to sentencing practice rather than attempt to influence sentencing practice by altering the maxima. They feared also that if a new framework were proposed, "the momentum for adopting a new system would be squandered in a welter of confused debate".[1] Details of the recommendations which the Advisory Council did make are discussed below.[2] Suffice it to say here that for the foreseeable future statutory maximum penalties, which may well be more influential than the Advisory Council believed,[3] will continue to be set and altered in a piecemeal fashion as a result of recommendations by law reform bodies and of political enterprise.

ii. *Common law.* In the cases of the surviving common law offences such as common law conspiracy[4] and public nuisance, the custodial punishment is imprisonment at the discretion of the Court. This means that, subject to the prohibition of cruel and unusual punishments contained in the Bill of Rights, any term of imprisonment up to a maximum of imprisonment for life is permissible for common law offences.

For some time before 1950 it was widely, though erroneously, believed that the maximum punishment for a common law misdemeanour was two years imprisonment. This belief was fostered by the Penal Servitude Act 1891 under which for any offence punishable with penal servitude, whatever the permitted maximum length might be, a maximum of two years imprisonment but no more could be imposed as an alternative. The validity of this belief was tested in *Morris*,[5] decided in 1950, by which time the distinction between imprisonment and penal servitude, for long obsolescent, had been abolished. A sentence of four years imprisonment for a common law conspiracy to evade Customs duties was upheld by the Court of Criminal Appeal; but the erroneous belief had already been influential and, from the point of view of what is theoretically possible, its influence may still be discerned. In 1947, in response to complaints from the judges about the inadequacy of two years imprisonment as

---

[1] Report, para. 164.
[2] See p. 204, *infra.*
[3] See pp. 41–43, *infra.*
[4] Part I of the Criminal law Act 1977 provides maxima for statutory conspiracy, but for other forms of conspiracy, such as conspiracy to defraud or conspiracy to corrupt public morals, the maximum penalty remains at large.
[5] [1951] 1 K.B. 394, affirmed by *Verrier* v. *Director of Public Prosecutions*, [1967] 2 A.C. 195.

the maximum punishment for the common law offence of attempted rape, Parliament passed the Attempted Rape Act. Under this statute seven years is the maximum for the crime in question. Accordingly, for the common law offence of an attempt to commit what is now the statutory crime of robbery of a woman or girl a man is liable to a maximum possible punishment of imprisonment for life, whereas he could, at most, be sent to prison for a mere seven years for attempted rape of the same woman or girl. There are a few similar anomalies where there are statutory maxima for attempts or conspiracies.[1]

iii. *Reservation of the maxima for the worst cases*. The maxima punishments are rarely imposed and, in some cases, never. This fact is judically recognised from time to time, but the best statement on the point is contained in Chapter III of the Dove Wilson Report on Persistent Offenders published as long ago as 1932.

> "In order that there may be a proper grading of sentences to fit the many degrees of gravity presented by the various cases which fall within the same legal category, it is necessary that the maximum sentence authorised by law should be reserved for the rare offences which are exceptionally heinous, that sentences approaching the legal maximum should be reserved for offences falling within the next degree of gravity,—and so on, with the result that, for ordinary offences (such as form the great majority of cases coming before the Courts) the heaviest sentence which the Court feels justified in imposing is usually far below the maximum sentence authorised by law for the category of offence in question. It is the duty of the Court to take into consideration all the circumstances and consequences of the offence."

It might be thought that, as the maxima are so rarely imposed, they are of no particular importance. Indeed, the Advisory Council on the Penal System took the view that, apart from a few offences for which the maxima are commonly believed to be too low (such as cruelty to children, indecent assault on a girl under 13, and some forms of corruption and of fraudulent trading),

> "the maxima do not affect the normal range of sentences passed by the courts, and thus scarcely have any bearing, let alone influence, upon the vital question of the relative severity of sentences."[2]

At least four points may be made against this sweeping view.

In the first place Law Reform Committees and Parliament attach importance to the judges having room to manœuvre so as to be able to reserve the maximum for the worst kind of case. This is a recurrent theme in the Eighth Report of the Criminal Law Revision Committee upon which the Theft Act 1968 was based. Parliament's

---

[1] See p. 151, *infra*.
[2] Sentences of Imprisonment: A Review of Maximum Penalties, para. 83.

interest in the matter is vividly illustrated by the debates in the House of Lords on the Suicide Act 1961. It was generally agreed that, suicide having been made lawful, there were arguments against having a crime of aiding and abetting another to commit suicide and that, if there were to be such a crime, the punishment would not normally have to be particularly severe. Nevertheless, a maximum of as much as fourteen years was accepted partly on account of the hypothetical case of the man who, having sickened of the younger girl with whom he had had an affair, basely encourages her to commit suicide and even falsely promises to do so himself.[1]

Secondly, it is thought that the maxima influence the judge by making him give a longer sentence for the offence with the higher maximum in cases otherwise similar.

> "If the Legislature considers that two years is a suitable maximum for indecent assault on a female and ten years is the proper maximum for indecent assault upon a male, then a Judge must and should regard the latter as an offence which deserves higher punishment than the former, circumstances being as nearly as possible equal."[2]

Thirdly, changes in the maxima may have an effect on conceptions of the gravity of an offence. Courts may have regard to an increase in the maximum punishment for a crime,[3] and an attempt to alter social attitudes may be made through changing the maximum penalty. Thus, para. 87 of the report of the Advisory Committee on Drug Dependence on cannabis in 1968 stated that they "wished to demonstrate (by reducing the maximum punishment for it) that taking cannabis in moderation is a relatively minor offence".

Fourthly, courts appear still to find it useful to "steer by the maximum" in cases which present difficult sentencing problems, relying on the notion that the statutory maximum may be taken as an indication of the penalty which Parliament believes appropriate for the worst manifestation of a particular crime. Thus in a judgment attempting to set out criteria for sentencing terrorists who commit offences with explosives, LAWTON, L.J., described the maximum penalty provided by the Explosive Substances Act 1883 as

---

[2] H. L. Debates Vol. 229 Col. 271. A further striking example of Parliamentary faith in the efficacy of high maxima is s. 28 of the Criminal Justice Act 1972 under which maxima for various offences under the Firearms Act 1968 were raised from fourteen years to life and from seven and ten years to fourteen. It is hard to believe that this will affect the conduct of criminals and the effect on the conduct of the courts is problematic.

[2] Report of a Committee of Justice on Legal Penalties, 1959. See also *English* p. 85, *infra*.

[3] *Cf. Sands* (1976), 63 Cr. App. Rep. 297 (anti-rabies laws), and the Home Office's Review of the Criminal Justice Policy 1976, para. 5(i)(a).

"the right starting point" and then proceeded to apply the "general sentencing principle that the maximum sentence provided for by statute should be reserved for the most serious type of case".[1] And in a later case of possession of explosives the Court of Appeal again emphasised the need to steer by the maximum.[2]

There are therefore several reasons for regretting the Advisory Council's decision not to embark upon a re-structuring of the system of maximum penalties. Their influence upon sentencing practice is surely greater than the Advisory Council allowed, and, whilst it may be true that there are other methods of influencing the length of sentences apart from the revision of statutory maxima, it is doubtful whether the recommendations in the Advisory Council's report deal satisfactorily with the difficult cases.[3] In the meantime the courts continue to reserve the maxima for the worst cases, and the principle has indeed been broadened. In *Ambler*,[14] where the Court of Appeal upheld the imposition of a two year maximum sentence for corruption of prison officers, LAWTON, L.J., remarked that courts

> "should not use their imaginations to conjure up unlikely worst possible kinds of case. What they should consider is the worst type of offence which comes before the Court and ask themselves whether the particular case they are dealing with comes within the broad band of that type."

The case was one in which the maximum was low, and LAWTON, L.J., added that "where the maximum is low, the band may be wide", but the new "broad band" principle has been applied in upholding a maximum sentence of ten years in *Sholanke*[5] for administering poison with intent to endanger life.

B. LIFE SENTENCES

The life sentence is wholly indeterminate in the sense that, when the person upon whom it is imposed is received into prison, he cannot be given a date of release. By contrast, one sentenced to a fixed term of immediate imprisonment can be told, on reception, the precise date when, if he conducts himself properly, he will be released. It is true that, thanks to parole, there is an element of indeterminacy in every fixed-term sentence of more than eighteen months, but even so a definite date can be given on reception as that on which the prisoner will become eligible for parole.

So far as parole is concerned, life sentences are governed by s. 61 of the Criminal Justice Act 1967 under which the Home Secretary

---

[1] *Byrne* (1975), 62 Cr. App. Rep. 159 at p. 163.
[2] *Wallace* (1978), 67 Cr. App. Rep. 291 at p. 299.
[3] See p. 209, *infra*.
[4] [1976] Crim. L.R. 266.
[5] (1977) 66 Cr. App. Rep. 127, C.A., discussed in the Advisory Council's report, para. 80.

may release a prisoner at any time on the recommendation of the Parole Board, but only after consulting the Lord Chief Justice for the time being, and, if he is available, the judge who imposed the life sentence. Some special cases (such as those involving mercy killing) are considered and reviewed at a very early stage, but the normal procedure now is that the cases of all life sentence prisoners who have served between three and four years of their sentence are considered by a joint committee consisting of the Board's chairman and vice-chairman (who is a High Court judge), a psychiatrist member and two senior Home Office officials. The joint committee either fixes a date for the first review by the local review committee or, if it is clear that the prisoner will not be released for several years or is not clear how soon he might be released, asks for the case to be brought before it again after a specified interval.[1] When a case comes before the local review committee, its recommendation goes to the Parole Board (before a panel which includes a High Court judge and a psychiatrist) and, if the Board recommends release, to the Home Secretary.

The release is on licence and, although the requirements of the licence may be relaxed from time to time, the offender is liable to recall for the rest of his natural life; moreover, the grounds of recall are not confined to the commission of another offence, but may, for instance, consist of conduct suggesting that another offence will be committed. An offender who is recalled has an opportunity of making representations to the Parole Board and, if he is not released forthwith, his case is reviewed from time to time.

Paragraph 47 of the Report of the Parole Board for 1970 contains the following passage:

"While the Board will always have in mind the gravity of the offence in dealing with determinate sentences, this is only of major importance where to grant parole would defeat the purpose of the sentence or would endanger the confidence of the public. In determinate sentences consideration by the Board is not a sentencing operation because the sentence has been fixed by the court. With life sentences, however, the sentence is indeterminate and our function assumes a sentencing character, because there is no fixed term. The question is not simply whether the conditions, bearing in mind the nature of the offence, are such as to justify granting parole. The primary question is whether the time served is appropriate to the crime."

This assumption of the role of a judge by the Parole Board is not to everybody's taste. There are those who argue that, if such matters as the appropriateness of the time served to the crime have to be considered, they should be considered by an independent judicial

---

[1] Report of the Parole Board for 1976, paras. 23–6.

body rather than by a Board so closely connected with the Home Office. On the other hand there are those who would argue that it is important not to become the slave of the doctrine of the separation of powers. Judges are members of the Parole Board and it is the practice for a High Court judge to be in attendance when a life sentence case is being considered. It is also necessary for the Home Secretary to consult the Lord Chief Justice and, when available, the trial judge, before releasing a life prisoner; it is rare for the Home Secretary to accept a recommendation of release from the Parole Board against the views of the Lord Chief Justice.

It is convenient to distinguish between two types of life sentence, the mandatory life sentence for murder and the discretionary life sentence which is the maximum for some other crimes.

Mandatory life sentence. Since the abolition of the death penalty for murder, a convicted murderer must be sentenced to imprisonment for life.[1] When imposing such a sentence the judge may declare the period which he recommends to the Home Secretary as the minimum period which in his view should elapse before the offender is released.[2] On the partial abolition of the death penalty for murder by the Homicide Act 1957 and, still more so, on its total abolition in 1969 after a previous experimental period, there was considerable public apprehension that the life sentence as currently administered would not be an adequate deterrent for potential murderers. Having regard to the fact that the procedure for paroling lifers mentioned above might often lead to the release of the offender in the eighth or ninth year it was argued that criminals may believe that they have nothing to lose in committing murder in order to avoid identification for some other serious offence, e.g. robbery, for which, if convicted, they may well serve a sentence at least as long as nine years.[3] The Home Secretary included the penalty for murder in the light of, and subject to, the then recent decision of Parliament to make permanent the abolition of the death penalty for that crime in his reference of the law relating to offences against the person to the Criminal Law Revision Committee in 1970. In an interim report the Criminal Law Revision Committee recommended retention of the mandatory life sentence,[4] but in their final report the Committee were almost evenly divided on the issue.[5] A small majority

---

[1] Unless he was under eighteen when the offence was committed, in which case he must be detained at Her Majesty's pleasure which comes to much the same thing.

[2] Murder (Death Penalty Abolition) Act 1965, s. 1(2).

[3] On the effect of this reasoning upon sentences for serious crimes such as robbery, see p. 183, *infra*.

[4] The Penalty for Murder (Cmnd. 5184, 1972).

[5] Fourteenth Report, Offences against the Person (Cmnd. 7844, 1980), Part IIIB.

favoured retention and, in the circumstances, the Committee felt unable to recommend any change.

The retentionists in the Committee took the view that, as the most heinous form of homicide, murder should "attract a unique penalty which demonstrates that society will not tolerate such grave criminal conduct"; and that the additional public protection provided by the indeterminacy of the life sentence and the power of recall was of "overriding importance". Similar reasons had led the Emslie Committee in Scotland to favour retention of the mandatory penalty.[1] The majority of the Criminal Law Revision Committee pointed out that the statistics on length of detention of lifers, reproduced as Table IV, *infra*,[2] refute the simplistic "life means nine years" argument by showing "that the number of murderers who have to be detained for twelve years or more is rising with the passing of the years as an increasing proportion of those whose crimes were such that they would formerly have been executed come into the field for release".

The abolitionists in the Committee argued that crimes of murder vary greatly in their gravity, and that the heinousness of a particular murder can only be marked by a sentence proportioned to its gravity. They also argued that it would be procedurally fairer for the judge rather than the Parole Board and the Home Secretary to determine release, since those authorities take their decisions in private, without hearing the offender and without appeal; and that the information available to them does not provide a sounder basis for predicting the offender's future behaviour than that available to the judge at the trial. These views, together with the fact that judges have for some years been entrusted with discretion in the sentencing of those who commit manslaughter upon diminished responsibility (who may be thought to be a most unpredictable group of offenders), led the Butler Committee to favour abolition of the mandatory life sentence.[3] The Advisory Council on the Penal System also aligned themselves with this view.[4]

There was also a division of opinion on the ability of the judges, if the mandatory sentence were abolished, to sentence for murder with the degree of consistency and public acceptance attained in sentencing for other crimes. The retentionists in the Committee thought it "virtually certain that sentences would vary considerably from judge to judge in cases of similar gravity" and that "discrepancy in sentences would be likely to lead to public disquiet" which the

---

[1] The Penalties for Homicide (Cmnd. 5137, 1972).
[2] P. 223, *infra*.
[3] Mentally Abnormal Offenders (Cmnd. 6244, 1975), paras. 19.8 to 19.16.
[4] Sentences of Imprisonment: A Review of Maximum Penalties (1978), Ch. 12.

appeal system would not allay. The abolitionists argued that judges are accustomed to dealing with crimes which vary widely in their gravity, such as manslaughter and wounding, and that consistency and public acceptability would present no greater problems than elsewhere in sentencing. The Advisory Council likewise referred to fears of wide disparities in sentencing for murder as "speculative" and "exaggerated"; yet, as a safeguard "against exceptionally long determinate sentences which might be passed primarily for their deterrent and retributive effect", they suggested that "every prisoner receiving a determinate sentence for murder or manslaughter should be eligible for parole after serving ten years, or one third of his sentence, whichever is the less".[1] Another compromise suggested by abolitionists is that of the New Zealand Criminal Law Reform Committee: they argue that the sentence for unlawful killing (which would include both murder and manslaughter) should be at the court's discretion, but that where a determinate prison sentence of more than two years is imposed the offender should be liable to recall for the remainder of his life.[2] This is an attempt to meet the retentionist argument that liability to recall is necessary for public protection. The New Zealand Committee argue that recall should be a judicial procedure, that the Minister of Justice should be able to terminate an offender's liability to recall, and that the offender should two years after release from prison be able to petition for termination and to have this petition heard in court.

It is regrettable that the Criminal Law Revision Committee's final report includes no discussion of the range of alternative approaches. Insofar as the legal distinction between murder and manslaughter implies that release of the murderer is more appropriately determined by the Parole Board whereas release of the manslaughterer can safely be determined by an upper limit set by a judge, it is unfortunate that the Committee fail to explore the consequences of that implication. The Parole Board accepts that when it comes to deal with lifers "the primary question is whether the time served is appropriate to the crime".[3] Yet, since the legal definition of the crime does not require proof of many of the matters which are relevant to culpability and since there is no post-conviction hearing to determine the extent of the offender's culpability where the sentence is mandatory, it is inevitable that the Parole Board is performing a function which for other crimes is performed by either judge or jury or both, and is attempting to do so without hearing evidence

---

[1] *Ibid.*, paras. 254–6.
[2] Report on Culpable Homicide (1976), para. 25.
[3] Report of the Parole Board for 1970, quoted *supra*, p. 44

and argument on the point.[1] Whatever view one takes of the general procedural adequacy of parole, the fact that in murder cases the Parole Board must also determine gravity and culpability strongly suggests that it is not in its present form the fairest mechanism for determining the release of a convicted murderer.

By s. 1(2) of the Murder (Abolition of Death Penalty) Act 1965 a judge is empowered, when sentencing a person convicted of murder to imprisonment for life, to recommend a minimum period which in his view should elapse before the offender is released. Such recommendations are made in about one out of every twelve murder cases. The Court of Appeal have held that no recommendation should be for less than twelve years,[2] and Table V below shows that one recommendation was for as long as 35 years. The Criminal Law Revision Committee accept that "the power to recommend has operated somewhat haphazardly in the past", but a majority argue for the retention of the power on the basis that it provides the public with reassurance in particular grave cases and that it furnishes the Parole Board and Home Secretary with a clear impression of the judge's view of the gravity of the offence. The Committee do, however, recommend a number of procedural reforms in an attempt to "reduce the element of chance in the making of recommendations": the judge who makes a recommendation should give reasons for doing so, an appeal against a minimum recommendation should be possible, and the practice of inviting counsel to make representations before a recommendation is made should be invariable.[3] Whilst these procedural improvements are to be welcomed, it must remain doubtful whether a power so uncertain in its status and so haphazard in its operation should continue to be available to the courts. The power recognises only in a small way the importance of a judicial determination of the term to be served by a murderer. The need is for a broader review of the proper allocation of functions in the actual determination of length of sentence for murder.

Discretionary life sentence. Life is the statutory maximum sentence for a few serious crimes such as robbery, wounding with intent contrary to s. 18 of the Offences Against the Person Act 1861, rape and manslaughter. There has been a substantial increase in recent years in the number of lifers in prison (see Table VI), and a Home Office study shows that in 1977 lifers imprisoned for manslaughter accounted for 9 per cent and lifers imprisoned for non-homicide offences accounted for 14 per cent of the total lifer population. The increase in non-homicide lifers may in part be attributable to the

---

[1] As cogently argued by D. A. Thomas [1980] Crim. L.R. 565.
[2] *Flemming,* [1973] 2 All E.R. 401.
[3] Fourteenth Report, paras. 64–74.

addition in 1964 of arson to the list of "life-carrying" offences, but the only general explanation seems to lie in a shift in sentencing practice.[1] Discretionary life imprisonment was imposed sparingly in the 1950s, but during the 1960s a relaxation in policy took place. The leading case of *Hodgson*[2] shows the influence of a variety of factors. The judge clearly had the protection of the public in mind when imposing a life sentence, although his language certainly does not suggest the total absence of punitive intent. The accused had been convicted of serious sexual offences, including two rapes and one buggery in respect of which he received life sentences, the judge saying

"Having heard the evidence it is difficult to know whether you are to be regarded as a man or a monster. It is quite clear that the public, in particular women and girls, must be protected against you."

The case is of importance because, in affirming the life sentences, the Court of Appeal laid it down that life is justified when the offence or offences are grave enough to require a very long sentence; it appears, from the nature of his offence or his history, that the offender is unstable and likely to commit such offences in the future; and that, if the offences are committed again, the consequences to others may be specially injurious as in the case of sexual offences or crimes of violence.

The *Hodgson* criteria were not always rigorously applied, and the extent of the relaxation of the first criterion is demonstrated by the decision in *Ashdown*.[3] The case involved a large number of offences arising out of blackmail; at the trial a life sentence was passed for robbery (committed with a toy pistol). The second and third *Hodgson* criteria were satisfied but from the words of the Court of Appeal in upholding the life sentence it was apparent that the first criterion was not, since the Court accepted that the offences would normally have attracted a prison sentence of only five years. Thus *Ashdown* suggested that "a high degree of probability of future offences could justify the use of life imprisonment where the instant offence was not of the first order of gravity".[4]

There is evidence now of a more rigorous application of the *Hodgson* criteria. The trend has coincided with, and may well have been influenced by, the express opposition to life sentences of the Advisory Council on the Penal System. In their 1978 report the Advisory Council argued that indeterminacy of sentence often leads

---

[1] *Life-Sentence Prisoners*, Home Office Research Study No. 51, p. 35.
[2] (1967), 52 Cr. App. Rep. 113.
[3] (1973), 58 Cr. App. Rep. 339.
[4] See the commentary by D. A. Thomas at [1974] Crim. L.R. 131, and Appendix P to the report of the Advisory Council (*infra*).

to an increase in the anxiety and insecurity of life sentence prisoners, to an "alternation between optimism and pessimism as hopes of release wax and wane", and generally towards introversion and institutionalisation.[1] The concept of life imprisonment as a merciful sentence should certainly be banished: "a realistic determinate sentence, where it is feasible for the court to impose it, would put an end to this needless uncertainty". However, the Advisory Council stopped short of recommending the abolition of life imprisonment as a maximum for non-homicide offences, recognising that "there will be a few cases — for instance, the psychopath convicted of a number of offences of rape, where the gravity of the offence and the mental instability of the offender raise acute problems" and maintaining that in these cases executive release is preferable. Appropriate cases for life imprisonment, the Advisory Council held, would be "very serious" and "where questions of the mental disability of the offender arise, [life] should be imposed only in cases involving a serious psychological or personality disorder or a dangerous instability of character".

The adoption of a much more restrictive policy by the courts is evident from *Hercules*,[2] where the Court of Appeal declared that "life imprisonment is a very severe sentence which should be avoided whenever possible". And in *Pither* the Court adverted to:

> "the anguish which must be felt, even by the most hardened of young thugs, if they are in prison, sentenced to life imprisonment, and have no idea, as the years go by, when (if at all) they will be released."[3]

In that case the Court quashed the life sentence, which had been passed for "merciful" reasons, and substituted a sentence of five years imprisonment.

The second *Hodgson* criterion, relating to instability and likelihood of future offending, has certainly been interpreted more restrictively: the Court of Appeal has emphasised the need for "clear evidence of mental instability"[4] and for evidence that the offender is likely in future to be a danger to society.[5] It must be said, however, that the *Hodgson* criteria are imprecise and the Advisory Council's suggested criteria no less so. If the life sentence were to cease to be available for non-homicide offences, some judges would see a need to impose

---

[1] Advisory Council on the Penal System, Sentences of Imprisonment: A Review of Maximum Penalties, (1978), para. 226 and Ch. 11 generally. Cf. the Australian decision in *Veen* v. *R.* (1979), 23 A.L.R. 281.

[2] [1980] Crim. L.R. 596.

[3] (1979), 1 Cr. App. Rep. (S) 209 at p. 213.

[4] *Blackburn* (1979), 1 Cr. App. Rep. (S) 205 at p. 27; cf. also *Robinson* (1979), 1 Cr. App. Rep. (S) 108 and *Headley* (1979), 1 Cr. App. Rep. (S) 158.

[5] *Mottershead* (1979), 1 Cr. App. Rep. (S) 45 at p. 47; cf. *Thornett* (1979), 1 Cr. App. Rep. (S) 1 and *Spencer* (1979), 1 Cr. App. Rep. (S) 75.

very long determinate sentences that would raise in open court the issue of the justification for lengthening a particular sentence on the basis of a prediction of dangerousness, an issue which in life sentence cases is now effectively determined behind the closed doors of the Parole Board once the judge has imposed life imprisonment. If the life sentence is to be retained, the present judicial movement towards restricting the grounds for the sentence must be continued, and an attempt made to sharpen the *Hodgson* criteria. No precise formula could ever be devised; but, since the passing of a life sentence results in the transfer of power to determine length of sentence entirely into the hands of executive bodies and since the sentence in itself carries the risk of the psychological effects which so impressed the Advisory Council, there are strong and urgent grounds for seeking a more clearly circumscribed approach.

C. EXTENDED SENTENCES

Extended prison sentences are governed by s. 28 of the Powers of Criminal Courts Act 1973 (substantially re-enacting s. 37 of the Criminal Justice Act 1967). The object of the section is to enable the Courts to pass a longer sentence on a persistent offender than would be merited by the offence[1] without obliging them to add to the period of incarceration as greatly as in the case of preventive detention.[2] The object of the additional period is the protection of the public rather than the punishment of the offender. Although the accused's record is a relevant consideration in determining the length of his sentence, quite apart from any special statutory provisions, it ought not to be allowed to play a dominant role in the absence of such provisions for the simple reason that it is considered improper to punish a man again for an offence for which he was sentenced in the past.

Section 28 of the 1973 Act reads:

"(1) Where an offender is convicted on indictment of an offence punishable with imprisonment for a term of two years or more and the conditions specified in sub-section (3) below are satisfied, then, if the court is satisfied, by reason of his previous conduct and of the likelihood of his committing further offences, that it is expedient to protect the public from him for a substantial time, the court may impose an extended term of imprisonment under this section.

"(2) The extended term which may be imposed under this section for any offence may exceed the maximum term authorised for the offence apart from this section if the maximum so authorised is less than ten

---

[1] I.e. longer than would have been imposed if s. 28 had not been enacted, and not necessarily a term of imprisonment beyond the statutory maximum for the offence: *Director of Public Prosecutions* v. *Ottewell*, [1970] A.C. 642.

[2] P. 34, *supra*.

years, but shall not exceed ten years if the maximum so authorised is less than ten years or exceeds five years if the maximum so authorised is less than five years."

The conditions specified in sub-s. (3) concern the criminal record which it is necessary that the offender should have in order to be liable to an extended sentence. The sub-section should be consulted for details.[1] The offence must have been committed within three years of a previous conviction or final release from custody, and the offender must have had three previous convictions involving at least two sentences of immediate imprisonment since the age of twenty-one.

Under s. 28(4) the Court must, on passing an extended sentence, issue a certificate stating that the sentence is an extended sentence. The effect is that the prisoner may be released on licence when he would have been entitled to be discharged under the remission rules, i.e. after he has served two-thirds of the sentence if he behaved properly; the licence will remain in force until the date of expiration of the sentence. A person serving an extended prison sentence is entitled to be considered for parole like any other fixed-term prisoner, but, if he is granted parole, his licence will remain in force up to the date of expiration of his sentence whereas the ordinary parolee only remains under supervision up to the date when he would have been entitled to be discharged under the remission rules. The fact that a person serving an extended sentence is, even after release, under supervision for the entire period of his sentence is regarded as an important part of the system.[2]

The extended sentence has not been much used by the courts. Although in 1970 some 129 extended sentences were passed, numbers soon declined and in 1976 a mere fourteen were passed. The lengths of extended sentences have also tended to decline, so that some two-thirds are now for five years or less.[3] The principal effect of certifying such terms as extended is to ensure that the offender remains on licence until the expiration of the full nominal sentence. The extended sentence has typically been used for property offenders, especially burglars. Thus, like preventive detention before it, the extended sentence has failed to capture the "real menaces" at whom it was supposed to be aimed; the ordinary powers of the courts are sufficient to deal with them. The Advisory Council on the Penal

---

[1] Details of sentencing policy under s. 28 may be found in Thomas, *Principles of Sentencing* (2nd Edn., 1979), Ch. 8.

[2] *Gordon*, [1970] 2 All E.R. 385.

[3] Advisory Council on the Penal System, Sentences of Imprisonment: A Review of Maximum Penalties (1978), Appendix K.

System concluded in 1978 that

> "the extended sentence is demonstrably inappropriate to the problem it was intended to solve and unwanted by the courts who have been empowered to use it. It should be abolished."[1]

The virtual obsolescence of the extended sentence and the Advisory Council's recommendation do not, however, mean that the problems of sentencing persistent offenders will be solved. Courts often pass longer sentences upon persistent offenders, even if they justify this technically by stating that they are merely withholding from the persistent offender the credit which would have been given to an offender of previous good character, and so the question arises:

To what extent is it proper to punish a man more heavily for the sake of the protection of the public than he would be punished if he was not a persistent offender?

In the old days this question could be avoided by a resort to semantics: "preventive detention" was not the same thing as "imprisonment". Part of the sentence at any rate was not punitive, a fact which was thought to be emphasised by the "double track" system under the Prevention of Crime Act 1908 under which a habitual criminal's sentences consisted of two parts, a period of penal servitude for his last offence to be followed by a period of preventive detention for the protection of the public. Section 28 of the Powers of Criminal Courts Act 1973 at least refrains from subterfuges of this nature (for they must necessarily be regarded as subterfuges) unless there is such a significant difference between the conditions under which sentences of imprisonment and preventive detention are served as to justify the description of the latter as non-punitive in any realistic sense of that word. It is commonly suggested that an offender who has served the sentence considered by the Court to be appropriate to his offence has "paid his debt to society"; but a rigid adherence to this purely retributive notion leads to the conclusion that persistent offenders should be treated in the same way as first offenders. Up to a point the heavier punishment of a persistent offender can be justified on deterrent grounds. Many a parent must have said to his child after punishing him "If you do it again there is more coming"; but the question posed by the persistent offender is "How much more is morally permissible?" Cast into the terms of chastisement, it may well be thought proper for a mother to say to the errant child after giving it one smack "Next time it will be two", but everyone would agree that a time must come when the implementation of a threat of "more" would be

---

[1] Ibid., para. 115.

immoral. The question is: to what extent can a period of incarceration which it is impossible to justify on retributive grounds be justified by preventive considerations?

The answer to this question must depend on the nature of the offence and the likelihood of its being repeated. To take the second point first, no sane person would object to the compulsory detention of someone who had not even committed any offence if he felt quite sure that the person in question would commit a serious offence within a very short time if left at large; but the evidence would have to be a great deal more cogent than such evidence as there is that someone who comes within the provisions of s. 28(3) of the Act of 1973 will commit another serious offence shortly after discharge from a sentence of imprisonment appropriate to the offence for which he has just been convicted.

As for the nature of the offence, it may be argued that one reason for the failure of the extended sentence was that the qualifying convictions might be for *any* offences punishable with two years imprisonment. The legislation did not confine the extended sentence to offenders with records of persistent violence or persistent sexual attack, although it must be said that legislation which confined the qualifying convictions to a particular kind of offending (such as violence or sexual attack) might place an inadvisable premium on versatility. It would certainly be a step forward if it were possible to establish criteria of "offence-seriousness" which might be acceptable grounds for lengthening a sentence for protective purposes, and the proposals of the Advisory Council are considered below.[1] In the meantime, the courts continue to maintain the principle that the gravity of the instant offence sets a ceiling beyond which the sentence even for a persistent offender may not go. Thus in *Harrison*[2] an offender with a long history of offending and upon whom almost every penal measure had been tried was convicted of a single burglary. He had broken into the house of an elderly woman, leaving empty-handed when challenged by a neighbour. The Court of Appeal stated that the public was entitled to be protected from someone with such a bad record, but regarded the sentence of five years imprisonment as too long and reduced it to three years. Since, as Tables XIV and XVI show, only just over half of the burglars sentenced at Crown Court are given immediate imprisonment and since no fewer than 86 per cent of those prison sentences are for two years or less, the least that can be said is that the principle of the "ceiling" set by the gravity of the particular offence leaves Courts

---

[1] See p. 209, *infra*.
[2] [1979] Crim. L.R. 262, with commentary by D. A. Thomas.

with considerable room for manœuvre, and that it may well be less liberal in its operation than it appears in the abstract.

D. SUSPENDED SENTENCES

Suspended sentences of imprisonment were introduced into English law by the Criminal Justice Act 1967; they are now governed by ss. 22–27 of the Powers of Criminal Courts Act 1973. Provided the sentence is for not more than two years, the Court imposing it may direct that it shall not take effect unless, during a period of not less than one nor more than two years (the operational period), the offender commits in Great Britain an offence punishable with imprisonment. If the offender is convicted of such further offence, the appropriate Court (usually that in which the second conviction takes place)[1] must "activate" the suspended sentence unless of opinion that it would be unjust to do so, having regard to occurrences since the suspended sentence was imposed including the circumstances of the new offence. If the Court does consider it "unjust" fully to activate the suspended sentence, it may either activate the sentence for a lesser period, or vary the period of suspension to one not exceeding two years from the date of variation, or make no order with regard to the suspended sentence.

A suspended sentence differs from a conditional discharge in that the penalty for the offence in respect of which it is imposed is fixed and will normally become operative on the commission of a fresh offence within the prescribed period; a suspended sentence also differs from a probation order in the absence of supervision. Both a conditional discharge and a probation order allow the Court, if an offender is reconvicted during the currency of such order, to sentence him additionally for the original offence for which the discharge or probation was imposed. The suspended sentence differs inasmuch as the term of imprisonment which the offender can expect to serve if he is reconvicted within the operational period is laid down at the outset, and hangs like a sword of Damocles over the offender's head. When the suspended sentence was first introduced, the predominant reason was to encourage courts to suspend sentences which would otherwise take effect immediately, and thereby to reduce the prison population. To this end the 1967 Act *required* a Court to suspend a sentence of imprisonment of six months or less except in specified types of case. Mandatory suspension was abolished in 1972, largely as a result of opposition from Judges and

---

[1] Unless the Court is a Magistrates' Court and the Court which passed the suspended sentence was the Crown Court when the offender may be committed in custody or on bail to that Court, or the Crown may simply be notified of the conviction (Powers of Criminal Courts Act 1973, s. 24(2)).

Magistrates to any restriction on their sentencing powers, and so the Courts have a discretion whether or not to suspend any sentence of imprisonment of two years or less.

Imposition. The Court of Appeal laid it down in *O'Keefe*[1] that the correct thought process before imposing a suspended sentence is for the judge first to consider whether it is appropriate to pronounce one of the non-custodial measures discussed in section 1 of this chapter; then, if the answer is in the negative, to fix the term of imprisonment that matches the gravity of the offence, and finally to decide whether the case is one in which the prison sentence can properly be suspended. Thus s. 22(2) of the 1973 Act expressly provides that a court shall not deal with an offender by means of a suspended sentence unless the case appears to be one in which a sentence of imprisonment would have been appropriate in the absence of a power to suspend.

There is, however, considerable evidence that this elaborate process of reasoning is not always followed by the Courts. Suspended sentences are, as we shall see from the statistics, probably still imposed on offenders who before 1967 would not have received a sentence of imprisonment. And some Courts, particularly Magistrates' Courts, tend to impose a longer term of imprisonment when suspending the sentence than they would impose if it were to take effect immediately. This practice was firmly disapproved by the Court of Appeal in *Trowbridge*,[2] a case in which three men had been convicted for a planned theft of meat from a butcher's shop. Two of the men were given immediate terms of imprisonment, of 12 months and 6 months respectively, but Trowbridge received a suspended sentence of two years imprisonment. The Court could only surmise that the reason why Trowbridge received the longest sentence was that it was suspended, and this went against the principle that Courts should fix the appropriate length of sentence before deciding whether to suspend.

There is scant authority concerning the principles on which the judge should act in deciding whether to exercise this power. A material consideration will obviously be the extent to which suspension would fail to protect the public either directly by leaving the offender at large, or indirectly by serving as an inadequate deterrent. The previous good character of the offender will equally obviously be a relevant consideration,[3] but it is not clear how much further a court can go in taking personal considerations into

---

[1] [1969] 2 Q.B. 29; [1969] 1 All E.R. 426.
[2] [1975] Crim. L.R. 295.
[3] In *Trowbridge*, above, the favourable social enquiry report was given as a reason for suspending this offender's sentence.

account. Indeed, if the Court has taken full account of mitigating factors in calculating the appropriate length of the prison sentence, then there will be, so to speak, no mitigation left to be taken into account when deciding whether or not to suspend.

A suspended sentence being punishment, though no more than potential punishment, cannot be combined with a probation order for the same offence on principles which have already been discussed.[1] There is a statutory prohibition against making a probation order for another offence of which the offender is convicted at the same time as the conviction in respect of which the suspended sentence is passed[2] and it has been held that a suspended sentence for one offence should not be combined with an immediate custodial sentence for another offence of which the offender has been convicted on the same occasion.[3]

A suspended sentence may be combined with a fine for the same offence in cases where the permitted penalty is both a fine and imprisonment. We saw earlier that this is proper where the offender has made a profit out of the offence[4] and, where the sentence is suspended rather than immediate, the offender may be able to continue earning money and may therefore be in a position to pay the fine. There are, however, three difficulties with combining suspended imprisonment with a fine. First, the offender with means or with a well paid job may be able to secure for himself a shorter term of suspended imprisonment than a less fortunate offender, which itself would be contrary to principle. Secondly, where an offender who received a combined sentence has already paid the fine and is then reconvicted within the operational period of the suspended sentence, the extent to which the Court should take account of the payment of the fine in deciding whether it is "unjust" to activate the whole of the suspended sentence is problematic. And thirdly, whilst it may be proper to add a fine to a suspended sentence, it is never proper to add a suspended sentence to a fine. This was the error made by the trial judge in *Ankers*,[5] who first stated that "with considerable hesitation" he had decided not to pass a custodial sentence, then imposed various fines, and then said that "in addition" there would be a suspended sentence of six months imprisonment. If the process laid down in *O'Keefe*[6] had been followed, this should not have happened. But *O'Keefe* does not prevent

---

[1] P.19, *supra.*
[2] Powers of Criminal Court Art 1973, s. 22(3).
[3] *Sapiano* (1968), 52 Cr. App. Rep. 674; *Baker* (1971), 55 Cr. App. Rep. 182.
[4] See p. 26, *supra.*
[5] (1975), 61 Cr. App. Rep. explained more fully by James, L.J., in *Genese* (1976), 63 Cr. App. Rep. 152, C.A. at pp. 604–605.
[6] P. 56, *supra.*

a Court which has formed the view that imprisonment is appropriate, from going on to suspend that sentence and to add a fine to that suspended sentence. For the reasons given in this paragraph, however, that is a course which should only be adopted with caution.

Activation. About one-quarter of those on whom a suspended sentence is imposed commit a further imprisonable offence during the operational period. The correct procedure is for the court before which the second conviction takes place to begin by deciding what is the appropriate sentence to pass in respect of that conviction; it should then consider the question of activating the suspended sentence. Although the question of the propriety of the suspended sentence cannot be reopened, the circumstances in which it was granted may have to be reviewed so that the court should have a complete picture of the situation.[1] If, as will usually be the case, the suspended sentence is activated, it should generally be made consecutive to whatever sentence is imposed for the fresh offence.[2] In what circumstances is it, in the terms of section 23(1), "unjust" fully to activate the suspended sentence? The comparative triviality of the fresh offence is a ground for not activating, or not wholly activating, the suspended sentence[3] but the mere fact that the second offence is different in kind from the first is not a reason for refusing activation. In *Saunders*,[4] for example, a suspended sentence of six months for larceny was held to have been rightly brought into full operation on convictions for driving while disqualified, dangerous driving and assaulting a constable. A further reason for not wholly activating the suspended sentence is that the second conviction comes very close to the end of the operational period: the Court may decide to activate the sentence only in part,[5] or to activate it concurrently with (rather than consecutively to) the sentence for the second offence.[6]

If a probation order is made on the second conviction, a suspended sentence cannot be activated because the conviction does not count as such for the purpose of activating such a sentence;[7] nor can a suspended sentence be activated when sentence is deferred on the conviction of the second offence because the deferment may ultimately result in a probation order or a discharge.[8]

---

[1] *Munday* (1971), 56 Cr. App. Rep. 220.
[2] *Ithell*, [1969] 2 All E.R. 449.
[3] *Moylan*, [1970] 1 Q.B. 143; [1969] 3 All E.R. 783.
[4] (1969), 54 Cr. App. Rep. 247.
[5] *Beacock* (1979), 1 Cr. App. Rep. (S) 198.
[6] *Kilroy* (1979), 1 Cr. App. Rep. (S) 179.
[7] *Tarry*, [1970] 2 Q.B. 561; [1970] 2 A,, E.R. 185.
[8] *Salmon* (1973), 57 Cr. App. Rep. 953.

The courts have set their faces against a mixture of sentences. It has therefore been held that a judge who passes a sentence of immediate imprisonment for eighteen months for an offence committed during the operational period of a suspended sentence ought not to prolong that period so that it will remain operative after the termination of the prison sentence;[1] the right course will usually be to activate the suspended sentence and make it consecutive to the sentence of immediate imprisonment. Of course there are situations in which a mixture of sentences is inevitable. The same offender may be given a sentence of six months suspended for two years in January and he may be convicted in March of an offence, committed in the previous December. If the appropriate sentence for that offence is six months immediate imprisonment, the judge must pass it, but then there is no question of activating the suspended sentence because the offence was committed before the imposition of the suspended sentence.

Use. The evidence that, when they were first introduced, suspended sentences were used in cases in which the offender would not have been sent to prison in the absence of a power to suspend is provided by Table VII. The Table is reproduced from para. 23 of the Home Office guide to the Criminal Justice Act 1972 where it is estimated that, in the initial stages, only 40 to 50 per cent of those receiving suspended sentences would formerly have gone to prison, and this way well remain true today. Suspended sentences obviously flourish at the expense of the fine and, to a lesser extent, of probation. Since, on reconviction, the Court must activate the suspended sentence unless it is "unjust to do so", the result is that a number of the offenders receiving these sentences finish up in prison for longer periods than would otherwise be the case. Someone given a suspended sentence of six months in 1980 might be sentenced to six months immediate imprisonment in 1981 for an offence committed during the operational period of the 1980 sentence. On the activation of this sentence, the offender would receive a total of twelve months imprisonment whereas, if he had only been fined in 1980, he would at most go to prison for six months in 1981, and it is not improbable that the 1981 sentence would be suspended.

Four practical difficulties with the suspended sentence[2] are therefore (i) that it has frequently (and understandably) been treated by sentencers as a "half-way house" between immediate imprisonment and non-custodial measures, rather than strictly as a mitigation of

---

[1] *Goodlad*, [1973] 2 A,, E.R. 1200; 57 Cr. App. Rep. 717.
[2] See R. F. Sparks, "The Use of Suspended Sentences" [1971] Crim. L.R. 384 and A. E. Bottoms, "The Advisory Council and the Suspended Sentence" [1979] Crim. L.R. 437.

what would otherwise be an immediate custodial sentence; (ii) that, despite the decision in *Trowbridge*,[1] there remains a tendency (especially in Magistrates' Courts) to fix a longer term of imprisonment when suspending the sentence than when imposing it immediately; (iii) that when an offender is reconvicted during the operational period the second Court is tightly constrained by s. 23(1) and usually has to activate the suspended sentence (as it does in three-quarters of the cases where there is a reconviction), whereas it might not choose to send the offender to prison if its discretion were unfettered; and (iv) as a consequence of these factors, the suspended sentence has made little contribution to the reduction in the prison population which was originally its primary aim.

Reform. It is difficult to see what legislative action might be taken to remedy these difficulties short of abolishing suspended sentences altogether, or seriously impairing their credibility by providing that, if there is a conviction within the operational period, the Court should have a full discretion whether or not to activate the suspended sentence. The Advisory Council on the Penal System thought that no significant change in the law on suspended sentences was called for,[2] but the case for abolishing suspended sentences has been strongly argued by Professor Bottoms,[3] and the Government has apparently moved towards this view in its proposal that suspended sentences should cease to be available for offenders aged 17 to 21.[4] It is, however, hard to predict the effects of abolition: how would Courts deal with offenders on whom they now impose a suspended sentence? If they would sentence half of them to an immediate custodial sentence, then, since only one-quarter of suspended sentences are now breached and in only three-quarters of those cases is the suspended sentence activated, to abolish the suspended sentence would lead to more offenders receiving custodial sentences and to an increase in the prison population. Abolition of suspended sentences must, therefore, as Professor Bottoms argues, be combined with a new strategy for non-custodial sentencing if the overall position is to be improved.

E. SUSPENDED SENTENCE SUPERVISION ORDERS

Section 26(1) of the Powers of Criminal Courts Act 1973 provides that,

---

[1] P. 56, *supra.*
[2] Sentences of Imprisonment: A Review of Maximum Penalties, Ch. 13.
[3] The Suspended Sentence after Ten Years: A Review and Reassessment (Univ. of Leeds, 1979), see also (1981) 21 Brit. Jo. Criminol. 1–26.
[4] Young Offenders (Cmnd. 8045, 1980), p. 83, *infra.*

"Where a court passes on an offender a suspended sentence for a term of more than six months for a single offence, the court may make a suspended sentence supervision order . . . placing the offender under the supervision of a supervising officer for a period specified in the order, being a period not exceeding the operational period of the suspended sentence."

An offender in respect of whom such an order is made must keep in touch with his supervising officer (a probation officer) in accordance with instructions and notify him of any change of address. If he fails to do so he is liable to be summoned to appear before a Magistrates' Court and fined up to £50; but the order remains in force until the expiry of the period for which it was made unless the suspended sentence is activated in the meantime, or the supervision order is discharged on the application of the offender or supervising officer.

A suspended sentence supervision order resembles a probation order in that the offender is placed under supervision; but there are important differences. The order is not made "instead of sentencing" the offender and his consent to its making is not required. In other words, just as the suspended prison sentence is a punitive measure, the suspended sentence supervision order is also punitive.

Under present conditions the order will be the prerogative of the Crown Court for there are few offences for which a Magistrates' Court can pass a prison sentence for a single offence of more than six months.[1] The number of suspended sentence supervision orders has declined since the mid-1970s, and only about one in every eight suspended sentences imposed by the Crown Court in 1978 was accompanied by a supervision order.

F. PARTIALLY SUSPENDED SENTENCES

Section 47 of the Criminal Law Act 1977 provides that a Court which imposes a prison sentence of between six months and two years may order that part of it be served immediately and the remaining part be held in suspense. The provisions of s. 47 are complicated, but the aim of the partially suspended sentence is to exploit "one of the few reliable pieces of criminological knowledge— that many offenders sent to prison for the first time do not subsequently re-offend."[2] The partially suspended sentence is intended to provide a penalty which lies between a medium term of immediate imprisonment and a wholly suspended sentence, and thereby to exert "a double deterrent effect—the deterrent element in actual

---

[1] One of the main exceptions, customs offences, is not likely to call for supervision. The Home Secretary has power under s. 26(2) of the Powers of Criminal Courts Act 1973 to make sub-s. (1) applicable to any suspended sentence.

[2] Advisory Council on the Penal System, Sentences of Imprisonment: A Review of Maximum Penalties, para. 282.

custody and a postponed deterrence during the suspension period."[1] The provision, however, fails to incorporate any safe-guards against the kinds of practical difficulty to which the sus-pended sentence itself has given rise,[2] and this, together with the inherent complexity of the partially suspended sentence, gives grounds for some relief that s. 47 has not been brought into force.

G. PROLIFERATION OF PENAL MEASURES AND TRENDS IN THE USE OF IMPRISONMENT

Anyone who has read the foregoing account of the courts' sentenc-ing powers or, to be more accurate, "powers of disposal", over offenders of and above the age 21 can hardly fail to have been struck by the increase in the variety of penal measures in recent years. Yet others are suggested from time to time. For example, there is the proposal for empowering the courts to order weekend detention, contained in the Advisory Council's 1970 report on non-custodial and semi-custodial penalties. It was suggested that an offender in regular employment might be spared the disruption of his work which a full custodial sentence causes if he could be committed to prison for ten consecutive weekends. Weekend detention has re-cently been considered again by the Government, and similar mea-sures are used in New Zealand and some European countries, but the present view is that staff shortages and financial stringency would make it difficult to introduce a measure which might not, in any event, be imposed only on offenders who would otherwise serve an ordinary prison sentence.[3] The question naturally arises whether this proliferation of penal measures is desirable. It is submitted that the answer is in the affirmative, provided the purposes of each measure and the respects in which it differs from that of other measures is clearly understood. Official guidance to the courts on these matters by means of booklets such as *The Sentence of the Court* is therefore to be commended, and the wise words of LAWTON, L.J., quoted on p. 16, should never be forgotten. Against this is another argument which the complicated provision for partially suspended sentences brings strongly to mind. This is that the existence of an ever increasing number of penal measures with varying purposes presupposes an ability on the part of the courts to identify with reasonable accuracy the right offender for each measure, and, in the present state of knowledge, this ability is possessed neither by the judges nor by the penologists who might communicate it to the judges.

---

[1] *Ibid.*, para. 268.

[2] P. 59, *supra.*

[3] White Paper, The Reduction of Pressure on the Prison System (Cmnd. 7948, 1980), para. 112.

The adoption of new penal measures by Parliament has to a large extent been in the hope that Courts will impose fewer custodial sentences. A comparison of Table I with Table III shows that since 1969 there has been an increase in the use by the Crown Court of suspended imprisonment, fines and, of course, community service (which was not available in 1969), accompanied by a decline in the use of imprisonment. But the clear lines of that change become blurred when Table II is brought into the comparison, for that shows that in 1973 Crown Courts imposed proportionately fewer sentences of imprisonment than in 1978 (44 per cent compared with 47 per cent), and in 1973 proportionately more offenders over 21 were fined or put on probation. The introduction of community service orders has therefore coincided with (and, probably, contributed to) a proportionate decline in the use of other non-custodial measures, whilst the marked decline in the use of imprisonment between 1969 and 1973 has been reversed. Terms of imprisonment are becoming shorter,[1] but they are also becoming proportionately more frequent again, even if they have not yet returned to the 1969 rate.

There are those, some High Court judges amongst them, who consider that the decline in the use of imprisonment has been a contributory cause of the increase in crime which has taken place since the second world war. It is suggested that offences such as theft, and even burglary, are ceasing to be regarded as the heinous crimes they were once thought to be because they are ceasing to be offences for which people are sent to prison to the same extent as was formerly the case. On the other hand, few people would now maintain that prison has a reformative effect, and there is no evidence that longer custodial sentences are more effective in preventing reconvictions than shorter terms, or indeed that custodial sentences are more effective in this respect than non-custodial sentences.[2] The policy of the Lord Chief Justice in attempting to being about a lowering in the level of prison sentences[3] therefore provides some ground for optimism, although this is to some extent offset by the proportionate increase in the use of imprisonment between 1973 and 1978.

Section 3.—**Ancillary orders**

To adapt a well worn statutory phrase, all the orders mentioned in this section are orders which the courts can make "in addition to

---

[1] See, for example, Tables XIV, XV and XVI.
[2] See p. 96, *infra*.
[3] See p. 174, *infra*.

dealing with the offender in any other way". They are ancillary to the powers of disposal mentioned in the two previous sections, a fact which must suffice to justify the brevity of the following account, especially in its later stages.

A. RESTITUTION

Under s. 28 of the Theft Act 1968 (as amended by s. 6 of the Criminal Justice Act 1972), where goods have been "stolen" (an expression which includes the obtaining of the goods by blackmail or deception), and a person is convicted of any offence with reference to the theft (e.g. theft, robbery, burglary, handling stolen goods), the court by or before which the offender is convicted may order him to restore the goods or their proceeds to the person entitled to them or to pay a sum, not exceeding their value, out of monies found in his possession on apprehension. It was held in *Lewis*[1] that a restitution order may properly be made in respect of money (£5,445) found in the possession of one of a group of persons convicted of robbery, even though the money exceeds that person's share of the proceeds of the robbery (£2,000), since liability to repay the sum stolen (in that case, £8,000) is joint and several. Though restitution orders are quite common and very useful, the courts rightly only make them in the clearest cases and are most unlikely to do so when third parties may have a claim to property found in the possession of the accused.[2] In such cases the problem of the respective rights of the parties is best left for solution by the civil courts.

B. COMPENSATION

Section 35(1) of the Powers of Criminal Courts Act 1973 provides that,

". . . a court by or before which a person is convicted of an offence, in addition to dealing with him in any other way, may, on application or otherwise, make an order (in this Act referred to as a "compensation order") requiring him to pay compensation for any personal injury loss or damage resulting from the offence or any other offence which is taken into consideration by the court in determining sentence."

A Magistrates' Court's order may not exceed £1,000 for any offence of which there has been a conviction, and must tend to be less for offences taken into consideration.[3] The practice of taking offences into consideration is explained in the next chapter.

The words "loss or damage resulting from that offence" are apt to cover damage to clothing resulting from an assault, although there is

---

[1] [1975] Crim. L.R. 353.
[2] *Ferguson*, [1970] 2 All E.R. 820.
[3] S. 35(5), as amended by Criminal Law Act 1977, s. 60.

no charge under the Criminal Damage Act 1971, or the loss of payment for a night's lodging provided for someone who obtains a pecuniary advantage by deception, although neither the person nor the property of the victim has been injured. No payments may be ordered for loss suffered by a person's dependants in consequence of his death, or in respect of injury, loss or damage due to an accident arising out of the presence of a motor vehicle on a road.[1] To this last restriction there is an exception in the case of damage to property which is returned under a restitution order made in accordance with the provisions of the Theft Act 1968. Compensation may be awarded in respect of such damage, however it was occasioned.[2]

In determining whether to make a compensation order, and in determining its amount if such an order is made, the court must have regard to the means of the person against whom it is made.[3] The mere fact that the person in question has no means is not conclusive against making an order because his earning capacity may be taken into account; but the Court of Appeal has emphasised that compensation orders must be realistic—they should not require payments which stretch over too long a period,[4] nor should they usually require payments to begin on the offender's release from a custodial sentence,[5] since that may act as a temptation to commit further crimes.[6]

The compensation order is properly considered as separate from and additional to the punishment for the offence.[7] Thus it is wrong to pass lower sentences on co-defendants who are able to pay substantial compensation than upon other co-defendants who are not.[8] Equally, the court should not allow an offer of compensation from an offender to enable him to "buy his way out of prison".[9] Where a court makes a compensation order on the same occasion as an order, breach of which renders the offender liable to a term of imprisonment (such as a suspended sentence or probation order), there is at present[10] no power in the court to revoke the compensation order when activating or imposing such a prison sentence, although this

---

[1] S. 35(3)
[2] S. 35(2).
[3] S. 35(4), see generally R. Brazier, "Appellate Attitudes towards Compensation Orders" [1977] Crim L.R. 710.
[4] *Bradburn* (1973), 57 Cr. App. Rep. 948; *Grafton* (1979), 1 Cr. App. Rep. (S) 305.
[5] E.g. *Shenton* (1979), 1 Cr. App. Rep. (S) 81.
[6] *Wilkinson* (1979), 1 Cr. App. Rep. (S) 69.
[7] *Inwood* (1974), 60 Cr. App. Rep. 70.
[8] *Stapleton and Lawrie*, [1977] Crim. L.R. 366.
[9] *Inwood, supra*; *Copley* (1979), 1 Cr. App. Rep. (S) 55.
[10] Such a power was recommended by the Advisory Council in Sentences of Imprisonment: A Review of Maximum Penalties, para. 267.

result may be achieved through the cumbrous procedure of an appeal against the original sentences and orders.[1]

Many crimes are also torts, and there are accordingly many criminal cases in which the victim can sue the offender civilly. In practice civil proceedings are probably not very common. The requirement that regard must be had to the offender's means shows that there is still a difference between compensation in criminal and civil proceedings, for the means of the defendant are theoretically irrelevant to the assessment of damages. In general, a compensation order should only be made where the offender's liability is clear:[2] disputes should be left to the civil courts. But, strangely, it is arguable that the Act does empower the court to make a compensation order where there would be no civil liability.[3]

If civil proceedings are brought for injury, loss or damage resulting from a crime, the amount of compensation ordered by the criminal court may be reduced *pro tanto* if the civil damages prove to be less than those awarded by the compensation order, or if any property in respect of which compensation was ordered is recovered.[4] Damages in the civil proceedings must be assessed without regard to the compensation, but credit must be given in the amount actually awarded for any payments made under the order.[5]

Research into the use of the new compensation provisions by Magistrates' Courts in 1974 showed that a compensation order was made in 90 per cent of cases of criminal damage, 60 per cent of dishonesty cases resulting in loss, and 9 per cent of cases of assault or wounding. Most orders were for relatively small amounts, but as many as one-quarter of the offenders had not completed payment after 18 months.[6] The low proportion of orders in cases of personal injury may have increased in later years: the Home Office has conducted an experiment with the use by Magistrates of "compensation guidelines" for personal injury cases,[7] and the Magistrates' Association has issued a list of suggested starting points for the assessment of compensation in such cases.[8] Proportionately fewer compensation orders appear to be made in the Crown Court, but this may be because more custodial sentences are imposed in the Crown Court.[9] There is certainly evidence that, where

---

[1] *Wallis* (1979), 1 Cr. App. Rep. (S) 168
[2] *Vivian*, [1979] 1 All E.R. 48.
[3] Atiyah, "Compensation Orders and Civil Liability" [1979] Crim. L.R. 504.
[4] S. 37.
[5] S. 38.
[6] Home Office Research Study No. 43, Compensation Orders in Magistrates' Courts.
[7] See Vennard, [1979] Crim. L.R. 510.
[8] (1978) 34 The Magistrate 137–8.
[9] See Tarling and Softley, [1976] Crim. L.R. 422.

a compensation order is combined with a custodial sentence, it is difficult to enforce.[1]

C. CRIMINAL BANKRUPTCY

Section 39(1) of the Powers of Criminal Courts Act 1973 provides that,

> "Where a person is convicted of an offence before the Crown Court and it appears to the court that—
>> (a) as a result of the offence, or of that offence taken together with any other relevant offence or offences, loss or damage (not attributable to personal injury) has been suffered by one or more persons whose identity is known to the court; and
>> (b) the amount, or aggregate amount, of the loss or damage exceeds £15,000, the court may, in addition to dealing with the offender in any other way (but not if it makes a compensation order against him), make a criminal bankruptcy order against him in respect of the offence or, as the case may be, that offence and the other relevant offence or offences."

There must be a conviction in respect of the other offences, or they must be taken into consideration.

The offender is treated as having committed an act of bankruptcy on the day of the order, and any creditor or "the official petitioner" (the Director of Public Prosecutions) may thereafter present a bankruptcy petition. The offender's assets will then be administered and divided among his creditors by the official receiver as on an ordinary bankruptcy. The provisions of the ordinary bankruptcy law with regard to the setting aside of dispositions made by the offender before the criminal bankruptcy order will apply.

There is no doubt about the soundness in principle of the provisions of the 1973 Act. They are symptomatic of the tendency shown by the new law with regard to compensation orders to allow the criminal courts to play their part in stripping offenders of their ill gotten gains. The time has probably come, however, to enable the courts to play a greater part than the present law allows. There is a case for simplifying the imposition of an order where the offender has committed a number of small crimes with a high total profit,[2] and indeed for reducing the lower limit for criminal bankruptcy from £15,000 to £10,000.[3] The practical difficulty of recovering money from offenders has proved considerable, especially with offenders serving substantial terms of imprisonment, and among the various recommendations for reform made by the Advisory Council

---

[1] Softley and Tarling, [1977] Crim. L.R. 720.

[2] *Per* Lord Wilberforce in *Director of Public Prosecutions* v. *Anderson*, [1978] 2 All E.R. 512 at p. 514.

[3] *Ibid.*, and Advisory Council, Sentences of Imprisonment: A Review of Maximum Penalties (1978), para. 303.

on the Penal System is a proposal that the bankruptcy receiver should invariably be asked to indicate to the Parole Board at the moment of eligibility for parole (and at intervals thereafter) what state a prisoner's bankruptcy has reached—thereby to an extent encouraging co-operation in the execution of the criminal bankruptcy order.[1]

D. MISCELLANEOUS

In addition to making one of the three ancillary orders mentioned above, the courts have power, in the appropriate circumstances, to make five others: an order depriving the offender of property used, or intended to be used for the purpose of crime,[2] an order disqualifying the offender from driving where a motor vehicle was used for the purposes of crime[3]; orders disqualifying the offender from holding, or for the indorsement of, a driving licence on conviction of a variety of road traffic offences;[4] an order for costs;[5] and a deportation order.[6] The last three types of order are beyond the scope of a work of this nature, but a few words may be added about the first two, each of which was introduced by the Criminal Justice Act 1972.

On conviction by any court of an offence punishable on indictment with imprisonment for two years or more, the offender may be deprived of any property which was in his possession or under his control at the time of apprehension provided the court is satisfied that it had been used for the purpose of committing any offence, or was intended by the offender to be used for that purpose. In this context, the facilitation of an offence includes the taking of steps to dispose of property to which it relates or to avoid apprehension. The order deprives the offender of his rights in the property and, if it is not already in their possession, the police may take possession of the property.

A number of statutes contain particular forfeiture provisions. Section 27 of the Misuse of Drugs Act 1971 empowers a court, on convicting a person of an offence under the Act, to order the forfeiture of anything which relates to the offence. The House of Lords held in *Cuthbertson*,[7] a case where the offenders had made vast profits from the manufacture of drugs, that this forfeiture provision did not apply to an offence of conspiracy to contravene s. 4 of the Act, since conspiracy was not "an offence under the Act"; that the notion of

---

[1] *Ibid.*, para. 301.
[2] Powers of Criminal Courts Act 1973, s. 43.
[3] *Ibid.*, s. 44.
[4] Road Traffic Act 1972, s. 93 and s. 101.
[5] Costs in Criminal Cases Act 1973. The prosecutor's costs may be ordered to be paid out of central funds as well as by the convicted offender.
[6] Immigration Act 1971, s. 3(5) and s. 3(6).
[7] [1980] 2 All E.R. 401.

forfeiture concerns tangible property and is inapt to cover choses in action, such as the bank accounts in this case; and that where conspiracy is the only charge, no tangible thing can be said to "relate to" the offence, since conspiracy consists merely of an agreement.

The order disqualifying from driving where a motor vehicle is used for the purposes of crime can only be made by the Crown Court, and then only if the offender is convicted of an offence punishable on indictment with imprisonment for two years or more. The court must be satisfied that the vehicle was driven by the offender, or someone else, for the purpose of committing, or facilitating the commission, of the offence of which there has been a conviction. Facilitation is defined sufficiently broadly to cover a "get away" car as well as a car used for getting to the scene of the crime.

Section 4—**Mentally disordered offenders**

The questions why we object to punishing someone who was insane at the time of the criminal act or omission, and whether it makes sense to talk of degrees of mental responsibility or, if it does make sense to do so, how those degrees are to be measured, are considered in Chapter III. The purpose of this section is to explain and illustrate the additional sentencing powers possessed by the Court in the case of the mentally disordered offender.

It is necessary to distinguish between the situations created by successful pleas of insanity at the time of the criminal act or omission and cases in which there is evidence of mental disorder at the time of sentence.

When an accused is found to have been insane at the time of the act charged, he must be ordered to be detained in a mental hospital at Her Majesty's pleasure. The hospital is selected by the Home Secretary. The defence of insanity is governed by the much discussed McNaghten Rules, but it is successful in only a handful of cases each year (three in 1978) and can safely be regarded as obsolescent.

Mental disorder at the time of the act charged is also relevant when diminished responsibility is pleaded as a defence to a charge of murder and in cases of infanticide. A successful plea of diminished responsibility leads to a verdict of manslaughter while persons convicted of infanticide are punished as though they had been found guilty of manslaughter. In both these cases the Court can employ any of the measures mentioned in Section 1 or imprisonment up to a maximum of imprisonment for life. These cases are really instances of murder in mitigating circumstances, and, as the annual average of diminished responsibility cases in the years 1968–78 was only slightly lower than that for murder convictions (see Table VIII), pleas of diminished responsibility are far from obsolescent.

Two special kinds of order that can be made on the conviction of someone who is shown to be mentally disordered at the time of sentence are probation orders with a requirement of psychiatric treatment under s. 3 of the Powers of Criminal Courts Act 1973 and hospital or guardianship orders under s. 60 of the Mental Health Act 1959. These orders can be made in all cases in which the sentence is not fixed by law, i.e. in all serious cases other than treason or murder.

A. PROBATION WITH PSYCHIATRIC TREATMENT

Section 3(1) of the Powers of Criminal Courts Act 1973 reads:

"Where the court is satisfied, on the evidence of a duly qualified medical practitioner approved for the purposes of section 28 of the Mental Health Act 1959, that the mental condition of an offender is such as requires and may be susceptible to treatment but is not such as to warrant his detention in pursuance of a hospital order under Part V of that Act, the court may, if it makes a probation order, include in it a requirement that the offender shall submit, during the whole of the probation period or during such part of that period as may be specified in the order, to treatment by or under the direction of a duly qualified medical practitioner with a view to the improvement of the offender's mental condition."

The rest of the section deals with such matters as the treatment that may be specified and the limitations on the powers of the probation officer while the treatment is in progress. The section concludes with a provision that a Court shall not make a probation order requiring a probationer to submit to treatment for his mental condition otherwise than in accordance with the terms of the section. Although the number of psychiatric probation orders has declined from its peak of nearly 2,000 in 1973 to around 1,500 per year, it remains the most-used court order for the mentally disordered.[1]

B. HOSPITAL AND GUARDIANSHIP ORDERS

Under s. 60 of the Mental Health Act 1959, the Court may, for any offence punishable with imprisonment other than murder, make a hospital or guardianship order on evidence that the accused is suffering from one of four types of mental disorder, the last three of which are defined in s. 4 of the Act. They are mental illness, subnormality, severe subnormality and psychopathic disorder. As both the degree of disorder required and the degree of intervention

---

[1] Cf. P. Lewis, *Psychiatric Probation Orders* (1980).

authorised by s. 60 of the Act of 1959 is considerably greater than that required by s. 3 of the Act of 1973, the provisions with regard to the necessary medical evidence are more stringent; there must be the written or oral evidence of two duly qualified doctors, whereas a probation order containing a requirement of psychiatric treatment may be made on the written report of one doctor.

Where appropriate a hospital or guardianship order may be accompanied by any one of the ancillary orders mentioned in the last section, but not by a fine, probation or imprisonment. Under s. 60(2) a Magistrates' Court may make a hospital order without proceeding to conviction where the medical reports show that the defendant is suffering from either mental illness or severe subnormality.

The effect of a s. 60 order is that the offender becomes a patient at a mental hospital for one year in the first instance. The order is renewable by the responsible medical officer for one year, and thereafter for two years at a time. Release may come about through the decision of the responsible medical officer, by applying successfully to a Mental Health Review Tribunal, or by absconding and remaining at large for a specified period. The s. 60 order does not guarantee detention, since most mental hospitals are neither designed nor operated as secure institutions; but, under s. 65 of the Act, the Crown Court can make a hospital order subject to the restriction that the accused cannot be discharged for a fixed or indefinite period without the consent of the Home Secretary. It has been said that the s. 65 order should be subject to restriction in all cases in which the public requires to be protected against violence or sexual molestation, and that the period of restriction should be indefinite except where it is clear that a cure can be effected within a fixed time.[1] Most s. 65 offenders are detained in the special hospitals, which are secure institutions. The procedure for approving the release of a person detained under s. 65 without limit of time was tightened in 1973.[2]

Under s. 72 of the Act of 1959 the Home Secretary may transfer someone serving a sentence of imprisonment to a mental hospital if there is evidence on which a Court could make an order under s. 60. A s. 72 transfer has the effect of a hospital order, the prison sentence ceases and release is effected by the same means as release from a s. 60 order. But under s. 74 the Home Secretary may, by warrant, give the transfer the same effect as a hospital order with restrictions. Under s. 75 he may, on being notified before the expiration of the

---

[1] *Gardiner*, [1967] 1 All E.R. 895; *Toland* (1973), 58 Cr. App. Rep. 453.
[2] Cf. Report of the Aarvold Committee (Cmnd. 5191, 1973).

sentence that the patient has been cured, direct him to return to prison until he would be entitled to be released. If someone transferred under s. 74 is still in hospital at the expiration of his sentence, he is treated as an ordinary mental patient so far as his rights to release and to have his case reviewed are concerned. However, he must wait until expiration of the full nominal sentence: no account is taken of the remission he would have received in prison.

The sentence of life imprisonment is sometimes imposed on mentally disturbed serious offenders, and in these cases the offender is, so to speak, almost as much in the hands of the Home Secretary as he is in the case of a hospital order with indefinite restriction; but the Courts have very properly insisted on the distinction between punitive and non-punitive detention. In *Cox*,[1] a case in which the evidence would have empowered the Court to make a hospital order, the accused had killed his wife when in a depressed state and was convicted of manslaughter on the ground of diminished responsibility. In passing sentence of life imprisonment the judge said:

> "You are not a man whom I regard as meriting punishment as such, but in the public interest I am not prepared to put you anywhere near a place where you could be at liberty. And I therefore pass a sentence of life imprisonment, which will put you in the hands of the Secretary of State for Home Affairs in the future."

A secure mental hospital was available, and the Home Secretary soon exercised his powers under s. 72 of the Mental Health Act 1959 to transfer the accused to it. Nevertheless, the accused appealed to the Court of Appeal on the ground that he should have been made subject to a hospital order. The Court of Appeal substituted a hospital order with indefinite restriction, WINN, L.J., saying:

> "In a sense today the issue involved is capable of being described as academic since it will make no difference to the appellant, so far as his treatment is concerned, nor, one supposes, the place where he will be detained, whether he is subject to s. 72 of the Act of 1959 or to s. 60 and s. 65, but the Court can well understand that he, feeling himself no criminal guilt for the death of his wife, though no doubt he bitterly regrets it, and having heard the trial judge say that he did not think that he merited punishment, would naturally think it an injustice that he should be subject to a sentence of life imprisonment from which it follows that hitherto at Broadmoor he had been detained as a criminal lunatic. He attaches a distinction, and the Court sees that there is a rightful distinction, between being in Broadmoor under s. 60 and being in Broadmoor under s. 72."

We have seen that the courts are now declaring more stringent

---

[1] [1968] 1 All E.R. 386; 52 Cr. App. Rep. 130.

criteria for the imposition of life imprisonment,[1] and Table IX shows the recent decline in hospital orders both under s. 60 and under s. 65. The accepted reason for this lies in the "increasing reluctance to admit offender patients to local hospitals", stemming largely from the unwillingness of hospital staff "to assume responsibility for treating patients who are, or who it is feared may be, disruptive or violent",[2] and in overcrowding in the special hospitals. The result is that courts have frequently been presented with the problem of dealing appropriately with an offender who is mentally disordered but for whom no satisfactory placement can be found. Judges have felt constrained to meet such problems by sending the offender to prison. Occasionally the problem is later resolved by notification that a place in a secure hospital has become available: this occurred in *Officer*[3] where the Court of Appeal observed that judges took a judicial oath to do justice to all men and when they had to send men to prison because no secure hospital beds were available their judicial consciences were strained almost to breaking point. There can be little doubt, however, that the numbers of mentally disordered offenders in prison have greatly increased in recent years.[4]

C. REFORM

The various proposals for reforming the defences of insanity and diminished responsibility and the doctrine of unfitness to plead are discussed in Chapter III.[5] The courts powers for dealing with mentally disordered offenders were reviewed by the Butler Committee,[6] and certain reform suggestions were advanced in the previous Government's White Paper.[7]

Two themes of the Butler report were more effective identification of mentally disordered offenders, and increased efforts to divert them from the criminal process. To these ends the report suggested greater vigilance in the preparation of social enquiry reports, a power to remand offenders to mental hospital for three to six months under an "interim hospital order" in order to assess suitability for hospital treatment, and a prosecution policy which avoided the "expensive and harmful formalities" of court appearance for the mentally disordered unless a "useful public purpose" would be served by prosecution. The Butler report recommended that the

[1] See p. 50, *supra*.
[2] Review of the Mental Health Act 1959 (Cmnd. 7320, 1978), Ch. 5.
[3] [1976] Crim. L.R. 698; cf. also *McFarlane* (1975), 60 Cr. App. Rep. 320.
[4] See the discussion by Ashworth and Shapland at [1980] Crim. L.R. 634–40.
[5] See p. 162, *infra*.
[6] Mentally Abnormal Offenders (Cmnd. 6244, 1975).
[7] Review of the Mental Health Act 1959 (Cmnd. 7320, 1978).

s. 60 order should be largely unchanged, except that no hospital order should be made on a psychopathic offender unless an identifiable disorder was present and a therapeutic benefit could be expected from treatment. The White Paper endorsed that "treatability" limitation, and also proposed to halve the duration of a s. 60 order, so that it would be for six months in the first instance and renewable for six months. As for s. 65 orders, the Butler report recommended that they should be used more sparingly (only where there is a threat of *serious* harm), that they should always be without limit of time, and that release procedures should be further tightened. The proposal that all s. 65 orders should be indeterminate was strenuously opposed by MIND (the National Association for Mental Health), who argue that in general

> "When a mentally disordered person has been convicted of a criminal offence, society is justified in protecting itself by holding him in custody for a period proportional to the gravity of his offence. During that period, society should do all that it can to rehabilitate him by offering treatment in a psychiatric hospital. Whenever possible, this treatment should be given on a voluntary basis. Society should not, however, use a label as a justification for holding the offender for indefinite periods, because we cannot change the character of a compulsory measure merely by calling it 'treatment'."[1]

The White Paper dismissed this argument by reference to the greater unpredictability of mentally disordered offenders, and to the resulting need for protective powers in order to prevent the release of persons believed still to be dangerous. It is already the position that the sentencer must consider whether to impose a s. 60 or a s. 65 order, and he is therefore to some extent making a prediction about future dangerousness. The argument of MIND is that the judge should go further, imposing an indefinite s. 65 order for "specified offences which involve serious violence against person or property" where appropriate, but in all other cases in which he believes a s. 65 order to be necessary the length should be proportionate to the gravity of the crime committed. In its argument that there is no relevant difference between detention for treatment and detention for punishment, MIND minimises the significance of the social aim of the detention and the effect that aim has on at least some offenders.[2] But the essence of its argument, that real progress is necessary towards defining the class of offenders for whom indeterminate s. 65 orders may be justified, deserves careful and further attention.

---

[1] *A Human Condition* (1977), by Larry O. Gostin, Vol. 2, p. 96.
[2] Cf. the discussion of *Cox*, p. 72, *supra*.

Section 5—**Offenders under twenty-one**

Offenders under 21 are divided into children (under 14), young persons (14–17) and young adults (17–21). Children and young persons are generally dealt with by juvenile courts, and may therefore be referred to collectively as juveniles. Young adult offenders are dealt with in adult courts, but for them, as for juveniles, the courts have available certain special methods of disposal.

Three schools of thought on juvenile delinquency may be distinguished. According to the "welfare" school, the problem of delinquency should be approached in the same way as the problems of juveniles requiring care or supervision: whether a juvenile commits an offence or is caught committing an offence may be a matter of chance, and it is important to concentrate on the underlying social and other reasons rather than upon the single incident of a crime. This approach led to the passing of the Children and Young Persons Act 1969. According to the "modified welfare" school, the general approach to juvenile delinquency is rightly based on welfare considerations but in respect of a small group of serious or persistent delinquents the courts should be able to take strong measures of social protection. This approach has been urged by some critics of the 1969 Act, particularly Magistrates. According to the "justice" school, which appears to be gaining strength in some circles, juveniles should be accorded the same right to protection from error and arbitrariness as adults; whilst it is proper to shield them from the full force of the criminal law and to ensure that they do not mix with older offenders in the criminal process, it is imperative that the same procedural safeguards should be available in Juvenile Courts as in adult courts and the juveniles should generally not be placed indefinitely in the hands of a "treatment" agency which takes decisions about their liberty on the basis of "welfare".

Although the Children and Young Persons Act 1969 adopted the welfare approach in dealing with offenders under 17, its provisions have never been fully implemented and those provisions which have been implemented depend on the spirited co-operation of various agencies outside the statutory framework. Implementation began in 1971, and one of the principal aims was to reduce the number of juveniles brought to court. Thus the police have been encouraged to use cautions more widely, and to develop juvenile liaison schemes. In 1978 some 69,256 juveniles were cautioned in respect of admitted indictable offences, compared with 96,072 who were found guilty of indictable offences by the Courts.[1] Another aim is to place in the

---

[1] *Criminal Statistics, England and Wales, 1978*, Tables 5.2 and 5.5

hands of the local authority, rather than the Court, the power to determine the precise form of the care appropriate for a juvenile upon whom the Court imposes a care order. It is this curtailment of the Juvenile Court's power to ensure that particular juveniles are removed from home which has drawn criticism from the "modified welfare" school. A further aim of the Act was to extend the welfare approach more fully to young persons (aged 14–17) by restricting the occasions on which they might be prosecuted for an offence and by phasing out attendance centres, detention centres and borstal for this group; this provision has never been implemented and, as we shall see, may soon be repealed.

It will be apparent from the foregoing paragraph that the Courts have available for offenders under 21 certain sentences which are not available for adult offenders. Two methods of disposal which apply only to children and young persons are the supervision order and the care order. The *supervision order* places the juvenile under the supervision of a local authority social worker or a probation officer.[1] The Court may impose conditions similar to those which may be inserted into adult probation orders,[2] with the addition that by s. 12(2) of the 1969 Act the Court may (in effect) empower the supervisor to require the juvenile to participate in "intermediate treatment". Intermediate treatment consists of residential and/or non-residential schemes to involve the juvenile in "recreational, educational or socially valuable activities". Participation may only be ordered if a scheme is available locally, and for a maximum period of 90 days during the currency of the supervision order, which may be for up to 3 years. The *care order* places the juvenile in the care of the local authority, vesting in them the rights and duties of a parent.[3] The local authority will, after observation and assessment of the juvenile, decide where he should live and what treatment he should receive. Among the alternatives are that the juvenile should be allowed to continue living at home; placed with foster parents; placed in a residential community home; or placed in a secure community home.

Three further forms of disposal are in varying degrees available to the courts in dealing with juveniles or young adults. If convicted of an offence punishable in the case of an adult with imprisonment, persons between the ages of 10 and 21 may be ordered by a Magistrates' Court to attend an *attendance centre* for a specified number of hours which may not exceed 24,[4] and is usually either 12 or 24.

---

[1] *Children and Young Persons Act 1969, ss. 11, 12 and 13.*
[2] *See p. 15, supra.*
[3] Children and Young Persons Act 1969, ss. 7, 20 and 21.
[4] Criminal Justice Act 1948, s. 19.

Attendance centres are for the most part run by police officers in their spare time in schools, youth clubs or police premises; the emphasis is upon discipline, and the regime normally includes physical training and instruction on matters relating to good citizenship (although some centres offer instruction on vehicle maintenance and "do-it-yourself" skills).[1] There are about 100 junior attendance centres for juveniles and four senior attendance centres for young adults, and the court may only make the order if a place is available locally. Persons between the ages of 14 and 21 who have committed offences punishable in the case of an adult with imprisonment and are thought to be in need of disciplinary treatment under a brisk and firm régime may be sent to a *detention centre* for three or, in some cases, six months.[2] Detention centres are whole-time custodial institutions, and on release the offender is subject to after-care supervision for one year. There are six junior detention centres for young persons and eleven senior detention centres for young adult offenders.

Borstal training (so called because of the village near Rochester at which the system originated) also takes place at whole time custodial institutions. The sentence is indefinite in the sense that the period of custody is not fixed by the Court. It can only be for less than six months with the leave of the Home Secretary and it cannot be for more than two years.[3] The normal period is now less than a year. On release, the offender is subject to supervision on licence for one year. The sentence is generally available only to the Crown Court (although a Magistrates' Court may commit an offender to the Crown Court with a view to borstal training). It applies to offenders aged 15 and under 21, but may not be imposed on an offender under 17 unless the court is satisfied that no other method of dealing with him is appropriate.[4]

A. CHILDREN

i. *Children under ten.* A child under ten cannot be convicted of any offence but he may be the subject of care proceedings under the Children and Young Persons Act 1969. These are civil proceedings and may be brought in a juvenile court (i.e. a specially constituted Magistrates' Court with informal procedure) by a local authority,

---

[1] Home Office Research Study No. 60, *Junior Attendance Centres*, by A. B. Dunlop (1980).
[2] Criminal Justice Act 1961, s. 4.
[3] Introduced by the Prevention of Crime Act 1908 borstal training is now governed by s. 20(1) of the Criminal Justice Act 1948 as amended by the Criminal Justice Act 1961.
[4] Criminal Justice Act 1961, s. 1(2).

constable or other authorised person on the grounds, *inter alia*, that the child is either exposed to moral danger or beyond the control of his parent or guardian and also in need of care or control which he is unlikely to receive unless the Court makes an order in respect of him. The commission by a child under ten of what would, in the case of an adult, be a criminal act, may no doubt be treated, on the facts of a particular case, as evidence of moral danger or lack of parental control.

The orders which may be made in care proceedings are an order requiring the parent or guardian to enter into a recognizance to take proper care of the child and exercise proper control over it, this order can only be made with the consent of the parent or guardian; a supervision order; a care order, and, provided the appropriate medical evidence is forthcoming, a hospital or guardianship order under the Mental Health Act 1959.

ii. *Children aged ten to fourteen.* The juvenile court has both a criminal and a civil jurisdiction over children between the ages of ten and fourteen. Dealing first with the criminal jurisdiction, such a child may be found guilty of any offence provided the prosecution overcomes the rebuttable presumption that children aged between ten and fourteen are incapable of crime, i.e. in addition to proving the ingredients of the offence which would have to be established in the case of people over fourteen, the prosecution must show that the child knew that what he or she did was morally wrong.

On a finding of guilt the juvenile court may: grant an absolute or conditional discharge or, in theory, bind the offender over; or, provided the offence is punishable with imprisonment in the case of an adult, make a care order, or a supervision order, or an attendance centre order; or fine the offender up to £50; or, assuming that the appropriate evidence is forthcoming, make a hospital or guardianship order. The juvenile court may also make a compensation order or an order depriving the offender of property used for the purpose or facilitation of crime if the offence is punishable with imprisonment for more than two years in the case of an adult. Subject to their consent the offender's parents or guardian may be ordered to enter into recognisances up to a maximum of £200 for a maximum of three years to take proper care of and exercise proper control over him. The parent or guardian must pay any fine or compensation unless he or she cannot be found, or can prove that the offence was not due to his or her default.

In the case of a charge of homicide, the juvenile court must commit a child over ten for trial and, if he is found guilty of murder, he must be detained at Her Majesty's pleasure under s. 53(1) of the Children and Young Persons Act 1933; if he is found guilty of attempted murder or manslaughter, he may be detained for a specified time (including life)[1] under s. 53(2) of that Act, but a care or supervision order are possible alternatives. The juvenile court may commit a child over ten for trial if he is charged with an offence punishable, in the case of an adult, with imprisonment of fourteen years or more. If he is found guilty, and the Crown Court is satisfied that none of the other methods of dealing with him is suitable, he may be sentenced to be detained at Her Majesty's pleasure for a specified time, not exceeding the maximum period of imprisonment permitted for the offence. In these cases, detention is in such place as the Home Secretary directs; in practice it may be in the young persons' wing of a prison, but no one under seventeen may be sentenced to imprisonment as such.[2]

Children between ten and fourteen years of age in need of care may be brought before a juvenile court, exercising its civil jurisdiction, by means of care proceedings and the court may make any one of the five orders mentioned above as possible orders in care proceedings brought in relation to a child under ten. Where a child has committed an offence other than homicide, care proceedings are an alternative to criminal proceedings. But if care proceedings are brought in reliance on what is known as the "offence condition", the child must also be shown to be in need of care or control which he is unlikely to receive unless the Court makes an order in respect of him. Although the jurisdiction is civil, the rules of the criminal law apply to the establishment of the "offence condition".[3] Hence the case of the local authority or constable bringing the care proceedings must be proved beyond reasonable doubt, and the rebuttable presumption of the child's incapacity to commit a crime applies. The offence condition is only one of the six conditions mentioned in s. 1(2) of the Act of 1969 upon which care proceedings may be based; three of the others are that the child is exposed to moral danger, that he is beyond the control of his parent or guardian, and that he is not receiving proper education.

iii. *Reform.* The 1969 Act provides for the abolition of criminal proceedings in respect of children between the ages of ten and fourteen, except for homicide cases. However, the relevant provisions, which would more fully implement the welfare approach by leaving care proceedings as the only means by which all children in trouble might be compulsorily dealt with, have not been brought into force.

---

[1] *Abbott*, [1964] 1 Q.B. 489; [1963] 1 All E.R. 738.
[2] Powers of Criminal Courts Act 1973, s. 19(1).
[3] Children and Young Persons Act 1969, s. 3.

B. YOUNG PERSONS

i. *The present position.* Young persons may be the subject of care proceedings before the juvenile court, exercising its civil jurisdiction, to the same extent as children. The same five orders can be made, and the same conditions have to be fulfilled before they can be made. One possible basis of care proceedings in respect of a young person is the offence condition, including the need for care and control.

A young person may also be charged in criminal proceedings with any offence. He is usually tried by a juvenile court. There are exceptions in the case of joint charges involving two accused, one of whom is over and one under seventeen, with regard to homicide, and, at the option of the magistrates, other crimes, provided they are punishable with fourteen years imprisonment or more as the maximum. A young person under eighteen found guilty of murder is detained at Her Majesty's pleasure under s. 53(1) of the Children and Young Persons Act 1933, and a young person convicted on indictment of an offence punishable with fourteen years imprisonment or more may be sentenced to detention for a specified time under s. 53(2) of the Act of 1933; but care or supervision orders are possible alternatives in these latter cases. Detention is regarded as something wholly different from imprisonment and the dominant consideration in fixing its length is the protection of the public by the incarceration of the child or young person until he can be safely released and no longer.[1]

The following are the orders which a juvenile court can make on the conviction of a young person: absolute or conditional discharges or a bind over, care or supervision, fine of not more than £200, hospital or guardianship orders, attendance centre, detention centre, and, if he is fifteen or over, Borstal training.

Deportation apart, all the ancillary orders mentioned in the previous section are theoretical possibilities where appropriate except that criminal bankruptcy orders can only be made in the Crown Court.

ii. *Reform.* The present Government proposes to repeal the provisions of the 1969 Act (as yet unimplemented) which would remove the court's power to order that a young person should go to an attendance centre, detention centre or borstal. In its White Paper on Young Offenders[2] it proposes to retain the detention centre, reducing the minimum period to three weeks and the maximum to four months. The Government has already introduced into one

---

[1] *Bosomworth* (1973), 57 Cr. App. Rep. 708; *Mustafa Fuat, Storey and Duignan*, [1973] 3 All E.R. 562; 57 Cr. App. Rep. 840; *Ford* (1976), 62 Cr. App. Rep. 303.
[2] Cmnd. 8045, 1980.

junior detention centre an even brisker regime, in what has become known as the "short, sharp shock experiment"; and it has increased the number of junior attendance centres from 71 to 100. The community service order is to become available for dealing with juveniles aged 16, and the provisions for making parents pay the fines of juveniles or enter into recognizances are to be strengthened. The welfare approach is also to be modified in two further significant respects. The principle that a care order places the juvenile entirely in the hands of the local authority is to be breached by giving to the court, where a juvenile already in the care of the local authority as an offender is found guilty of a further imprisonable offence, the power to add a "residential care order" with the effect that for a fixed period of up to six months he must be removed from his home. Magistrates have long campaigned for such a power; the previous Government refused to concede it.[1] A second modification of the welfare approach is to be found in the proposal for a power in the court to specify the programme of activities which a juvenile under supervision should undertake. At present the court may empower the supervising officer to require the juvenile to undertake intermediate treatment and other activities; the new order would allow the court itself, on the recommendation of the supervising officer, to direct that the juvenile should undertake intermediate treatment.

C. YOUNG ADULT OFFENDERS

i. *The present position.* In spite of suggestions that they should be tried in special Courts in order to avoid contamination by mixing with older offenders and to render greater informality possible, young adult offenders are tried in the ordinary Courts. On conviction they are liable to any of the non-custodial orders mentioned in section 1 of this chapter; indeed, in 1978 the community service order was used more frequently for young adult offenders than for adult offenders. They are liable to be sentenced to attend at an attendance centre, to go to a detention centre or to receive Borstal training; but there is an important and much controverted restriction on the power of the higher Courts to sentence them to prison. Under s. 3(1) of the Criminal Justice Act 1961, a sentence of imprisonment shall not be passed by any Court on a person within the limits of age which qualify for a sentence of Borstal training[2] except

(a) for a term not exceeding six months, and

---

[1] White Paper, Children and Young Persons Act 1969 (Cmnd. 6494, 1976), paras. 23–30.

[2] Now 15–21, but s. 19(1) of the Powers of Criminal Courts Act 1973 contains an absolute prohibition on imprisonment for persons under 17.

(b) for a term not less than three years;
the latter figure is reduced to eighteen months in s. 3(3) in the case of someone who has served a previous sentence of imprisonment of not less than six months or of Borstal training.

The policy of the Act of 1961 was to abolish imprisonment for less than six months altogether in the case of persons under twenty-one provided sufficient detention centres became available, leaving Borstal training for those who merit a longer period in custody and reserving imprisonment for three years or more for really serious cases. However, sentences of six months imprisonment or less were to remain available until sufficient detention centres were built, which has never happened. The 1961 Act therefore imposes upon judges a rigid framework, which has been resented since its introduction. If the judge takes the view that the punishment should be greater than six months imprisonment but that the crime is not sufficiently serious to warrant three years imprisonment, he may be compelled to impose Borstal training even if he regards it as inappropriate. An illustration of such a situation is provided by *English*, set out at the beginning of the next chapter.[1] If a judge seeks to avoid the restrictions of the 1961 Act by imposing a sentence of three years imprisonment where the crime does not justify it, the Court of Appeal will reduce the sentence as being wrong in principle.[2] The Borstal sentence thus has to serve as the standard tariff sentence for offences which warrant a custodial sentence of longer than six months but less than three years. Yet the courts continue to use it in some cases for the purpose which was before 1961 regarded as its primary aim—as a rehabilitative, training sentence for an offender whose current offence would not normally justify a custodial sentence of this length but who might be expected to benefit from the Borstal regime. Thus in *Coleman*[3] the courts were confronted with the problem of a boy of 15 who had a history of institutional placements, two findings of guilt, and seriously disturbed behaviour including signs of violence to his mother and to himself. Whilst at an assessment centre he broke a pane of glass valued at £5. Finding him guilty of criminal damage, the juvenile court committed him to the Crown Court with a view to borstal training. The Crown Court received reports which indicated the suitability of Borstal, and the Court of Appeal upheld the sentence. It was urged on the Court that it was wrong to impose a penal sanction simply on the basis that it would be "good for the offender", but the Court replied by re-asserting that

---

[1] See also *Caird* (1970), 54 Cr. App. Rep. 499.
[2] *Lowe*, [1964] 2 All E.R. 116.
[3] (1976), 64 Cr. App. Rep. 124.

"There are times when although an offence is slight, an apparently disproportionate sentence is correct and, in the view of this Court, this is one. It is not only in the interests of society but in the interests of the offender himself that this particular appellant should be where he is."

This conclusion was made easier by the fact that Borstal is still regarded as a potentially rehabilitative sentence (this offender had been sent to Feltham Borstal, which has a "therapeutic" regime), and by the fact that in any event s. 31 of the Children and Young Persons Act 1969 would give a Court power to order the removal to Borstal of a juvenile whose behaviour was such that his accommodation in a community home would be detrimental to other residents.

   ii. *Reform.* In recent years there have been three sets of reform proposals. In its Report on Young Adult Offenders in 1974, the Advisory Council on the Penal System recommended that there should be a single custodial sentence for young adult offenders, the Custody and Control Order, together with a new Supervision and Control Order.[1] A principal aim of these proposals was to entrust greater control over the form, content and minimum duration of sentences to those in day-to-day contact with the offender, such as probation officers and prison authorities. The proposals met with widespread criticism, particularly on the ground that there is little evidence that penal administrators are able to select the "best" treatment for an offender or the "best" time to release him from custody.[2] The proposal that there should be a single generic sentence to replace detention centres, Borstal and imprisonment did, however, survive in the previous Government's Green Paper,[3] which also suggested that the category of young adult offenders should be extended to cover those aged 16. The present Government has abandoned the idea of a single generic sentence. Detention centres are to be retained as a separate and indeed the sole custodial sentence of four months or less for young adults, according to the White Paper on Young Offenders.[4] Sentences of over four months will be called youth custody: in a sense it will be a generic sentence combining Borstal and imprisonment for young adults, but Courts will be "guaranteed" that sentences of (provisionally) 18 months or less will be served under Borstal conditions. The court's discretion in sentencing will be restored by the long-awaited abolition of s. 3 of the Criminal Justice Act 1961. The period of supervision of those

---

[1] The Advisory Council's proposals were outlined and discussed in the second edition of this work, at pp. 73–5.
[2] See the debate between Professor Walker and Dr. Hood in [1975] Crim. L.R. 540–52.
[3] Youth Custody and Supervision—a New Sentence (Cmnd. 7406, 1978), discussed at [1979] Crim. L.R. 125–8.
[4] Cmnd. 8045 of 1980, discussed at [1980] Crim. L.R. 753.

released from detention centres and youth custody will be reduced to between three and twelve months, depending on length of sentence. The Government has already opened two new senior attendance centres, and three more are planned. One significant but unsung proposal is that the suspended sentence should be abolished for young adult offenders: the effect of this on the general use of sentences in this age-group, and in particular whether it leads to an increase in immediate custodial sentences, remains difficult to predict.[1]

---

[1] See p. 60, *supra*.

II

THE SYSTEM IN OPERATION

Someone of imprisonable age has been convicted of an offence punishable with imprisonment. In the last chapter we saw what choices lie before the judge; the purpose of the early part of this chapter is to indicate certain matters which will influence his choice. One such matter is that the offender asks for other offences to be taken into consideration; another is the information possessed by the judge about the offence and the offender; a third is the existence of fetters on a discretion which is sometimes wrongly thought of as limited only by the maximum term of imprisonment permitted for the offence. If, after considering other possibilities, the judge decides that imprisonment is the only thing, what considerations affect his decision on length? Is he entitled to take the possibilities of remission and parole into account? If the offender has been convicted of more than one offence, should the sentences be concurrent or consecutive? Other aspects of the problem of fixing the length of a prison sentence are considered in Chapter IV. Heads B–F of this chapter deal respectively with taking other offences into consideration, the information available to the judge, limitations on judicial discretion in the matter of sentencing, the effect of the possibilities of remission or parole, and the question of concurrent or consecutive sentences where there has been a conviction for more than one offence. The chapter concludes with some miscellaneous points in order to complete the picture of the English sentencing system in operation, but first let us consider the judgment in *English*. It is not a leading case, although it does illustrate very clearly some characteristic judicial thought processes.

A. THE JUDGMENT IN *ENGLISH*[1]
    English, a boy of 20, pleaded guilty to a charge of concealment of

---

[1] (1967), 52 Cr. App. Rep. 119.

birth. At the age of nineteen he had become responsible for the pregnancy of a girl. They discussed an abortion but decided against it; they also considered matrimony but decided against that because English thought that it would have an adverse effect on his prospects of a university education, a matter with which, according to the Court of Appeal, he displayed an unduly selfish concern. In the end they rented a flat in which the girl gave birth to a child with no one to assist but English. He said that his first concern was for the girl and that he wrapped the child up in a blanket and placed it by the fire. He later went home for the night and, when he returned in the morning, the child was dead. He took its body to his home and concealed it, but it was subsequently discovered by his mother; a charge of manslaughter was dropped. The trial judge sentenced English to Borstal training, taking the view that a prison sentence of six months, the maximum he was permitted to impose in consequence of s. 3 of the Criminal Justice Act 1961 mentioned at the end of the last chapter, was inadequate. The Court of Appeal substituted six months imprisonment.

The following is an extract from the judgment of the Court of Appeal delivered by WIDGERY, J. as he then was:

"This Court thinks that the proper approach is that taken initially by the learned trial judge, namely, had this matter arisen before the 1961 Act was passed, it would have been proper for the Court to consider whether any sentence other than imprisonment was appropriate. The Court would, we think, have dismissed without hesitation such matters as conditional discharge and probation, because this is a case which should be treated seriously, and a case in which punishment of some kind was undoubtedly merited. We think that the Court would also have dismissed at this stage the possibility of Borstal training, because this is not on the face of it a case in which Borstal training is likely to be advantageous to the appellant or to assist him in building his character and putting him on the right lines hereafter. We feel, therefore, that the Court would have been driven to the view that a sentence of imprisonment was the only appropriate sentence. Then comes the crucial question; what length of sentence would have been regarded as appropriate? In this connection the Court has had regard to the maximum permissible sentence for this offence, it is a maximum of two years imprisonment only. It is an offence which varies considerably in culpability; of its kind this is a bad example. Nevertheless we have here an appellant who is young, nineteen when the offence was committed; we also have an appellant who was previously of good character in every respect and, even allowing for the unhappy question of the selfish attitude, to which I have already referred, we have come to the conclusion that if one looks at this case apart from the 1961 Act, a sentence in excess of six months was not called for."

The judgment of the Court of Appeal shows how the first question the sentencer puts to himself tends to be "Can imprisonment be avoided in this case?"[1] The possibility of a fine was not mentioned. This may have been due to the defendant's lack of means but, in any event, the case was probably one which any Court would have considered to be of too serious a nature for a fine. The maximum permissible length of imprisonment evidently affected the Court of Appeal's view concerning the appropriate sentence. English's youth and good character told in his favour, but the case shows that it is a mistake to suppose that first offenders do not get sent to prison.

B. TAKING OTHER OFFENCES INTO CONSIDERATION

The practice of taking other offences into consideration originated at the beginning of this century in order to prevent the re-arrest of a prisoner at the prison gates immediately after his release. A man might be convicted of theft and sentenced to six months imprisonment for that offence, only to find a police officer waiting for him on his release with a warrant for his arrest on charges which either had not or else could not have been brought against him at his former trial. These might be charges to which he was always willing to plead guilty and which had been "hanging over" him to his great perturbation during his period of incarceration. That man's chances of rehabilitation were obviously the poorer for this treatment. Accordingly a practice evolved whereby it became possible for an offender to ask the sentencing judge to take other admitted offences into consideration when fixing sentence.

Obviously the practice can be abused by the police if, in their anxiety to get offences cleared up, they urge the defendant to "claim" offences he did not commit. The practice may also be abused by the offender who, secure in the knowledge that his sentence will not be vastly increased in consequence of his doing so, asks for offences which were in reality committed by someone else to be taken into consideration. These possibilities have led the courts to insist on a measure of formality in the practice of taking offences into consideration, and the House of Lords has declared that

> "If justice is to be done, it is essential that the practice should not be followed except with the express and unequivocal assent of the offender himself. Accordingly, he should be informed explicitly of each offence which the judge proposes to take into consideration; and should explicitly admit that he committed them and should state his desire that they should be taken into consideration in determining the sentence to be passed on him."[2]

---

[1] In consequence of s. 19(2) and s. 20 of the Powers of Criminal Courts Act 1973, the sentencer must ask himself this question at some stage in the case of an offender under 21 and an offender of any age who has not previously been sentenced to imprisonment. .

[2] *Per* Lord DIPLOCK in *Director of Public Prosecutions* v. *Anderson* [1978] 2 All E.R. 512 at pp. 515–16.

When taking other offences into consideration a Court cannot impose a sentence higher than the maximum for the offence of which the accused has been convicted. Thus, in *Tremayne*[1], the accused had been convicted of obtaining credit by fraud for which the maximum punishment was a year's imprisonment. He asked for twelve other offences to be taken into consideration. Six of these were thefts for which the maximum punishment was then five years penal servitude. It was held nevertheless that he could not be sent to prison for more than a year. The increase in the maxima for offences under the Theft Act 1968 will tend to prevent the recurrence of oddities of this nature, but there can be little doubt that, in many cases in which other offences are taken into consideration, the over-all result is far more favourable to the offender than the accumula-tion of sentences which would have resulted if he had been tried and convicted for every single offence. The number of offences taken into consideration is frequently great, amounting in one reported case to 513 other offences,[2] and requests with regard to numbers of offences in the '80's or '90's are by no means rare. There is no doubt that judges regard other offences taken into consideration as a ground for an increase in the sentence they would otherwise have given, although there are reported cases in which appellate Courts appear to have taken the view that one extra offence would not have made any difference.[3] The precise effect of the taking of other offences into consideration would be an interesting, though difficult, subject of statistical research.

The practice is in complete opposition to a rigid penal theory which prevailed in some quarters in the nineteenth century accord-ing to which there is an exactly correct punishment for every offence, and it is right that that punishment should be suffered in every case. The proponents of the theory did not add "even at the cost of all chance of the rehabilitation of the offender", but they might have done so. Something like the present practice is undoubtedly desir-able, but it is sometimes argued that the practice is too informal. It is, in general, wrong for other offences dissimilar to that for which there has been a conviction to be taken into consideration, but it can hardly be said that there is a fixed rule to this effect. The taking of an offence into consideration does not rank as a conviction; hence, it is the better view that there can be no plea of *autre fois convict* in respect of such an offence.[4] It is most unlikely that there would be a prosecution for an offence taken into consideration as long as the

---

[1] (1932), 23 Cr. App. Rep. 191.
[2] *Coplin*, [1964] Crim. L.R. 483.
[3] *Ames and Carey*, [1938] 1 All E.R. 515.
[4] *Nicholson*, [1947] 2 All E.R. 535; 32 Cr. App. Rep. 127.

conviction on which it was taken into consideration stands, but what if that conviction is quashed?[1] Points such as those which have just been mentioned have led to the suggestion that an offence taken into consideration should count as a conviction;[2] at any rate it is arguable that the time has come for an indubitably beneficial practice evolved by that judges to be regulated by legislation, but it must be admitted that, since the Criminal Justice Act 1972 made it possibe for compensation, criminal bankruptcy and restitution orders to be made with regard to offences taken into consideration, the need for legislation on the subject is not an urgent one; formerly such orders could only be made where there had been a conviction.

C. INFORMATION AVAILABLE TO THE JUDGE

i. *The offence.* Although the modern tendency towards individualisation of punishment has led sentencers to concentrate considerably more then they did in the past on the circumstances of the offender, the circumstances of the offence must always be of the utmost importance. Indeed there are cases in which they will be decisive. Notwithstanding its highly retributive overtones and rather "loaded" nature, the majority of English judges would probably agree with the following passage from a lecture by an Australian judge. After referring to the Streatfeild Report of 1960 which stressed the desirability of sentencers having the fullest possible information about the offender, he said:

> "It is pertinent to ask, however, what real effect information about the offender, however extensive, can have, by way of mitigation, upon the sentence of the Court where the prisoner has been convicted of a manslaughter little short of murder, or an outrageous rape, or a brutal and unprovoked assault involving grave injuries to the victim, or an armed robbery in company that yielded a large haul, or a carefully planned counterfeiting of the note issue, or a cunning and heartless fraud involving widespread loss among persons of small means. In such cases law abiding citizens look to the Courts to retaliate on behalf of the community. They expect that criminals who prey on the community or violate its fundamental values or, by their aggressive and rapacious conduct, imperil the average citizen's sense of security and confidence in law and order, should be made themselves to suffer in requital for the harm they have done to others."[3]

Where the judge takes account in sentencing of the fact that a particular offence is "rampant" or "rife", either in the country as a whole or in a particular locality,[4] he will rarely hear sworn evidence

---

[1] See for example *Brandon* (1969), 53 Cr. App. Rep. 466.
[2] See White, Newark and Samuels, "Taking Offences into Consideration" [1970] Crim. L.R. 311.
[3] *The Courts and Criminal Punishment* by Sir John Barry, p. 53.
[4] See p. 185, *infra.*

on the point and is most likely to take judicial notice of the state of affairs. As for the offence charged, the judge will probably learn as much as he needs to know about that where the defendant pleaded not guilty and the facts have been tried. Most defendants, however, plead guilty and so the question of the proper procedure for establishing a factual basis for sentencing arises; indeed, the question is also raised in some cases where the plea was not guilty, since the verdict may not be sufficiently precise for the sentencer.[1] Four examples of the problems which arise may be considered:

(a) *Ambiguous verdict*: where the accused has pleaded not guilty and has contested the case on a particular version of the facts, the jury's verdict (although satisfactory in law) may not be sufficiently informative for the sentencer. "Guilty of manslaughter", for instance, may sometimes mean either diminished responsibility, provocation or killing by unlawful and dangerous act. In *Hudson*,[2] for example, the prosecution case on an indictment for murder was that the accused had knocked the victim down and then kicked him. The defence case was that the accused had merely struck out in self-defence, and that death resulted from the victim's head striking the pavement. The jury returned a manslaughter verdict and the judge passed a sentence of seven years imprisonment. But the Court of Appeal held that in this type of case the jury "must be taken to have accepted the less violent of the two alternative versions of the struggle", and reduced the sentence. In such cases there seems to be no objection to the judge's asking the jury to state their view of the facts, although resort to this course was once criticised by the Court of Criminal Appeal[3] and there could be complications where the verdict was not unanimous.

(b) *Ambiguous plea of guilty*: a similar problem may arise where the accused pleads guilty but wishes to dispute the version of the facts put forward by the prosecution. In drug offences and strict liability crimes, for example, the accused's knowledge of certain facts may be irrelevant to conviction but crucial to the sentence. Thus in *Lester*[4] the accused pleaded guilty to seven strict liability offences under the Trade Descriptions Act 1968 arising from the sale of second-hand cars with false mileometer readings. The trial judge sentenced him to imprisonment on the basis that he "knew very well what had been done", but no evidence had been heard on the issue. The Court of Appeal held that this was wrong and quashed the sentence. If the

---

[1] See D. A. Thomas, [1970] Crim. L.R. 80 and *Principles of Sentencing*, pp. 366–72.
[2] (1979), 1 Cr. App. Rep. (S) 130.
[3] *Larkin*, [1943] K.B. 174; but see *Doherty* (1887), 16 Cox C.C. 306 and *Matheson*, [1958] 2 All E.R. 87.
[4] (1975), 63 Cr. App. Rep. 144.

trial judge had been minded to draw an adverse inference of this kind, the proper course would have been

"to indicate to counsel for the appellant what was provisionally in his mind, to point out the basis of the suggested inference, and most important of all, to offer counsel the opportunity, if he was so minded, to call his client to give evidence about this matter, as to which of course he would have been open to cross-examination by the Crown."

Indeed, the judge may be said to have a duty to clarify the facts where such a disagreement is apparent, and he may himself call witnesses for this purpose.[1] The principle in *Lester* ought equally to apply where a judge is minded to sentence one offender on the basis of evidence emerging from the trial of a co-defendant.[2]

(c) *Specimen charges*: where the prosecution bring only a few specimen charges against an accused whom they believe to have committed a series of offences, he should be sentenced only for the offences of which he is convicted, unless the other alleged offences are put to him and he consents to their being taken into consideration.[3] Thus in *Huchison*[4] a father pleaded guilty to an indictment charging him with a single act of incest with his daughter. Her deposition alleged more than one act, and the judge heard evidence on this question from her as well as from her father. The judge disbelieved Huchison and sentenced him to four years imprisonment. The Court of Appeal reduced the sentence to two years because Huchison had, in effect, been deprived of his right to trial by jury on the further allegations which he disputed. The right course would have been for the judge either to have allowed a voluntary bill of indictment to issue with regard to the further allegations, or to have given leave to amend the existing indictment so that it could refer to them. It is true that either procedure would be cumbersome, would lengthen proceedings and might be impractical if the allegations were not precise on such matters as dates; but where allegations are disputed by an accused, he should be entitled to a fair trial on the matter.[5]

(d) *Course of offending*: the same principle ought to hold where the prosecution invite the sentencer to treat the offence of which the defendant has been convicted not as an isolated lapse but as part of a course of offending. As HUMPHREYS, J., said in a case where the police alleged the commission of further offences:

---

[1] *Gravell*, [1978] Crim. L.R. 438; *Campbell*, [1980] Crim. L.R. 248.
[2] *Depledge*, [1979] Crim. L.R. 733.
[3] *Per* Lord DIPLOCK in *Direction of Public Prosecutions* v. *Anderson*, [1978] 2 All E.R. 512 at p. 516; cf. also *Wishart* (1979), 1 Cr. App. Rep. (S) 322.
[4] [1972] 1 All E.R. 936.
[5] Cf. the suggestions of Geoffrey LANE, L.J. in *Mills* (1979), 68 Cr. App. Rep. 154 at p. 163.

"Either the police could prove that statement, in which case they ought to have prosecuted the appellant, or at least have given him the opportunity of asking for those offences to be taken into consideration, or they could not, in which case they ought not to have invited the presiding Judge to increase the appellant's sentence in respect of felonies with which he had never been charged, and therefore had never had the opportunity of disproving."[1]

The fairness of this approach was overlooked in *Robinson*,[2] where the trial judge had sentenced a man convicted of possessing three grammes of cannabis on the basis that he was a large-scale supplier of drugs, having allowed police officers to state that their investigations led them to this conclusion. The Court of Appeal did not condemn this practice: they merely seemed concerned that safeguards were built into it. Thus WIDGERY, L.J., laid down that such allegations should be based on the first-hand knowledge of the person making them,[3] must be sufficiently particularised to enable the defendant to challenge them, and must be notified to the defence beforehand.

It appears that this practice of hearing evidence after conviction and before sentence, in order to settle not only disputed matters concerning the offence itself but also allegations of wider lawbreaking, has now established itself as part of the procedure of the English sentencing system. Perhaps it is justified to allow expedition thus to triumph over formal justice; but it is essential to ensure that adequate safeguards for the defendant are provided. It has been held that the judge is not bound to accept the defendant's version of disputed facts, but that he ought to do so if there is reasonable doubt about the prosecution's version,[4] and that he should not base the sentence on allegations from a victim which are uncorroborated in respect of certain points of difference.[5] The extent to which the ordinary rules of evidence apply to the presentence hearing remains unsettled; the greater the extent to which they apply, the less the advantage of such hearings from the point of view of expedition, but the fuller the protection for the defendant.

ii. *The offender.* Generally speaking, there are three types of report with which a court may be provided in order to assist it in passing sentence: a social enquiry report made by a probation officer, a medical or psychiatric report and a report made by a police officer on the offender's antecedents.

Section 45(1) of the Powers of Criminal Courts Act 1973 empowers

---

[1] *Burton* (1941), 28 Cr. App. Rep. 89 at p. 90.
[2] (1969), 53 Cr. App. Rep. 314.
[3] This requirement had been breached in *Wilkins* (1977), 66 Cr. App. Rep. 49.
[4] *Taggart* (1979), 1 Cr. App. Rep. (S) 144; *Kerr*, [1980] Crim. L.R. 389.
[5] *Long*, [1980] Crim. L.R. 315.

the Home Secretary to make rules requiring a court to consider a social inquiry report before passing sentence in specified classes of case. Such a report is defined as "a report about [the offender] and his circumstances, made by a probation officer or any other person authorised to do so by the rules". But, both before and after the coming into force of the Criminal Justice Act 1967 which contained a similar provision, the Home Secretary has preferred to make recommendations to courts by a series of circulars.[1] These circulars were originally designed to give effect to the report of the Streatfeild committee on the Business of the Criminal Courts published in 1960. As part of the movement towards the individualisation of punishment, it made a number of recommendations designed to give sentencers more information about offenders.

A social inquiry report should give information concerning the character and personality of the offender, his social background, educational record, employment and prospects. The Streatfeild report was to some extent innovatory in its unqualified approval of the inclusion in these reports of the probation officer's opinion on the likely effect of various sentences on the offender, even when such an opinion was not requested by the court.

"Some courts have encouraged probation officers to express explicit opinions on these lines but others have deprecated them on the ground that the probation officer was usurping the function of the court or might appear to others to be doing so."[2]

"Opinions of this sort, however frank and comprehensive they may be, relate to only one of the possible considerations in the court's mind: how to stop the offender from offending again. The court has still to consider the nature of the offence and the public interest, and it has the sole responsibility for the sentence which is ultimately passed. The probation officer should never give his opinion in a form which suggests that it relates to all the considerations in the court's mind. It is not a recommendation, but an informed opinion proffered for the assistance of the court on one aspect of the question before it. Provided that this is understood by all concerned, there can be no grounds for thinking that in expressing a frank opinion on the likely effect on the offender of probation or other forms of sentence the probation officer is in any way usurping the functions of the court."[3]

Probation officers have generally accepted this invitation to assist the courts: research suggests that around two-thirds of reports contain what the Home Office circulars, despite Streatfeild, refer to as "recommendations", and that in some two-thirds of those cases the

---

[1] See Home Office Circulars 28/1971, 195/1974 and 118/1977; cf. Brian Harris, "Recommendations in Social Inquiry Reports" [1979] Crim. L.R. 73.
[2] Para. 343.
[3] Para. 3346.

sentence of the Court accords with the recommendation.[1] The Court of Appeal has on occasion criticised a probation officer for including in his report a recommendation which is "unrealistic" in view of the gravity of the crime,[2] but such criticisms overlook the Streatfeild Committee's point that the officer's opinion relates only to one of the possible considerations in the Court's mind.

Social inquiry reports may be and, subject to the consent of the accused, often are, prepared before trial. The adoption of such a course has the advantage of avoiding an adjournment which, apart from the inconvenience it occasions to all concerned, tends to flout what is commonly regarded as an underlying principle of the English sentencing system, viz. the principle that sentence should follow speedily on conviction for all and sundry to observe. But pre-trial, as opposed to post-conviction reports have their disadvantages, especially when the accused intends to plead not guilty for, in many instances, the report should refer to the offender's attitude to his offence.

Social inquiry reports are obligatory in the juvenile court except in trivial cases,[3] any court can request a report in any case, ordering an adjournment where necessary, and both the Crown Court and Magistrates' Courts are recommended to procure social inquiry reports before sentencing an offender to a detention centre, to borstal, to imprisonment (even if the sentence is suspended) when he has not previously served a prison sentence, and before making a community service order or deferring sentence. If the offender is a woman a social inquiry report is recommended before she is sent to prison, whatever her past record may be, and such a report is also recommended as a normal course before putting an offender on probation. The liaison officer attached to the Crown Court notifies probation officers in the neighbourhood when offenders in certain categories are coming up for trial, so that the possibilities of a pre-trial report can be investigated. The categories are mainly traceable to the Streatfeild report and include anyone beneath the age of 31 at the date of committal for trial, anyone who has not served a custodial sentence since the age of 17, any woman and anyone subject to a suspended sentence.

Social enquiry reports have been the subject of much research in recent years,[4] and the optimism of the Streatfeild era can no longer

---

[1] Home Office Research Study No. 48, *Social Inquiry Reports: a Survey*, Chs. 2 and 6.

[2] *Blowers*, [1977] Crim. L.R. 51; *Smith and Woolard* (1978), 67 Cr. App. Rep. 211.

[3] Children and Young Persons Act 1933, s. 35(2); see also Children and Young Persons Act 1969, s. 9, dealing with information from local authorities.

[4] Most of the relevant research in summarised in Ch. 2 of Home Office Research Study No. 48, *Social Inquiry Reports*.

be sustained. Considerable variation has been found in the points on which reports comment, and this has led to the suggestion that social enquiry reports should be presented on a standard form which (whilst allowing further and broader opinions) would at least provide information on certain standard matters. This would reduce the selectivity which the Home Office research confirms:

> "It seemed that from the mass of information an officer collects, that which supports his argument or will benefit his client, is selected. Variations exist because of the needs of individual cases, the court for which the report is prepared, and the views of the report authors."[1]

There remains the vexed question of whether probation officers are qualified to express opinions about the effect of various sentences on the defendant. Officers may feel that from experience they are able to predict a defendant's reaction to probation or to community service, but it is doubtful whether they are equipped to give an "informed opinion" on his probable response to other measures, let alone on the question of whether one sentence is likely to be more effective than another.[2] Yet if the primary role of the social enquiry report were viewed, more conservatively, as providing the court with information about the offender, other questions would arise: Is it possible to lay down the matters on which information is and is not required? Might there not be a danger of overloading the probation officer with investigations, and the court with information? Can information gathered by probation officers be regarded as sufficiently reliable? Ought social enquiry reports to be subject to the same safeguards as other information tendered at the sentencing stage (including the ban on hearsay and the opportunity for examination of the officer in court), particularly if officers continue to be allowed to make recommendations for custodial sentences?

Medical and psychiatric reports may also be made before trial, and they too may comment on the accused's probable reaction to treatment. Cases often have to be adjourned in order that these reports may be obtained because the need for them may not become apparent before the trial.

The "antecedents" report is really a proof of the evidence which the police officer in charge of the case can give if called upon to do so after conviction. So far as the Crown Court is concerned the contents of the report are largely dictated by a *Practice Direction* of the Court of Criminal Appeal.[3] It should refer to the age, education, employment and domestic circumstances of the offender. It should

---

[1] *Ibid.*, p. 16.
[2] See para. iii, *infra.*
[3] [1966] 2 All E.R. 929.

summarise the previous criminal career of the offender, if any, and may contain statements about the accused's general reputation if known; but any other allegations of a general nature, particularly allegations of other offences, should be proved by the evidence of the maker according to the procedure described earlier.[1]

In some cases there will be a report from the governor of the prison where the offender has been awaiting trial and, in most cases, the judge may glean a few further details from the plea in mitigation made by the offender or his legal representative.

iii. *General efficacy of sentences.* What do sentencers know about the general effect of the sentences they choose? There are facilities recommended by the Streatfeild Report for judges to find out about the subsequent history of offenders they have sentenced. It does not appear that great use is made of them, and, in any event, the result of such inquiries could only be a highly impressionistic approach to the problem of efficacy. The general effectiveness of the different kinds of sentence can only be determined by research. The first edition of the Home Office handbook, *The Sentence of the Court*,[2] reported research into the effectiveness of sentences from which the fine emerged as by far the most effective (in terms of being followed by fewest reconvictions). Since then, however, the shortcomings of such research have increasingly been emphasised. The latest edition of *The Sentence of the Court* acknowledges that the earlier research was "rather crude" and points out that, if reconvictions are to be taken as a measure of effectiveness, then there is no evidence that longer custodial sentences are more effective than shorter periods, no evidence that the different custodial regimes (e.g. Borstal, detention centre, or a special therapeutic regime) are more effective than any others, little evidence that custodial sentences are more effective than non-custodial disposals, and little evidence that special forms of non-custodial supervision are more effective than ordinary supervision.[3] All these conclusions are carefully stated in terms of "no evidence" or "little evidence": as a Home Office study has shown,[4] the lack of evidence may to some extent be the result of insufficiently precise or crudely designed research methods and does not inexorably lead to the view that no penal measure is ever any more effective than another. For the practical purposes of the sentencer, however, the point is that it will assuredly be rare that either he, or a probation officer in his report, or indeed anyone else,

---

[1] See the discussion of *Robinson*, p. 92, *supra.*
[2] H.M.S.O., 1964, Part VI and Annex.
[3] 3rd Edn., H.M.S.O., 1978, Part VI.
[4] Home Office Research Study No. 35, *The Effectiveness of Sentencing* (by S. R. Brody), Part III.

can be confident that one sentence will be less likely to be followed by further convictions than another.

D. LIMITATIONS ON JUDICIAL DISCRETION AS TO LENGTH OF PRISON SENTENCES

It is all too easy to form a picture of the judge as someone who enjoys a complete discretion in the matter of the length of a prison sentence, subject only to the restriction imposed by the maximum permitted for the offence. Further limitations on judicial discretion in the matter of length of sentence have already been mentioned. At this stage it may be convenient to collect them together and to mention others. Those mentioned under the first two heads reflect the growing tendency to keep youthful offenders and offenders who have not been there before out of prison.

i. *Young offenders.* Section 19 of the Powers of Criminal Courts Act 1973 provides that no Court may imprison someone under seventeen, and that no Court shall sentence someone under twenty-one to imprisonment unless of opinion that there is no other way of dealing with the offender. Before doing so the Court must obtain and consider information about the circumstance and character of the offender. Magistrates' Courts must state reasons for their action; this is not a very exacting requirement because it is frequently satisfied in practice by the inscription of one word "gravity" in the appropriate register.

Section 3 of the Criminal Justice Act 1961 has already been discussed. It prohibits a prison sentence on someone between seventeen and twenty-one, even when the Court is of opinion that there is no other way of dealing with the offender, of more than six months or under three years. The intermediate sentence must be Borstal training. As mentioned at the end of the last chapter, s. 3 of the Act of 1961 is likely to be repealed in the near future.

ii. *First imprisonment.* Section 20 of the Powers of Criminal Courts Act 1973 provides that no court shall pass sentence of imprisonment on a person of twenty-one or over who has not previously served a sentence of imprisonment, unless of opinion that no other method of dealing with him is appropriate. Section 20 applies to a person on whom a suspended sentence of imprisonment has previously been passed, if that sentence was never activated. Before passing sentence of imprisonment in these cases, the court must obtain and consider information about the circumstances, and take into account any information relevant to the offender's character and physical or mental condition. A Magistrates' Court must give reasons for its opinion that no other method of dealing with the offender is appropriate.

Under s. 21 of the 1973 Act, no court may pass a sentence of imprisonment, Borstal training or detention in a detention centre, on someone who is not legally represented and has not previously been sentenced to imprisonment by a court in the United Kingdom unless he has applied for legal aid and been rejected on the score of his means, or refused to apply for such aid.

iii. *Miscellaneous statutory provisions.* The Bill of Rights of 1688 prohibits cruel or unusual punishments. The reference of course is to the excessive whippings and finings of Pym and Milburne; it is doubtful whether a prison sentence within the statutory maximum for the offence would ever be held to be within this prohibition. On the other hand, if *per impossibile* a judge were to sentence someone to imprisonment for life or for fifty years for the common law offence of public nuisance, it is conceivable that the punishment would be held to be cruel and unusual within the Bill of Rights just as it would undoubtedly be treated as cruel and unusual by common sense.

Section 18(2) of the Powers of Criminal Courts Act 1973 prohibits the imposition of a prison sentence (or fine) for an attempt in excess of the maximum permitted for the main crime, and s. 3 of the Criminal Law Act 1977 applies the same restriction to sentences for conspiracy to commit a crime.[1] And, as we saw in Chapter I, s. 23 of the Powers of Criminal Courts Act 1973 requires a court to activate a suspended sentence when the offender commits a further offence during the operational period, unless "of the opinion that it would be unjust to do so".

iv *Future developments.* Should sentencers be further restricted by legislation? There is little doubt that most sentencers resent statutory restrictions on their discretion, and there is equally little doubt that most of the above provisions have only a slight effect on sentencing practice. Indeed, the only device which appears to exert a restrictive influence is the last-mentioned, the "unjust to do so" formula relating to the activation of suspended sentences. If progress is to be made towards restricting the use of imprisonment, there is surely a case for re-drafting ss. 19 and 20 of the Powers of Criminal Courts Act in a similar way, and thereby leading the Court of Appeal to develop more explicit criteria for the imposition of the first custodial sentence.[2] Thomas has cogently argued that "the most effective device is that of the required disposition subject to excepting circumstances".[3] Yet amongst all the recent reports and proposals relating to the sentencing system there is hardly a trace of

---

[1] Sentencing for attempts and conspiracy is discussed in Ch. III, *infra.*
[2] A. J. Ashworth, "Justifying the First Prison Sentence" [1977] Crim. L.R. 661.
[3] D. A. Thomas, "The Control of Discretion in the Administration of Criminal Justice in R. G. Hood (ed.), *Crime, Criminology and Public Policy*, p. 147.

any suggestion that any of the statutory provisions mentioned above calls for reconsideration.

v. *The tariff.* The propriety of describing the system according to which offences tend to be graded according to gravity and to the circumstances in which the offences were committed as a "tariff system" is considered in Chapter IV. The point that is relevant here is that no judge would think of exceeding certain limits so far as length of prison sentence is concerned in the vast majority of cases. He knows of these limits in consequence of observing the practice of other judges when hearing appeals or dealing with applications for leave to appeal against sentence, and in consequence of conversations with other judges and attendance at sentencing conferences organised by the Lord Chief Justice. The judge of a superior Court also knows that any serious infringement of the tariff limits will be put right by the Court of Appeal if the case comes before it.

E. THE EFFECT OF REMISSION AND PAROLE

To what extent is it proper for a judge to allow for the possibilities of remission and parole when fixing the length of a prison sentence? The decided cases give a clear answer to this question. These matters should not be considered when punishment is the object of the sentence, but they may be considered when therapy or the protection of the public is the main aim.

In *Maguire*,[1] when sentencing the accused for a number of offences involving dishonesty, the Deputy Chairman of Quarter Sessions said:

> "In order to secure that you should be removed from criminal circulation for four years and eight months, owing to the provision that you automatically receive a remission of one third of your sentence for good behaviour, we have to sentence you to seven years concurrent."

The Court of Criminal Appeal reduced the sentence to one of five years because:

> "The business of a criminal Court is to consider what is a proper length of imprisonment to impose for a particular offence."

The exception to this general principle was established in *Turner*,[2] where the Court of Appeal approved a sentence of five years in a case in which the judge had been told that three years mental treatment was necessary. Four and a half years was, if allowance were made for remission, the minimum sentence that would achieve

---

[1] (1956), 40 Cr. App. Rep. 92.
[2] (1967), 51 Cr. App. Rep. 72; see further Ch. III, p. 160, *infra.*

that object:

> "It is no doubt true that when one is considering punishment, it is quite wrong for the Court to take into consideration matters of remission, but it has long been recognised that when one is considering not punishment, but considering reform or mental treatment, something which is in the interest of the prisoner, it would be obviously right for the Court to take remission into consideration."

A similar distinction applies to the possibility of release on parole,[1] which in any event is not a "right" in the same way as one-third remission.

F. CONSECUTIVE AND CONCURRENT SENTENCES

When someone has been convicted of more than one offence and the judge is minded to pass sentence of immediate imprisonment for each one, should the sentences be concurrent or consecutive? The answer is that the judge has a discretion, but the sentences must be concurrent when the offences arose out of the same transaction, and they are frequently made concurrent in other cases out of mercy. The Courts' notion of "the same transaction" varies somewhat,[2] but in principle offences committed on the same occasion or as part of a single enterprise will be so regarded, and a series of offences against the same victim may be so regarded. As we shall see, however, the Courts depart from the general principles in some types of case.

At one time a certain amount of uneasiness seems to have been felt over the question of the validity of consecutive prison sentences, although they were upheld in the eighteenth century.[3] Thus Lord HALSBURY once said:

> "What earthly right has a Judge to say 'You shall be sentenced to seven years penal servitude, the sentence to begin in ten years time'? If you cannot do that how does another sentence for another offence justify you in doing it?"[4]

He was referring to *Castro*[5]. In that case the Tichborne claimant was held by the House of Lords to have been rightly sentenced to two consecutive periods of seven years imprisonment for different perjuries against an argument that consecutive sentences for more than one instance of the same category of offence could not be made to total up to more than the maximum permitted for the offences

---

[1] *Eaton* (1969), 53 Cr. App. Rep. 118; *Cash* (1969), 53 Cr. App. Rep. 483; *Black*, [1971] Crim. L.R. 109.

[2] Compare the relative orderliness of the principles described in Appendix M of the Advisory Council's Report, Sentences of Imprisonment: A Review of Maximum Penalties, with the decisions discussed by Thomas, *Principles of Sentencing*, pp. 52–61.

[3] *Wilkes* (1769), 4 Burr 2527 at p. 2577.

[4] R. Heuston, *Lives of the Chancellors* 1885–1940, p. 14.

[5] (1880), 6 App. Cas. 229.

which, in the case of perjury, was seven years. The very same argument was raised and rejected in *Blake*[1] where three consecutive sentences of fourteen years imprisonment for offences under the Official Secrets Acts were upheld by the Court of Criminal Appeal.

Blake's case, together with *Wilson*[5] in which sentences of thirty years imprisonment on the principal participants in a gigantic train robbery were upheld, raises the question of the possible objection to very long prison sentences on the ground that they are inhumane. In Chapter III we will be considering various theories of punishment and questions of justice and desert will arise. It is important to remember, however, that particular types of punishment may be objectionable, not because they are unjust or undeserved, but simply because they are inhumane. If an arsonist who had deliberately burnt the inhabitants of a house alive were condemned to be burnt alive himself, one would not be inclined to say that the punishment was either unjust or undeserved, but it would none the less be wholly unacceptable by contemporary standards of humanity. As more evidence of the psychological deterioration resulting from long periods of incarceration becomes available,[3] very long sentences such as those passed on Blake and on Wilson and his fellow train robbers may come to be regarded as inhumane and unacceptable.

Be that as it may, humanitarian considerations certainly lie at the root of the courts' practice of making sentences concurrent in spite of the fact that the offences in respect of which they are passed cannot, by any stretch of the imagination, be said to form one transaction.

> "When a man is being sentenced at the same time for a number of different crimes, it is necessary, when fixing the length of each sentence, to take into account whether it is going to be made consecutive to or concurrent with other offences. Thus when a man is being sentenced for, say, four separate burglaries, it is not unusual for him to be sentenced to three years on each count concurrent. While each count, considered alone, merits three years imprisonment, twelve years would be too severe a punishment for the whole course of crime."[4]

Some of the reported cases on multiple sentences suggest, at first sight, that there is an excessive concentration by the Court of Appeal on keeping the record straight, and that some appellants are very lucky in consequence; but meticulous care where the liberty of the subject is involved and even an occasional error on the side of mercy can hardly be strongly condemned.

---

[1] [1962] 2 Q.B. 377.
[2] [1965] 1 Q.B. 402, p. 197, *infra*.
[3] E.g. Home Office Research Study No. 51, *Life Sentence Prisoners*, pp. 40 and 41 and references thereat.
[4] CAIRNS, L.J., in *Bentham*, [1973] 1 Q.B. 357; [1972] 3 All E.R. 271; 56 Cr. App. Rep. 618 at p. 626.

In *Smith*[1] the accused pleaded guilty to 15 offences of taking conveyances, obtaining by deception and forgery, and asked for a further 5 to be taken into consideration. He used skeleton keys to get into one car, which he took. He then took another car, from which he stole a credit card and cheque book. And then he used the credit card and cheques to obtain goods. The trial judge sentenced him to three years imprisonment concurrent on each of the counts, but the Court of Appeal held that this was the wrong approach. Although a total of three years was correct as a reflection of the overall gravity of the course of lawbreaking, it would have been fairer to impose a three year sentence in respect of the most grave offence and lesser concurrent sentences in respect of the others. The Court pointed out that it certainly would have been wrong to have imposed a large number of short consecutive sentences, a course which this judge did not take. But it was equally "not fair for an offender to have his record saddled, albeit concurrently, with a number of lengthy sentences merely because they did not increase the total". Not only, therefore, must the judge correctly assess the overall gravity of the offences and set a realistic total for the sentences; he must also fix the length of each of the concurrent sentences so that the seriousness of each individual offence is fairly reflected. Even though this second task does not affect the period served in prison by the offender, it ensures that his criminal record gives a reasonably accurate impression of the gravity of his offences.

Apart from the general principle that sentences for offences which do not form part of a single transaction should be consecutive, and the limiting effect of the requirement that the judge should not allow the total period of imprisonment to exceed what is proportionate to the overall gravity of the lawbreaking, the courts have developed the policy of imposing consecutive sentences in particular kinds of case for deterrent reasons. For example, a consecutive sentence will generally be imposed, despite the "same transaction" principle, where someone is convicted of committing an offence and carrying a firearm with intent to commit an offence[2] (otherwise the threat of additional punishment for the firearms offence would lose credibility), and where someone has been convicted of an offence and of a later offence upon a police officer in an attempt to avoid arrest.[3] It should also be borne in mind that the sentence will usually be consecutive where imprisonment is imposed for an offence for which an offender was conditionally discharged, put on probation or given

---

[1] [1975] Crim. L.R. 468.
[2] *Faulkener* (1972), 56 Cr. App. Rep. 594.
[3] *Kastercum* (1972), 56 Cr. App. Rep. 298.

a community service order, in cases where the offender is later brought before the court for committing a further offence. Where the original sentence was a suspended sentence, the court must activate it consecutively unless it would be "unjust to do so".

G. OBSERVATIONS OF THE JUDGES

Judges almost invariably make some remarks to the accused beyond announcing his sentence. Specimens of such remarks are scattered throughout this book and four examples are given below.[1] The remarks vary considerably in quality from what are almost certainly rare instances of sheer abuse[2] or mere fatuity[3] to statements which are obviously helpful as an explanation to the accused of what the judge is doing, or as an assurance to the local inhabitants that the law is doing its best, or as an explanation by the judge to the Court of Appeal and others who may be interested of the reasoning on which his sentence is based.[4]

If the offender is put on probation, granted a conditional discharge, given a community service order or made the subject of a suspended sentence, the Court is obliged by statute to explain to him in ordinary language the effect of its action. If that action is likely to be regarded as lenient, there may be those in Court (including reporters) who ought to know why it was taken, and the same is true of a sentence which might, at first sight, seem to be inordinately harsh.

i *Examples*. It seems probable that the nature of the judges' observations when passing sentence have undergone a subtle change. They used, in the main, to take the form of moral exhortations, whereas they now tend to be more in the nature of down to earth explanations.[5]

None the less the exhortation is by no means unheard of today. The following observations were made by an Assize Judge in 1969 to someone who had been convicted of robbery:

"You know if only you could avoid crime you would be a great deal happier. You are here, a young man with the world at his feet, and you

---

[1] We are indebted to the late Lord Justice James, to Lord Justice Lawton and to the Registrar of the Criminal Division of the Court of Appeal for having supplied the material from which the four examples are taken.

[2] "You are just an idle scavenger who is not fit to live in civilised society" (Stockdale, *The Court and the Offender*, p. 32); see also *Hodgson*, p. 49, *supra*.

[3] "What makes it all the worse is that you committed this beastly offence under one of London's most beautiful bridges" (*ibid.*, p. 34).

[4] For an interesting collection of judicial remarks on passing sentence, see the article by Spreutes, [1980] Crim. L.R. 486.

[5] We owe this suggestion to the Registrar of the Criminal Division of the Court of Appeal.

start and continue committing crime, coming before courts, having people condemn you, criticising you, and you going away with a chip on the
shoulder and then coming back again. I am going to send you to prison, I
have to for this offence, but I think it is time you reflected and said to
yourself, 'Well, it would be rather nice to go to a football match on a
Saturday afternoon and enjoy myself and not have to worry about police
and judges and crime'. You did not have a happy childhood, I feel sorry
for you. In many ways you did not get a lot of chances, and it is a terrible
pity to see there a good looking man with plenty of health and strength go
to prison for a long time. There is an after care service who if you go to
them will help you a lot, but unless you take my advice you are going to
be facing long periods of imprisonment throughout your life. I am going
to send you to prison for three years."

It is, however, probably true to say that the following laconic
observations to a recently divorced man of 62 convicted at
Snaresbrook Crown Court in 1979 of arson are more typical of
current practice:

"Stand up please. I take into account your age. I take into account the
fact (and I am prepared to regard you as such) that you are a man of
hitherto good character despite one appearance in 1977 of a petty nature
which I wholly disregard. I take into account your war service, and the
fact that this is an offence under section 1, sub-section 3 and not sub-
section 2 of the Act [sub-section 2 creates a more serious offence, involving known danger to the lives of others]. I take into account the fact that
you were depressed at the time of this offence because of the break-up of
your marriage and I take into account, lastly, the fact that in my view you
had taken alcohol at the time that this offence was committed. I give
you credit for all those matters. The fact remains that arson is a very
serious offence and there can only be one outcome. I am able to mitigate
the sentence that I must pass in view of those factors, but setting fire to a
terraced house and causing serious damage is a grave matter indeed. The
very least sentence I could pass upon you is one of two years imprisonment."

The following remarks made by an Assize Judge by way of explanation of a life sentence to someone convicted of manslaughter
who was probably mentally disordered are indicative of the importance attached, perhaps rather optimistically, by the judges to a
thorough explanation to the accused of what is happening. It is
understood that the enlistment of the aid of the accused's counsel in
these matters is becoming increasingly common.

"You have pleaded guilty to killing your little daughter who was not quite
two years of age. One has only to read the evidence in this case about the
injuries which she had suffered and your statement which accounts for the
injuries to be horrified that such a thing could happen in these days. The
reason why it happened is now tolerably clear. It is obvious that you
suffered from a tension home, tension between you and your wife, tension
between you and Collette, the sort of tension which the normal father puts
up with and can overcome. Unhappily in your case you suffer from an

inborn emotional instability and that instability it is quite clear was aggravated, made worse, by the blow which you had on your head during the fight in which you were involved whilst you were in the Army. Those factors brought about indirectly this dreadful crime. To that extent your moral guilt is made the less. Unfortunately, I have two duties to perform: one is the duty to find the correct punishment and sentence for you, and the other one is a duty to the public to protect them from people who cannot control themselves. I very much hope that in the course of time your particular disability will improve, as I am sure it will. I hope that some form of treatment for what you suffer from may be found. What I am going to do may sound harsh to you but in the end it is the best from your point of view, but it is a sentence which can continually be reviewed year by year, and that is a sentence of life imprisonment. The sentence of the Court is you go to prison for life. [To the accused's counsel], I have no doubt you will have the opportunity of seeing your client and perhaps explaining to him in less emotional surroundings the significance of that sentence."

The following observations were made after convictions on some 14 counts relating mostly to the obtaining of money and property by deception, some from the Department of Health and Social Security but mostly by passing worthless cheques for building materials and other goods. Before passing sentence at Southampton Crown Court in 1979 the judge heard evidence and read statements as to what the offender did with the money and property he obtained,[1] and his remarks on passing sentence included the following passage:

"There are two things to be said in your favour. The first is that you pleaded guilty to everything and the second is that you have been out of trouble since you were released from prison in 1973, and I give you full credit for that and I take it into account in the sentence that I pass upon you. You have set out in a statement, Exhibit 28, your account of where this money went. I am sorry to say I do not believe a word of it and I will tell you why. This is the third occasion in a case before me during the last year or so that I have been told the same story and it seems to have got round that that story is an explanation which may be accepted by a Court for the disappearance of large sums of money. I do not believe a word of it. I do not know where the money has gone really; you are the only person who knows. I am much more concerned with the people who have been deprived of it than who has had the benefit of it. As I say, you have been a successful defrauder over this period and I must send you to prison as the only proper way of dealing with you. . . The net result is that you will go to prison for three years."

ii. *Reasons for sentences.* Mr. D. A. Thomas suggested in an important article published in 1963[2] that judges should be obliged to give reasons for their sentences. He supported his suggestion by reference to four points. The first was natural justice, for every party is

---

[1] See the discussion at p. 92, *supra*, of the problems of establishing the factual basis for sentence.
[2] [1963] Crim. L.R. 243.

entitled to know the reasons for a decision; the second was rationalisation, for the necessity of giving reasons will add to the assurance
which we already have that the judge's choice of sentence will be a
rational one; the third point related to consistency in sentencing,
which would be enhanced by the obligation to give reasons; and the
fourth related to the right of appeal for "the giving of reasons is no
less important to the offender who wishes to appeal against sentence
than to the party affected by the decision of an Administrative
Tribunal or a Minister", and reasons are usually required in such
cases. Mr. Thomas conceded that it would be a waste of time to
require Magistrates' Courts to give reasons for imposing small fines,
but it is noteworthy that since 1972 they have been required to
record their reasons for imposing a sentence of imprisonment upon
an offender who has not previously served such a sentence.[1] An
amendment to the 1972 Bill which sought to extend the requirement
to Crown Courts in such cases was defeated, Lord Widgery (then
Lord Chief Justice) remarking that in nine cases out of ten the
gravity of the offence was the obvious reason. So far as the Crown
Court is concerned, a more difficult question is what a judge can be
expected to say by way of a reason for imposing a prison sentence of
a particular length. Cases where the judge can "steer by" the
statutory maximum for the offence will be relatively rare. Where
special circumstances, such as the offender's youth or previous
character (good or bad) are present, it is right for the judge to
indicate that he has taken them into consideration and it seems that
he usually does so, but what is he to say apart from this? The idea of
giving reasons for length of sentence only makes sense if there is an
accepted norm for each offence independent of special factors affecting the gravity of the offence or of mitigating or aggravating circumstances peculiar to the offender. It will be submitted in Chapter
IV that such norms do exist. Whilst the norms may not always be
precise, they surely form a sufficient basis for a judge to explain why
a particular sentence is placed at what the judge believes to be the
top, the middle or the lower end of the normal range. The argument
that in nine cases out of ten the gravity of the offence explains
everything is gradually losing force as the moral distinctions underlying sentencing practice are more clearly articulated and as sentencing principles become more sophisticated.[2] The fairness and
the consistency of the English sentencing system would surely be
improved if the giving of reasons for sentence were an obligation in
all Crown Court cases, and indeed in all cases where Magistrates'

---

[1] P. 97, *supra.*
[2] Pp. 174–6, *infra.*

Courts impose a sentence of imprisonment. To recite the fact that most judges in the Crown Court now do give reasons as an argument against imposing the obligation to do so in all cases is surely inadequate: if the practice has merit, as it does, then it ought to be universal.

H. SENTENCING IN MAGISTRATES' COURTS

Limited powers. The Magistrates have power to employ all the non-custodial measures, apart from the common law bind-over mentioned in section 1 of Chapter I, but their fining powers are limited by a vast number of statutes. It is impossible to make a useful generalisation with regard to the extent of these limitations; the prescribed maximum often does not run into double figures; but, in what is admittedly a most exceptional instance, it is as much as £50,000.[1] Where someone over seventeen has been convicted summarily of an offence "triable either way"[2] in accordance with the provisions of s. 16 of the Criminal Law Act 1977 he cannot be fined more than £1,000; where such a person is convicted of a summary offence in accordance with the provisions of s. 23 of that Act, he cannot be fined more than £500. The tendency of most recent legislation is to allow for the decrease in the value of money by increasing the magistrates' fining powers,[3] but many people think that the only way of dealing with this problem would be to relate fining powers to the cost of living index or the average daily income of a person in the position of the offender.[4]

The powers of imprisonment of a Magistrates' Court are likewise limited by numerous statutes. Maxima of two, three and four months are not uncommon, but the general position is that magistrates may not impose more than three months imprisonment for a summary offence or more than six months for an offence triable either way.[5] Consecutive sentences are possible and, where imposed on summary trial of offences triable either way, they may amount in the aggregate to a year's imprisonment.[6]

If, after convicting someone who has attained the age of seventeen of an offence triable either way, a Magistrates' Court is of opinion that the offender's character and antecedents are such that greater punishment should be inflicted than it has power to inflict, it may

---

[1] Prevention of Oil Pollution Act 1971, s. 2.
[2] This notion is explained in the Introduction, p. 2, *supra.*
[3] Criminal Law Act 1977, ss. 28–32.
[4] Schemes of this nature were rejected by the Advisory Council's Report on Non-Custodial and Semi-Custodial Penalties.
[5] Criminal Law Act 1977, ss. 29 and 28.
[6] Magistrates' Courts Act 1980, s. 133.

commit the offender in custody to the Crown Court for sentencing.[1] This does not oblige the Crown Court to pass a heavier sentence than that which the Magistrates' Court could have passed but it has all the sentencing powers it would have had if the offender had just been convicted before it on indictment.

Sitting as a juvenile court, a Magistrates' Court can make all the orders with regard to children and young persons mentioned in section 5 of Chapter I except an order for detention at Her Majesty's pleasure in the case of homicide and other grave crimes and an order for Borstal training. If a juvenile court is of opinion that there is no other method of dealing with him, it may commit an offender between the ages of fifteen and seventeen to the Crown Court with a view to a Borstal order being made.[2]

So far as offenders between the ages of 17 and 21 are concerned it is possible for a Magistrates' Court to commit them to the Crown Court if it considers that a Borstal sentence is appropriate. This is, however, subject to any legislation that may emerge in consequence of the recommendations contained in the White Paper on Young Offenders, discussed at the end of Chapter I.

The grounds on which a Magistrates' Court can make hospital and guardianship orders in the case of mentally disordered offenders differ from those of the Crown Court. In particular, a Magistrates' Court can make a hospital order upon a mentally ill or severely subnormal person without proceeding to conviction, and, for a hospital order subject to restrictions, there must be a committal by the Magistrates to the Crown Court.

Use of powers. Nearly 98 per cent of the criminal cases dealt with annually in England and Wales come before Magistrates' Courts. Therefore it is to be regretted that all the judicial citations in this book are taken from the Crown Court, Court of Appeal, their predecessors and the House of Lords; but, as the statements of magistrates when sentencing do not appear in law reports, they are difficult to collect and authenticate. These statements are, however, of considerable importance in the locality in which the magistrates sit. When published in the local press, they are read by the local inhabitants, and form the basis of much discussion, informed and uninformed, public and private. In fact such knowledge of our sentencing as is possessed by the ordinary man may well be largely based on what he knows of the doings of the local magistrates, eked out perhaps by occasional consideration of a sensational case.

The omission from this book of anything in the nature of a full and

---

[1] *Ibid.*, s. 38.
[2] *Ibid.*, s. 37.

separate discussion of sentencing in Magistrates' Courts is rendered less regrettable by the fact that the leading works[1] on the subject suggest that the system resembles in essentials that of the Crown Court. Within the permitted maxima, fines are imposed on a tariff basis according to the gravity of the offence and there is a statutory obligation to take the offender's means into consideration.[2] Within the permitted maxima, prison sentences are fixed on a similar tariff basis, and magisterial thinking on the length of sentence is apt, like that of some Crown Court judges, to begin with the maximum. As these are low there is little question of magistrates using imprisonment for reformative or incapacitative reasons, and considerations of individual and general deterrence are liable to be uppermost in a magistrate's mind when sending an offender to prison.

A comparison of Tables I, II and III shows that, for indictable offences, there was a fall in the proportionate use of immediate imprisonment between 1969 and 1973 but the rate had begun to rise again by 1978. The use of fines rose between 1969 and 1973, and was maintained at that level in 1978. The use of probation continued to decline, and the advent of community service has so far made little impression on patterns of sentencing adults in Magistrates' Courts.

Most of those convicted in Magistrates' Courts are fined—more than nine out of every ten non-indictable offenders and more than six out of every ten adult indictable offenders. Consistency in the levels of fines imposed by different benches has long been a matter of concern, and the Magistrates' Association has in recent years issued lists of suggested basic penalties for motoring offences. These lists, which deal principally with the level of fines, endorsement of driving licences and disqualification from driving, are merely put forward as starting points: as such, they may be modified by local benches and, when used, will often be increased or reduced to take account of any aggravating or mitigating circumstances in the particular case. The sentencer's discretion is thus preserved, whilst the use of starting points must certainly be welcomed as a contribution to consistency.

There has also been concern about variations in the proportionate use of imprisonment by Magistrates' Courts. It is doubtful whether this can be explained, wholly or even largely, by variations in the types of offence and offender with which different benches have to deal, and it is more likely that different penal philosophies play a

---

[1] For the law and the principles, see Brian Harris, *The Criminal Jurisdiction of Magistrates* (7th Edn., 1980); for empirical studies see p. 110, n. 1, *infra*.
[2] Magistrates' Courts Act 1980, s. 35.

significant role in explaining the variations.[1] Some take the view that the matter is so serious that the only suitable remedy would be to deprive lay magistrates of the power to pass sentences of imprisonment, requiring them to commit to the Crown Court offenders for whom they believe a custodial sentence to be necessary (as they now do when they believe that Borstal is necessary for an offender under 21), but this would certainly go against Parliament's intention to reduce the workload of the Crown Court, as manifested in Part III of the Criminal Law Act 1977. A less sweeping but more practical approach might be to attempt to draw up guidelines for the use of imprisonment by Magistrates' Courts along the lines of the Magistrates' Association's list of basic penalties for motoring offences. Such guidelines could not hope to deal with all kinds of offences and offender, but by suggesting starting points for certain common types of case they might perform a useful function. Direct guidance to Magistrates' Courts from the Court of Appeal is rare, largely because that Court only hears appeals from defendants who allege that a Crown Court sentence is too severe: the Court therefore has little opportunity to consider short sentences and, on matters of direct concern to magistrates such as when a sentence of imprisonment ought to be suspended, the guidance given by the Court has been less helpful than it might have been. The point is well illustrated by one of the line of recent decisions aimed by the Court of Appeal at reducing the length of terms of imprisonment. In *McCann*[2] the offender was discovered crouching at the rear of a shop whose burglar alarm was sounding, and he had tried to force open the shop door. The offender had only one previous conviction, which had resulted in a conditional discharge, and the Court of Appeal held that the sentence of two years imprisonment was too long "in view of the fact that this was a comparatively trivial type of burglary, not a burglary of a private house, and that the appellant did not seek to remove large quantities of goods and in view of the fact that the appellant showed some promise of not offending in the future". Yet, remarkably, the sentence was reduced only to nine months imprisonment—more than a Magistrates' Court could impose for a single offence. Does the Court of Appeal seriously expect Magistrates' Courts to commit to the Crown Court all those who commit equally trivial types of burglary, and of course all those who commit more serious varieties of the offence? Evidently the Court was not

---

[1] See the two studies by Roger Hood, *Sentencing in Magistrates' Courts* (1962) and *Sentencing the Motoring Offender* (1972), and Home Office Research Study No. 56, *Sentencing Practice in Magistrates' Courts* (1979), by Roger Tarling.
[2] [1980] Crim. L.R. 734, with commentary by Mr. D. A. Thomas; cf. p. 174, *infra*.

directing its attention towards Magistrates' Courts when determining this appeal; that, however, makes the decision more, rather than less, lamentable.

I. APPEALS AGAINST SENTENCE

i. *From Magistrates' Courts.* An appeal lies against the sentence of a Magistrates' Court to the Crown Court by the person convicted, whether his sentence was passed on his conviction of a summary offence or of an offence triable either way after a summary trial. The Crown Court may award any punishment which could have been awarded by the magistrates, whether it is more or less severe than the sentence actually imposed by them.[1] The Crown Court's decision is final except that there is an appeal by either the prosecutor or the offender by way of case stated to a Divisional Court of the Queen's Bench Division of the High Court on the ground that the order of the Crown Court was wrong in law.[2] Such an appeal lies directly from the magistrates to the High Court, an example being a case in which it was contended that they had erred in treating, or not treating, certain facts as special reasons for not disqualifying certain road traffic offenders from driving.[3] There is an appeal by either party against the decision of a Divisional Court on a case stated to the House of Lords subject to the leave of either court, and the certification by the Divisional Court that a point of general public importance is involved.

If the magistrates commit the accused to the Crown Court under s. 38 of the Magistrates' Courts Act 1980 on the gound that their sentencing powers are inadequate, or, under s. 37 of the Act, with a view to a Borstal sentence, the offender may appeal against the sentence of the Crown Court with the leave of the Criminal Division of the Court of Appeal, provided the sentence is of more than six months imprisonment or includes activation of a suspended sentence.[4]

ii. *From the Crown Court to the Court of Appeal (Criminal Division).* Anyone convicted on indictment by the Crown Court may appeal against sentence to the Criminal Division of the Court of Appeal, except where the sentence is fixed by law. The leave of the Court of Appeal is necessary, and it is sought in the first instance by means of an application to a single judge of the court, in practice to one of the

---

[1] Courts Act 1971, s. 9(4).
[2] *Ibid.*, s. 10.
[3] Administration of Justice Act 1960, s. 1.
[4] Criminal Appeal Act 1968, s. 10(3). There may also be an appeal against a deportation order or a disqualification from driving under the Road Traffic Act 1972.

Queen's Bench judges, and the consideration of these applications is one means by which the judges learn of each other's sentencing practices. An application may be made to the full court against the refusal of leave by a single judge.[1]

The Court of Appeal may vary the sentence to any other which the Crown Court could have passed but, and here there is an important contrast with the powers of the Crown Court on hearing appeals against magistrates' sentences, not so that, taking the case as a whole, the offender is dealt with more severely on appeal than in the Crown Court. For example, if, on charges of theft, the sentences were two and three years concurrent, and the conviction resulting in the three years sentence was quashed, the two years sentence could be increased to three years. The words "more severely" are those of s. 11(3) of the Criminal Appeal Act 1968 and they give rise to difficulty. Is a very large fine more severe than a very short term of imprisonment? Is a very long fixed term more severe than life imprisonment? Is Borstal more severe than eighteen months imprisonment? One suggestion is that it should be left to the appellant to decide questions of this nature: the Court should inform him of the sentence which they believe to be proper, and this sentence should be substituted for the original order only if the appellant consents.[2] The Butler Committee recommended that this procedure should be followed in cases where the Court of Appeal was minded to substitute a hospital order for a sentence of imprisonment, and *vice versa*,[3] and there is certainly an argument for applying the procedure to other cases, such as the substitution of a long fixed term of imprisonment for life imprisonment.

The issue might be less controversial if the powers of the Court of Appeal and the role of the prosecution in sentencing were different. Under the Criminal Appeal Act 1907 the Court of Criminal Appeal had power to increase sentence. The power was exercised sparingly. It was regarded by many as a useful sanction against vexatious appeals, but it is doubtful whether it is a proper means to that end, since it might also discourage genuine appeals.[4] A further question concerns the desirability of giving the prosecution a right of appeal against sentence. It has such a right in some Commonwealth jurisdictions. A point in favour of granting the right is that the Court of Appeal tends only to vary sentences where a question of principle is involved.

---

[1] *Ibid.*, s. 31.
[2] Cf. Stephen White at (1973) 36 M.L.R. 396.
[3] Mentally Abnormal Offenders (Cmnd. 6244), paras. 13.23 to 13.26.
[4] Cf. Stephen White, "Deterrence and Criminal Appeals" (1975) 38 M.L.R. 369.

"This Court never interferes with the discretion of the Court merely on the ground that the Court might have passed a different sentence; for this Court to revise a sentence there must be some error in principle."[1]

Errors in principle can lead to undue leniency just as much as they can lead to undue severity, and some judges certainly think that a fair amount of "under-sentencing" goes unnoticed because the offender does not and the prosecution cannot appeal. A point against granting a right of appeal against sentence to the prosecution is that it might militate against the image of the detached prosecuting counsel which is usually counted among the blessings of the English criminal process. If the prosecution were to have a right of appeal against sentence, why should prosecuting counsel not urge the judge to pass a particular sentence at the trial? This would surely be a logical development, however momentous a departure from the English tradition it might appear. Many English lawyers would find repulsive the idea of a judge having to hold the ring between a prosecuting counsel pressing for a substantial term of imprisonment and defence counsel arguing for a probation order or suspended sentence. But, as the principles of sentencing become more highly developed and as reference to decided cases on sentencing becomes more straightforward, it surely becomes easier to regard counsel as performing the same function at the sentencing stage as they perform during the trial. The present system permits defence counsel to engage in this exercise but prohibits the prosecution from doing so; if there is an imbalance, at least that imbalance redounds to the advantage of the individual defendant.[2]

On a point of law either the prosecution or the defence has a right of appeal from the Criminal Division of the Court of Appeal to the House of Lords, but this is subject to the leave of either of those Courts, and to the certification by the Court of Appeal that a point of general public importance is involved. An example of a point of law in the matter of sentencing is that taken by the defence in *Verrier* v. *The Director of Public Prosecutions*,[3] namely, where a conspiracy to commit a crime can be punished by a longer term of imprisonment than the maximum permitted for that crime. The question of the justification of the affirmative answer given by the House of Lords is considered in the next chapter.

To what extent are appeals against sentence a necessity in the sense that a system which fails to make allowance for them can be

---

[1] Lord HEWART, C.J. in *Gumbs* (1926), 19 Cr. App. Rep. 74.
[2] For extended argument on these points, see D. A. Thomas, [1972] Crim. L.R. 288; A. J. Ashworth, [1979] Crim. L.R. 480, and G. J. Zellick, [1979] Crim. L.R. 493, and M. King, [1979] Crim. L.R. 775.
[3] [1967] 2 A.C. 195.

justly criticised? There may be no doubt of the necessity of appeals against sentences under a system like the present English one. In the first place the supervisory jurisdiction of the Court of Appeal where matters of principle are concerned is essential in the interests of uniformity; secondly, the appeal from a single trial judge to the Court of Appeal is one to a tribunal of at least three and there is a lot to be said for the possibility of a resort to a multiple tribunal. Save in the case of a Stipendiary Magistrate, there is no question of a resort from the one to the many in the case of appeals from Magistrates' Courts, but, again with the exception of appeals from Stipendiary Magistrates, it is an appeal from laymen to lawyers. Should a time ever come when sentencing, or a large part of it, was done by boards consisting of prison governors, psychiatrists and the like as well as judges, it is by no means obvious that an appeal against sentence would be a necessity. It could only be to another board, and there is no particular reason for supposing that the second bite at the cherry would be better than the first.

J. THE PREROGATIVE OF MERCY

For the sake of completeness it should be pointed out that the exercise of the royal prerogative of mercy in relation to sentencing is not, as some students appear to imagine, confined to the commutation of the death sentence to imprisonment for life. To quote from the late Sir Frank Newsam's book on *The Home Office*:[1]

"A prisoner who comes to the assistance of a prison officer attacked by other prisoners may be rewarded by some reduction of sentence; a man who is nearing the end of a long sentence may be released a few weeks before his normal date in order to be with his dying wife; or a Bench of Magistrates may find that they were inadequately informed about a defendant's means when they imposed a fine and ask the Home Secretary to involve the prerogative to reduce the fine to the amount which they now think appropriate. The Home Secretary is always ready to consult the Court which passed the original sentence, but in many of these cases the considerations which governed the original decision of the judicial authority have little relevance to questions which the Home Secretary has to consider in advising on the exercise of the prerogative of mercy."

The general accuracy of this statement is confirmed by the criminal statistics for 1978. There were 92 free pardons, 183 remissions of parts of custodial sentences and 35 remissions of fines. Some 30 of the free pardons related to convictions for speeding on two roads which turned out not to be restricted, while the remissions of imprisonment included cases in which assistance had been rendered to

---

[1] *The Home Office* by Sir Frank Newsam, p. 121.

the authorities and releases on medical or other compassionate grounds.

K. PLEA BARGAINING

In the context of sentencing practice a "plea bargain" refers to any case in which the accused pleads guilty after something said by or on behalf of the judge or prosecution which led him to believe that he would receive a lighter sentence than would have been the case if he had pleaded not guilty. It has been declared by Lord SCARMAN that "Plea-bargaining has no place in the English criminal law",[1] but a constant stream of appeals in recent years shows that a number of judges think (or, at least, have thought) otherwise. The Court of Appeal laid down in *Turner*[2] the rules to which the words and deeds of judge and counsel at this stage of the criminal trial ought to conform. Turner originally pleaded not guilty to a charge of theft; but, on the second day of the trial, his counsel advised him in strong terms to change his plea to one of guilty. Turner demurred, but he ultimately did so after much discussion and after his counsel had spoken privately to the judge. The Court of Appeal ordered a *venire de novo* because Turner may have been led to suppose that the judge had intimated that he would receive a lighter sentence if he pleaded guilty. The Court laid down four rules of which the third and fourth are of particular importance in the present context.

1. Counsel must be completely free to give the accused his best advice, albeit in strong terms. This will often include the advice that a plea of guilty, showing an element of remorse, is a mitigating factor which may well enable the court to give a lesser sentence than would otherwise be the case.
2. The accused, having considered counsel's advice, must have a complete freedom of choice whether to plead guilty or not guilty.
3. There must be freedom of access between both counsel for the prosecution and the defence and the judge. Any discussion that is to take place must be between judge and counsel for both sides. It is desirable that such discussions should, so far as possible, be in open court, but it is sometimes necessary that they should be in the judge's room; for example, "counsel may by way of mitigation wish to tell the judge that the accused had not long to live,[3] is suffering, maybe from cancer, of which he should remain ignorant. Again counsel on both sides may

---

[1] *Atkinson*, [1978] 2 All E.R. 460 at p. 462.
[2] [1970] 2 Q.B. 321; [1970] 2 All E.R. 281.
[3] The ethics of this conduct have been questioned in an interesting article by J. E. Adams in [1971] Crim. L.R. 252.

wish to discuss with the judge whether it would be proper, in a particular case, for the prosecution to accept a plea to a lesser offence."

4. Subject to one single exception the judge should never indicate the sentence he is minded to impose. "A statement that, on a plea of guilty, he would impose one sentence, but that, on a conviction following a plea of not guilty, he would impose a severer sentence is one which should never be made . . . ." Under the exception it is permissible for a judge, if he feels able to do so, to indicate that, whatever the accused's plea may be, the sentence will or will not take a particular form.

The third and fourth requirements are intended to ensure that a defendant is not subjected to the pressure which might arise from a belief that the judge has indicated that he might impose one sentence if there is a guilty plea and another sentence if there is a conviction following a not guilty plea; and the pressure is no less if the judge conveys that impression in open court.[1] From the defendant's point of view, however, there is evidence that the conduct permitted by the first *Turner* rule—that his counsel may give him advice, in strong terms where appropriate—exerts considerable pressure to change the plea to guilty.[2] If counsel believes that the evidence against the defendant is so compromising as to make a guilty verdict probable, and if he believes (from his knowledge of the Court, or even of the particular judge) that a guilty plea will result in a much lighter sentence, he may well phrase his advice in strong terms. This, indeed, is the inevitable result of various practices which have evolved over the years—those of taking other offences into consideration, the rule that a plea of guilty should lead to a reduction of sentence and the acceptance from time to time of pleas of guilty to the lesser of two offences charged or which could be found against the accused on the indictment.

The practice of taking other offences into consideration has already been discussed. The court must be satisfied that the accused really did commit the offences and freely admits it; but it would be idle to pretend that there are no cases in which the police have enlarged on the advantages of his doing so before the accused signs the list of other offences handed to him, and all parties concerned know perfectly well that the sentence the accused will receive for the offence of which he is convicted plus all the offences taken into consideration is going to be nothing like the aggregate sentence which would have been passed had all those offences been contested.

---

[1] *Atkinson*, [1978] 2 All E.R. 460. Cf. the Australian decision in *Tait and Bartley* (1979), 24 A.L.R. 473.
[2] Baldwin and McConville, *Negotiated Justice* (1977).

The sentencing "discount" for pleading guilty is well established. In *de Haan*[1] sentences for receiving totalling four and a half years were reduced to three years because the judge had made insufficient allowance for the accused's change of plea.

"It is undoubtedly right that a confession of guilt should tell in favour of an accused person and that it is clearly in the public interest."

In *Harper*[2] sentences of five years for receiving were reduced to three years because the judge had made remarks which were critical of the manner in which the defence had been conducted.

"This court feels that it is very improper to use language which may convey that an accused is being sentenced because he has pleaded not guilty or because he has run his defence in a particular way. It is, however, proper to give an accused a lesser sentence if he has shown genuine remorse amongst other things by pleading guilty."

No doubt there are cases in which the plea of guilty is indicative of contrition and the possible justifications of this particular ground of reducing sentence are considered in Chapter IV. More frequently, however, the guilty plea will be based on hard-headed realism, and there are at least two reasons of expediency why some credit should be given for a plea of guilty. In the first place, there are cases, of which charges of sexual offences against children and girls are an example, in which prosecution witnesses are spared much pain by the accused's plea as they do not have to give evidence at the trial; secondly, it is greatly in the interest of the smooth working of the present English judicial system that, provided they are in fact guilty, accused persons should plead guilty. This second reason has been recognised by allowing a sentencing discount for pleading guilty even to the most serious forms of robbery, where mitigating factors usually count for little:[3] the discount will generally be of the order of one-quarter to one-third.[4]

Provided it is clearly understood to refer only to those who are guilty, moderate encouragement to plead is, as the Court of Appeal put it in *de Haan*, "clearly in the public interest". The sentencing discount does, however, give rise to three major difficulties. The first is that, since it is widely known, it inevitably exerts an influence on the choice of plea. The *Turner* rules appear to prohibit the judge from stating the obvious,[5] but the defendant may himself know of

---

[1] [1968] 2 Q.B. 108; [1967] 3 All E.R. 618n.
[2] [1968] 2 Q.B. 108; [1967] 3 All E.R. 618n.
[3] *Davies*, [1980] Crim. L.R. 598.
[4] *Ibid*; cf. Baldwin and McConville, (1978) 41 M.L.R.
[5] Cf. *Davis*, [1979] Crim. L.R. 327, and the article by R. D. Seifman at [1976] Crim. L.R. 556.

the sentencing practice and if he does not know his legal advisers will soon make it known to him. The very fact that the sentencing discount is common practice therefore places defendants under considerable pressure. This leads on to the second major difficulty, which is that the encouragement to plead guilty inevitably stretches beyond those who are in fact guilty — to those who protest their innocence but against whom the evidence is compromising, or who have an arguable point of law or a debateable question of degree (such as questions of dishonesty or reasonableness). Defendants in this position may be strongly tempted by the likely difference in sentence, particularly if they are advised that the plea may make the difference between an immediate custodial sentence and a suspended or non-custodial sentence, and there is some authority that such a change in the type of sentence may be permissible.[1] The third difficulty is that any notion of a right to have any criminal charge tried in open court is diluted by the inevitable concomitant of a discount for pleading guilty, which is that those who are convicted after pleading not guilty receive a heavier sentence than they would if they had pleaded guilty. It has been held that a person who elects Crown Court trial rather than summary trial should not be given a heavier sentence on that account,[2] although any costs awarded against him will inevitably be greater in the Crown Court.[3] But the difficulties stemming from the discount for pleading guilty are largely an inseparable part of it.

It is by no means uncommon for persons charged in the Crown Court with murder or wounding with intent to plead guilty to manslaughter or unlawful wounding, and for persons charged in a Magistrates' Court with reckless driving to plead guilty to driving without due care and attention. The prosecutor's acceptance of such pleas has to be approved by the judge, and the judge's approval is by no means a formality. If he is hearing a charge in the Crown Court, the depositions and statements which led to the accused's committal for trial will indicate the nature of the prosecution's evidence, and, if that evidence appears to be sufficient to sustain the more serious charge, the judge may insist on it being tried.[4] In any case, the judge or magistrates may require the prosecutor to indicate why he is prepared to accept a plea of guilty to the lesser charge. It would, however, be idle to deny that the prosecution's acceptance of

---

[1] Cf. *Tonks*, [1980] Crim. L.R. 59 with *Hollyman*, [1980] Crim. L.R. 60, and commentary.
[2] *Jamieson* (1975), 60 Cr. App. Rep. 318.
[3] *Bushell*, [1980] Crim. L.R. 444.
[4] *Soanes*, [1948] 1 All E.R. 289; 32 Cr. App. Rep. 136; *Broad* (1978), 68 Cr. App. Rep. 281.

the plea to the lesser charge is often the outcome of a bargain in which the representatives of the accused have stressed certain weaknesses in the Crown's case, but, at the same time, made it plain to their client that he will probably get a considerably lighter sentence if he pleads guilty to the lesser charge than he would get if he were found guilty of the more serious one. Once again, there are in this practice dangers similar to those outlined in the previous paragraph.

III

THEORIES OF PUNISHMENT

Section 1.—**Introduction**

The object of the first two sections of this chapter is to provide an account of the different theories of punishment which will be adequate for a consideration of the general questions relating to certain aspects of our sentencing practice discussed in section 3. Reference will also be made to the different theories of punishment when the manner in which the lengths of prison sentences are fixed is considered in the next chapter. The upshot may well be thought to be nothing but a series of glimpses of the obvious—our sentencing practice is not explicable on any one theory of punishment; the behaviour of the Courts is often justified by every theory of punishment; some sentences are only to be explained in the light of one theory, and much that happens is not attributable to any theory of punishment but to a variety of considerations most of which can be described as "expediency". But, notwithstanding the obvious nature of these conclusions, a discussion of the different theories of punishment is essential to a proper understanding and criticism of the sentencing system, while the discovery that some features of that system can only be accounted for on the footing of expediency is in no way fatal to the merits of those features, it is a sign of the presence of something requiring special justification.

In many ways it is a pity that the word "theories" ever came to be employed to describe the moral justifications of the practice of punishing with varying degrees of severity about to be discussed. As punishment by definition entails the deliberate infliction of pain, it certainly needs to be justified morally, but the use of the word "theory" is unfortunate for at least two reasons. In the first place, it suggests that one theory must be right to the exclusion of all others whereas, as will appear shortly, it may well be the case that neither retributive theories standing alone nor utilitarian theories standing alone can provide an adequate answer to any of the major questions that are commonly raised with regard to punishment. The second objection to the use of the expression "theories of punishment" is that it tends to produce interminable and inconclusive discussions concerning the correctness of any one of them, to the exclusion of considerations of what, to a lawyer at least, seem the more interesting and more important attempts to answer concrete questions of the kind raised in section 3 and in the next chapter.

It has become common to divide philosophical discussions of punishment into three main questions. Why punish? Who should be punished? How much punishment should be inflicted? Any account of the theoretical basis of a sentencing system must necessarily be primarily concentrated on the third of these questions, although some of the concrete questions raised in section 3 of this chapter such as Why not Punish the Mentally Disordered? require consideration of the question Who Should Be Punished? An answer to the first question is offered at this stage. It is dogmatic and brief because it is not intended to provide anything more than a basis for the ensuing discussion of some sentencing practices. The answer is also limited because it is confined to punishment by the State, whereas a full answer would have to concern itself with punishment by parents, schoolmasters and others.

A. THE GENERAL OBJECT OF STATE PUNISHMENT

This book is written on the assumption that the aim of the penal system is to reduce crime by making as many people as possible want to obey the criminal law. It follows that the general practice of punishment by the State is only justified if it has two objectives, the reduction of crime, and the promotion of respect for the criminal law. Each is essential. Although it is a mistake to suppose that the practice can be justified without stressing the objective of the reduction of crime, it is also a mistake to suppose that the reduction of crime can be treated as an adequate objective without reference to the promotion of respect for law.

The first mistake, that the reduction of crime is not essential to the justification of punishment, was made by Kant:

"Even if a civil society were to dissolve itself by common agreement of all its members (for example, if the people inhabiting an island decide to separate and disperse themselves around the world), the last murderer remaining in prison must first be executed, so that everyone will duly receive what his actions are worth and so that the blood guilt thereof will not be fixed on people because they failed to insist on carrying out the punishment; for if they fail to do that, they may be regarded as accomplices in this public violation of legal justice."[1]

Thus for Kant it was intrinsically right, quite independently of any consequences of the transaction, that offenders should be given their deserts. It was also essential for him that the State should endeavour to insure that offenders receive their deserts, for we have already seen that his theory of punishment does not allow for any abstention from punishment in the name of expediency such as that which happens daily in this country when an offender is discharged or put on probation.[2] The weakness of Kant's position is that it does not follow from the fact that State action would be intrinsically right that it must be carried out. No doubt the execution of the last murderer could be described as "just" and he could properly be said to have had his deserts, but how could this last act of the hypothetical State be said to have been justified?[3] To this question Kant would have had to give some such unconvincing reply as "In order to prevent the population from sharing in the murderer's condoned guilt" or "In order to prevent the perpetration of an injustice because all previous murderers have been executed". Surely most people would say that if, *per impossibile*, they were certain that a convicted criminal would never commit another crime, that failure to punish him would not in any way weaken the deterrent effect of the threat or example of punishment, and that it would not militate in any degree against the condemnation by society of the convict's crime, punishment would not be justified for, by inflicting it, the State would be allocating to itself the role of the Deity. There is force in the remark attributed to a judge "I don't punish, that is done by a higher power; I only protect society."

The second mistake about the general object of State punishment, that the reduction of crime can be treated as an adequate objective without reference to the promotion of respect for the law, is made by Professor Nigel Walker in *Sentencing in a Rational Society*. His conclusion is that the reduction of prohibited conduct must be the only aim of any penal system, although he concedes that it must be tempered both by economic considerations and by humanity if the system is to be practicable and tolerable. "No society can afford a policeman at everyone's elbow." Even if such a society were economically feasible, it would be a great deal more unpleasant than a society with less coercion and more crime. The criminal law can only work successfully if the practice of punishing for its breach as well as the nature

---

[1] *The Metaphysical Elements of Justice*, translated by John Ladd (Bobbs-Merrill U.S.A.) p. 102.
[2] P. 8, *supra*.
[3] See "Justified and Deserved Punishment", by Max Atkinson, (1969) 78 Mind 354.

and extent of the punishment is accepted by a very substantial part of society; and it is reasonable to assume that such a majority would, in general, approve of punishments which are deserved, no more, no less.

The importance of the dual nature of the assumption made in this book concerning the general nature of State punishment should now be apparent. It is possible for the same person to assert on the same occasion both that the justification of the practice of punishment is that it reduces crime (either by deterring potential offenders, by deterring the individual offender, or by reforming the individual offender), and that the justification of punishment is the meting out to offenders of their deserts (the aim being to reduce crime by a means which commands the respect of the majority of society). The first assertion is commonly associated with preventive theories (utilitarian or rehabilitative) and the second with retributive theories, and the Danish jurist Alf Ross maintains that the two sets of "theories" are concerned with different questions, retribution supplying only a justification for imposing penalties on particular persons and being incapable of amounting to an *aim* of State punishment.[1] But in reality, prevention and retribution are mutually dependent. If punishment is to deter it may only do so by giving offenders their deserts; but the only reason for giving offenders their deserts is that it deters.

B. PUNISHING THE INNOCENT

The dual nature of the assumption made in this book also assists in the solution of a theoretical problem which recurs in philosophical discussions of punishment. It is said that, unless one accepts Kant's view that giving offenders their deserts is the sole justification of State punishment, one is forced to accept a theory which could, on occasions, condone the punishment of a man known to be innocent. Two situations are envisaged. The first is the situation in which it is thought necessary to find a scapegoat, the second is that in which it is thought necessary to restrain someone who has not committed an offence because it is believed to be very highly probable that he will do so in the near future.

The first situation may be illustrated by an imaginary scene in one of the Southern States of the U.S.A. in the days about which Mark Twain wrote. A white woman has been raped by an unidentified negro; the mob is about to take the law into its own hands and indulge in an orgy of lynching. To prevent this the governor causes a negro, who is known to have committed some other crime, to be

---

[1] Ross, *On Guilt and Punishment* (1975), pp. 44 and 63.

arrested, tried on perjured evidence, and publicly executed for the rape. Much bloodshed and many other crimes will have been prevented at the cost of one not wholly innocent life. Why is the procedure utterly unacceptable? Kant's answer was simple:

> "Judicial punishment can never be used merely as a means to promote some other good for the criminal himself or for civil society, but instead it must in all cases be imposed on him only on the ground that he has committed a crime; for a human being can never be manipulated merely as a means to the purposes of someone else and can never be confused with the objects of the law of things."[1]

It is said, however, that those who justify punishment on the ground that it tends to reduce crime, should find it difficult if not impossible to answer the question why, if crime will be reduced thereby, a man should not occasionally be punished for an offence although there is no evidence that he committed it. Even someone who believes, without any such qualification as is adopted in this book, that the practice of punishing is justified if and only if it tends to reduce crime has several answers to the question concerning the punishment of those known to be innocent. The procedure is not "punishment" at all because punishment is, by definition, the infliction of pain on someone who has committed the particular offence in question, or is at least believed to have done so. The procedure is inhumane and the most ardent reductivists must accept the limiting factor of humanitarian considerations. But some people prefer to define State punishment as the pain inflicted on those who have been convicted of an offence, and others would prefer to limit the objection to inhumane punishments to those which are, on other grounds, just and deserved.[2] For those who hold these views, the most satisfactory answer to the question, "Why should we disapprove without exception of the punishment of someone who has not committed the offence for which he is being punished?" is "Because the object of State punishment is to reduce crime by means which will command the respect of most citizens". Most citizens would not respect the reduction of crime by means of the punishment of those known to be innocent. If it be said that most citizens would not know that an innocent man was being punished, the correct retort is "truth will out and confidence in the legal system as a whole would be undermined".[3]

The other situation in which it is argued that, unless one accepts something like Kant's view, one is obliged to condone the

---

[1] Kant, op. cit., p. 100.

[2] Atkinson, op. cit., and see p. 101, supra.

[3] If the secret could be kept, we would be left with the question whether expediency can ever justify wholesale deception and the killing of one for the sake of the many.

punishment of someone known to be innocent, may be illustrated by a hypothetical case put by Professor Walker. That is:

> "Imagine a situation in which it is as certain as it can be that a man will commit serious and irreparable harm—such as murder or mutilation to another person (he may for instance be a jealous and violent husband whose wife has eloped with another man). The only method of ensuring that the harm is not done may well be to put him in custody for a while."

It is not clear what Kant's attitude to non-punitive detention in such a situation would have been; but, for him, anything in the nature of punishment would have been out of the question. However, one does not have to be a pure Kantian in order to reach a similar conclusion. The detention of the hypothetical husband would not be "punishment" within the meaning of that word as used in this book and, assuming that he has not even committed a preparatory offence (such as carrying an offensive weapon, or loitering with intent) he would not deserve to lose his liberty. There is a case for detaining him if the evidence of his intentions is so clear, but the detention must be non-punitive. In other words the case is analogous to that of the innocent person who has not committed an offence. Professor Walker suggests that the distinction between punitive and non-punitive detention in these contexts is a form of "double think"; but Cox[1] shows that the distinction was regarded as significant by at least one detainee and by the Court of Appeal. A legal system which at least endeavours to preserve the distinction is entitled to more respect than one which does not.

C. PUNISHMENT AND DESERT

It is not enough, however, to argue that the innocent should not be punished. The commission of an offence as defined by the criminal law is certainly a necessary condition of punishment, but it may not be sufficient—the law itself may be iniquitous, or the principles on which criminal liability is imposed may conflict with moral notions of desert.

Punishment may be undeserved on the first ground if the offence for which it is imposed fails to correspond with more fundamental principles of justice. If the law of the road were changed with retrospective effect, we would want to say that the punishment of those who had driven on the left-hand side of the road before the law was changed would be unjust, since it is grossly unfair to convict and punish someone for conduct which was lawful when it was done. If a statute imposed severe penalties on parents who did not kill their

---

[1] P. 72, *supra*.

mentally handicapped children, we would want to join issue with
someone who said that the imposition of the penalties on parents
who disobeyed the statute was deserved, since the notion of "deserved punishment" goes wider than "legally justified punishment"
and allows moral conceptions of justice to influence judgments of
desert. Thus punishment is only deserved if it is imposed for an
offence, but even if it is imposed for an offence we may still on some
wider moral ground describe it as undeserved.[1]

Punishment may also be undeserved if it is imposed despite the
absence of fault on the defendant's part. English law contains a
number of offences of "strict liability" for which no fault is required.
A publican may be convicted of supplying drink to a drunken
customer although he believed, on reasonable grounds, that the
customer was sober; a shopkeeper may be convicted of selling
adulterated food although he had no means of knowledge of the
adulteration; an undischarged bankrupt may be convicted of obtaining credit of more than £10 without disclosing the bankruptcy
although the failure to disclose was that of his agent through whom
the credit was obtained. In all these cases punishment is undeserved, not merely in the sense that the offender's conduct is morally
blameless, but also in the sense that there has been no deliberate or
negligent breach of the law. If punishment can be justified in these
cases, it can only be on the ground of the expediency which underlies
arguments in favour of the imposition of strict liability such as the
avoidance of the risk of bogus defences and the need to goad those
who embark on certain undertakings to maintain the utmost vigilance at all times. This is not the place for a consideration of the
merits of these arguments, but it is essential to the present discussion
to observe that strict liability is only acceptable, even to its most
ardent proponents, on the basis that the punishment to be meted out
will be minimal, a moderate fine at the most. Something of great
value is sacrificed in these cases, namely the principle that punishment should only be inflicted on those who deserve it. Infringe-
ments of the principle may have to be tolerated at various points in
the sentencing process, but the infringement must be as slight as
possible and the justification for it must be susceptible of the clearest
possible statement.

A similar sacrifice could be said to be made where the law
penalises negligence, inasmuch as the negligent offender does not
knowingly risk bringing about the proscribed consequence. The
question whether it is proper to punish negligence has been much

---

[1] Cf. J. D. Mabbott, in *The Philosophy of Punishment* (ed. H. B. Acton), p. 45, with
C. W. K. Mundle, *ibid.*, p. 77.

debated,[1] and will not be reviewed here. Suffice it to say that negligence can be regarded as a species of fault, the basis of liability being the offender's failure to make the effort to ensure that his conduct conformed to reasonable standards. So long as he was capable of making that effort and so long as the standards were known or knowable, then not only may there be good social reasons (as in driving offences) for penalising negligence but it may also be fair to say that punishment is deserved because the offender was at fault.

Punishment may be said to be most clearly deserved where the offence is committed intentionally, knowingly or recklessly. The concept of mens rea in English criminal law encompasses these three states of mind, which are considered in some detail below.[2] The fault in these cases resides in the offender's choice to bring about, or at least to risk bringing about, the result or state of affairs prohibited by law. So clear is the element of fault where intention or knowledge is present that in some preparatory crimes, such as attempts, loitering with intent and carrying an offensive weapon without excuse, the law penalises persons who have not got as far as doing any harm. But in the first two crimes by definition, and in the third by assumption from the absence of lawful excuse, the offenders intended harm, sometimes of considerable magnitude. It cannot therefore be said that their punishment was undeserved. Someone who intends the kind of harm contemplated by these offences is morally blameworthy and he has gone far enough towards committing a crime to justify intervention on the part of the law. The reason why the law does not punish evil intentions in cases in which the agent has not moved a fairly long way towards executing them, is expediency based on the difficulty of proof, the undesirability of vexatious prosecutions, and the fact that people often form criminal intentions without carrying them out. It is difficult to dissent from the spirit of Sir James Stephen's statement when he said that to punish bare intention:

"would be utterly intolerable: all mankind would be criminals, and most of their lives would be passed in trying and punishing each other for offences which could never be proved."[3]

Section 2.—**The different theories of punishment and the general aims of sentencing**

Granted that the general justification of the State's practice of

---

[1] J. Hall, *General Principles of Criminal Law*, Ch. IV; H. L. A. Hart, *Punishment and Responsibility*, Ch. VI.

[2] P. 146, *infra*.

[3] *History of the Criminal Law of England*, Vol. II, p. 78.

punishment is that it reduces crime by giving offenders what they deserve, is it possible to carry the analysis a stage further and find more specific justifications under each of these heads? An affirmative answer to this question is provided by the different grounds put forward for believing that punishment reduces crime or for giving offenders their deserts. Some of them are advanced as justifications on their own account of the entire practice of punishment, but they may also be treated as complementary. The grounds connected with the reduction of crime are usually described as "utilitarian", while those related to the giving to offenders of their deserts are described as "retributive". It will be convenient to begin with the latter after a word has been said about the distinction.

The usual way of distinguishing between retributive and utilitarian theories of punishment is to say that the former are concerned with the relation of the punishment to a past event, the crime, whereas the latter are concerned with the consequences of the punishment; but this distinction is unsound because the satisfaction of the victim's demand for vengeance is commonly regarded as a typical retributive justification, although it lays stress on a particular consequence of punishment. A sounder basis of distinction is that between theories which stress the accountability of the offender to his victim and others and those which stress the effect of the punishment on the offender and others. The essence of retributive theories is that punishment is justified because the offender is in some sense made to "pay" for what he has done, whereas the essence of utilitarian theories is that punishment is justified because it tends in some way to prevent the occurrence of future crimes.

A. RETRIBUTIVE THEORIES

Vindication in the sense of society's claim to amends for the harm done, or for outraged feelings, fairness to the law abiding and proportionality of punishment to the seriousness of the offence may respectively be treated as the bases of retributive theories. The first two provide partial or total answers to the question: why punish at all? The third is concerned with the question: how much should we punish?

i. *Vindication.* In its crudest form the first kind of vindication justifies punishment on the ground that it tends to satisfy the victim's need for vengeance. More refined notions are the satisfaction of the victim's sense of justice or the satisfaction of the feelings of resentment of the victim, his friends and relations, or others who are aware of the crime. It would be a mistake to ignore these feelings for to do so altogether would discourage respect for the law. But this type of vindication cannot be treated as a justification of punishment on its own account. What has to be justified is the deliberate infliction of pain by the State, and there is force in the Benthamite point that the satisfaction engendered by the spectacle of punishment will never equal the pain caused by that punishment. It is noteworthy, however, that Bentham was not unaware of the importance of this aspect of vindication.

> "A kind of collateral end, which it [punishment] has a natural tendency to answer, is that of affording a pleasure or satisfaction to the party injured, where there is one, and, in general, to parties whose illwill, whether on a self-regarding account, or on account of sympathy, or antipathy, has been excited by the offence. This purpose, as far as it can be answered gratis, is a beneficial one. But no punishment ought to be allotted merely to this purpose, because (setting aside its effects in the way of control) no such pleasure is ever produced by punishment as can be equivalent to the pain. The punishment, however, which is allotted by the other purposes, ought, as far as it can be done without expense, to be accommodated to this. Satisfaction thus administered to a party injured, in the shape of a dis-social pleasure, may be styled a vindicative satisfaction or compensation."[1]

We shall see that some features of our sentencing system can only be explained on the basis that the sentence, or part of it, is allotted to the purpose of vindicative satisfaction without being allotted to any other obvious purpose.

Examples of the second kind of vindication are provided by the cases of *Williams* and *Llewellyn Jones*.

In *Williams*[2] the two accused, who had been drinking, pleaded guilty to buggery of a sheep. When sentencing them to a year's immediate imprisonment the trial judge said,

> "I fully appreciate that it is going to be a matter of comment about you for years to come and I think the kindest thing I can do is to visit upon you the outrage which I think anybody with decent feelings would feel about it so that nobody can say, in your village, that you haven't paid for it."

Having regard to the circumstances (which no doubt included the drink), to the fact that the accused showed remorse, and to the fact that they had been in custody for six weeks, the Court of Appeal suspended the sentences for an operational period of two years.

In *Llewellyn Jones*[3] a deputy County Court Registrar was convicted of offences involving the conversion of funds under his control belonging respectively to a crippled infant and a mental patient. The trial judge sentenced him to four years imprisonment. On appeal it was argued that heavy punishment was not called for on deterrent

---

[1] *Principles of Morals and Legislation* (ed. Hart and Burns), pp. 158–9, note a.
[2] [1974] Crim. L.R. 558.
[3] [1968] 1 Q.B. 429; [1967] 3 All E.R. 225; 51 Cr. App. Rep. 204.

grounds, it was unlikely that the accused would ever again be in a position to commit such offences, and other deputy County Court registrars scarcely needed a powerful warning by example in order to deter them from converting funds under their control. The retort of the Court of Appeal to these arguments was:

"This Court is quite satisfied that this is not a deterrent sentence. It is a sentence which is fully merited, in the opinion of this Court, as punishment for very grave offences, and as expressing the revulsion of the public to the whole circumstances of the case."

For the reason stated in the above quotation from Bentham, the visitation upon the offender of the outrage at his offence experienced by people with decent feelings cannot by itself be a sufficient justification of punishment, although it may serve a useful collateral purpose. We shall, however, shortly see that there is a utilitarian version of this type of theory according to which the denunciation of the offender's conduct involved in punishment is essential to the maintenance of social disapprobation of the offence. If this is the case, the pain occasioned to the offender by the punishment may be outweighed by the disadvantages which would accrue to society in consequence of the failure to punish.

ii. *Fairness.* There is a sense in which the criminal gains an advantage over the law abiding every time he commits an offence. This is obviously so in the case of successful acquisitive crimes, but there is an intangible gain in other cases for the law abiding might have derived some satisfaction, however ephemeral, from the commission of the offence, and yet they abstained; in some cases they may even have wished to commit the offence. Punishment may therefore be justified by the need to show the offender and the law abiding that the threats of the law will be carried out, and that those who unfairly take advantage of the self-restraint of others cannot do so with impunity. Inasmuch as punishment aims at depriving the offender of his gain, or at least counter-balancing the advantage obtained unfairly through the offence, this justification may be seen as retributive.

This question of fairness, like the question of State punishment as a whole, is entirely one between the offender and the State (representing the general public). Fairness and consistency are the concern of the State and the offender, and punishment for a serious crime should therefore not be determined by, for example, the wishes of a particular victim.[1] In the case of offences against person or prop-

---

[1] In some circumstances, however, the wishes of the victim may lead to a decision not to prosecute the offender: D. J. Steer, *Police Cautions—a Study in the Exercise of Police Discretion* (Oxford, 1970), pp. 27–9; A. F. Wilcox, *The Decision to Prosecute* (1972), pp. 79–81.

erty, if the sole justification of punishment were the vindication of the victim's injury, punishment ought never to be inflicted where the victim forgives the offender. But, generally speaking, the Courts consider the attitude of the victim irrelevant to the accused's punishment because he has to be punished for having flouted the law. This point is vividly illustrated by *Hampton*.[1] Hampton, aged twenty-three, had been convicted of rape of a girl of eighteen. She had permitted familiarities on the occasion in question, but clearly did not consent to intercourse and reported the incident to the police immediately afterwards. On hearing that Hampton had been sentenced to three years imprisonment, the girl wrote to the Court of Criminal Appeal saying that she was shocked by the result, that she had no idea that this would be the consequence of her action, and that she had told the accused, before the incident, that she would have intercourse with him some time in the future. The sentence of three years was nonetheless upheld.

> "It might well be true that she had no idea of the serious view that the Courts take of the crime of rape on young girls. But her misgivings could not afford any justification for altering a sentence which was right in principle and in fact well deserved."

Similar reasoning led the Court of Appeal to uphold a sentence of two years imprisonment in *Buchanan*[2] for wounding with intent the woman with whom the appellant had been living, despite her expressed forgiveness and willingness to resume her life with him. In general, neither the offender's wickedness nor his danger to others is reduced by the forgiveness of this particular victim, and the Courts are usually right to approach these cases with the interests of society as a whole as the primary consideration.

iii. *Proportionality*. We saw earlier that the notion of desert has an important bearing on the question, Who should be punished? We turn now to a question on which it has an equally important bearing, namely, How much punishment should be inflicted? The general answer to this question is: As much as is deserved for the offence, no more, no less. But there may be exceptions. At the upper extreme, those exceptions should be closely circumscribed: the sentence of life imprisonment violates the norm of proportionality in the name of increased public protection against an unusually dangerous offender, and the conditions for imposing it[3] need careful justification. At the lower extreme, rehabilitative considerations may be allowed to reduce a sentence or to avoid a punitive sentence

---

[1] [1965] Crim. L.R. 564; *cf. Pritchard* (1973), 57 Cr. App. Rep. 492.
[2] [1980] Crim. L.R. 317.
[3] See p. 49, *supra*.

altogether (as by probation or discharge), and this is surely right when the offence is not so serious as to require a punitive sentence. Two questions may fairly be raised at this point. Is the proportionality in terms of which sentencers think, entirely one of the relationship between the quantity of punishment and the moral deserts of the offender? How is the proportionality measured?

The answer to the first question is "not entirely". Sentencers think in terms of a complex notion which they frequently describe as "the gravity of the offence". This certainly includes wickedness and, to the extent that punishment is measured proportionately to the wickedness implicit in the definition of the offence, or indicated by the particular circumstances, the sentencer is thinking in terms of proportionality to the moral deserts of the offender; "gravity" also includes a reference to the amount of harm done by the offender and to the extent that such harm was inflicted intentionally or negligently, the proportionality with which the sentencer is concerned is again proportionality to moral desert. Some retributive theories measure punishment according to the amount of harm actually done, but the proper measure of moral desert is surely the amount of harm that the offender intentionally inflicted, knowingly risked or (perhaps) negligently caused.[1] Additionally, "gravity" sometimes refers to features which have a social rather than a moral significance. These include the alarm caused by the particular category of offence and the belief that the conduct in question encourages crime. Burglary and handling stolen goods are not morally worse offences than theft, but the maximum punishment is higher in each case.

It is often said to be an incurable defect in any form of retributive theory of punishment that an attempt to inflict pain commensurate to the crime is a futile endeavour to equate incommensurables. What sense is there, it is asked, in talking about the proportionality of a fine or term of imprisonment to an assault or theft? In spite of the fact that it was expressed in the terms of his own difficult philosophy, the first and most important step towards an answer to this question was taken by Hegel more than one hundred and fifty years ago; the second step can be taken with the aid of a very elementary consideration of the practice of the Legislature and the Courts.

Hegel's point was simply that, though they may differ greatly in form, crime and punishment resemble each other in that they are each a species of injury.

---

[1] See further discussion p. 127, *supra* and p. 146, *infra*.

". . . the universal feeling of nations and individuals about crime is and has been that it deserves punishment, that as the criminal has done, so should it be done to him . . . .

But a point of great difficulty has been introduced into the idea of retribution by the category of equality, . . .

. . . it is easy enough from this point of view to exhibit the retributive character of punishment as an absurdity (theft for theft, robbery for robbery, an eye for an eye, a tooth for a tooth—and then you can go on to suppose that the criminal has only one eye or no teeth) . . . . Value, as the inner equality of things which in their outward existence are specifically different from one another in every way, is a category which has appeared already in connection with contracts, and also in connection with injuries that are the subject of civil suits . . . . In crime, as that which is characterised at bottom by the infinite aspect of the deed, the purely external specific character vanishes all the more obviously, and equality remains the fundamental regulator of the essential thing, to wit the deserts of the criminal, though not for the specific external form which the payment of those deserts may take. It is only in respect of that form that there is a plain inequality between theft and robbery on the one hand, and fines, imprisonment, etc., on the other. In respect of their 'value', however, i.e. in respect of their universal property of being injuries, they are comparable."[1]

In the above passages Hegel was referring primarily to offences against person and property, but the concept of injury can be applied to society and that of desert to the deliberate flouting of the law, with the result that crimes in which there is no obvious personal victim may be included.

Even if crime and punishment are each regarded as species of injury, there remains the question of the feasibility of measuring the proportionality between them in terms of the magnitude of a fine or the duration of a prison sentence. The procedure would be entirely unfeasible if its object were thought of as the production of a precisely correct sentence for each offence in isolation from all others. But the procedure is perfectly feasible if the object is recognised to be a rough attempt to equate the size of the fine or the length of imprisonment to the gravity of the particular category of offence as contrasted with offences of other categories (theft contrasted with murder, for example), and the gravity of the circumstances in which the offence was committed as contrasted with those in which other offences of the same category are committed (for example, rape where the victim acted to some extent as a temptress as contrasted with a rape in which the victim was waylaid and subjected to great violence). Although the sphere is admittedly one in which historical accident is more influential than policy, the English Legislature may be said to attempt the first half of the above equation with fixing the maximum punishment for each offence while the Judiciary attempts

---

[1] Hegel's *Philosophy of Right* translated by T. M. Knox, pp. 71–2.

the second when grading the circumstances of the different offences according to gravity.

Hegel was fully conscious of the difficulty which has just been mentioned.

> "Reason cannot determine, nor can the concept provide any principle whose application could decide whether justice requires for an offence (i) a corporal punishment of forty lashes or thirty-nine, or (ii) a fine of five dollars or four dollars ninety-three, four, etc., cents, or (iii) imprisonment of a year or three hundred and sixty-four, three, etc., days, or a year and one, two, or three days. And yet injustice is done at once if there is one lash too many, or one dollar or one cent, one week in prison or one day, too many or too few."[1]

Hegel conceded that allowance has to be made for an element of arbitrariness, a decision simply has to be taken one way or another within certain fairly clearly defined limits. This is certainly the attitude of our judges who, as we shall see in the next chapter, tend to think in terms of ranges of appropriate sentences. The Court of Appeal is quick to react when the limit has been exceeded. Thus, in *Disbrey*[2] a sentence of three years imprisonment for receiving and fraudulently using a stolen excise licence was reduced to six months notwithstanding the bad record of the appellant and the fact that he had committed the crimes in the course of his employment. Speaking for the Court of Appeal SALMON, L.J. said:

> "This Court does not want to minimise the seriousness of the offences of receiving excise licences and using them fraudulently, but to send a man to prison for three years for doing that seems to this Court to be beyond all reason."

The same Lord Justice, speaking for the same Court, subsequently drew attention to an instance of gross under-sentencing in *Riddle and Stevens*[3] in which appeals against convictions for assaults causing actual bodily harm were dimissed. Speaking of the sentences, fines of £20 against which there were no appeals, SALMON, L.J. said:

> "No doubt there are crimes against property which, in exceptional circumstances, enable justice to be tempered by mercy and first offenders to be treated with extreme leniency. But crimes of violence are altogether different in kind. These appellants were members of a gang which in brutal and cowardly fashion, set on a man standing alone, and proceeded to kick him as he lay unconscious . . . . In such circumstances the appellants would, or should, have been sentenced to long terms of imprisonment . . . . They are all young with no previous convictions. Even so in circumstances such as these to impose the most derisory fines of £20 and £25[4] is a travesty of the proper administration of justice."

---

[1] *Op. cit.*, pp. 37–8.
[2] [1967] Crim. L.R. 431, C.A.
[3] (1970), 114 Sol. Jo. 492.
[4] The fine imposed upon another member of the gang.

   In recent years the Court of Appeal has paid increasing attention
to questions of proportionality and grading. In two judgments, for
example, LAWTON, L.J., has set out various factors which make
certain sexual offences more or less serious,[1] and in two other
judgments LORD LANE, C.J., has given indications of a general
scaling-down of prison sentences for what might be called "run-of-
the-mill" offences.[2] The grading of offences is further considered in
Chapter 4.[3]

B. UTILITARIAN THEORIES

   The assumption underlying the utilitarian theories of punishment
is that crime must be prevented as economically in terms of the
suffering of the offender as possible. Prevention, deterrence and
reform may be treated as the three bases of these theories, although
deterrence has to be sub-divided into individual deterrence, general
deterrence and long term deterrence.

   i. *Prevention.* According to the prevention theory, the object of
punishment is to incapacitate the offender from committing further
crimes. The protection of society from the offender's maraudings,
even for a comparatively short time, is a frequent judicial justification of a sentence, but there are limiting considerations. Thus in
Clarke[4] the Court of Appeal criticised a sentence of 18 months
imprisonment upon a mentally disturbed young recidivist for breaking a flower pot valued at £1, holding that such a sentence was
"wholly inappropriate" for the crime committed, and varied it to a
fine of £2. It has already been noted[5] that the sentence of life
imprisonment breaches the principle of proportionality, but the
rarity of such sentences suggests that the Courts recognise that any
preventive sentence should generally be limited by considerations of
proportionality.

   ii. *Deterrence.* The idea common to deterrent theories of punishment is that the experience, threat or example of punishment dis-
courages crime.

   (a) *Individual deterrence.* In the case of individual deterrence, the
idea is that the offender should be given such an unpleasant time
that, through fear of a repetition of the punishment, he will never
repeat his conduct. Again there are limiting considerations. The
retributivist insists that the punishment must not be disproportionate to the offender's deserts, the utilitarian insists that the

---

[1] *Willis* (1974), 60 Cr. App. Rep. 146; *Taylor*, [1977] 3 All E.R. 527.
[2] *Upton* (1980), 71 Cr. App. Rep. 102; *Bibi*, [1980] Crim. L.R. 732.
[3] Pp. 173–177, *infra.*
[4] (1975), 61 Cr. App. Rep. 320, supported in *Tolley* (1978), 68 Cr. App. Rep. 323.
[5] P. 131, *supra.*

punishment must be no more than is necessary to achieve its deterrent effect, sheer expediency insists that the punishment shall not be such as to make the offender an object of public sympathy. Even the Rev. Sydney Smith (1771–1845), whose views on these matters were notoriously harsh, was very much alive to this latter point.

> "When we recommend severity, we recommend, of course, that degree of severity which will not excite compassion for the sufferer and lessen the horror of the crime. That is why we do not recommend torture and amputation of limbs."[1]

In our own day, the wholly lamentable tendency on the part of some sections of the public to make heroes of the participants in the great train robbery of 1964[2] may be due in part to the length of their sentences as well as to the daring nature of the crime and the size of its proceeds.

The current penological view is that one sentence of imprisonment is enough for the majority of offenders: "it is the first prison sentence in an offender's life which is widely held, though largely on conjectural grounds, to have the most traumatic effect".[3] The initial impact of prison life is therefore thought to be a powerful individual deterrent, and sentencers have frequently in recent years been urged to make the first prison sentence reasonably short. Lord LANE, C.J., stated in *Upton* that "sentencing judges should appreciate that overcrowding in many of the penal establishments in this country is such that a prison sentence, however short, is a very unpleasant experience indeed";[4] as we shall see, the point about the shortness of the first prison sentence was also made by LAWTON, L.J., some six years earlier.[5]

(b) *General deterrence.* When reliance is placed on general deterrence, the aim of punishment is thought of as the discouragement of others minded to commit crime by the threat of punishment and the example of the punishment of the offender. For Bentham this was the principal aim of punishment, but there is growing scepticism about the deterrent effect of either the threat or the example of punishment, and the difficulties of conducting satisfactory research into the deterrent effect of a particular sentencing policy have been

---

[1] Cited in *The Modern Approach to Criminal Law* by Radzinowicz and Turner, p. 40.
[2] *Wilson*, [1965] 1 Q.B. 402.
[3] Advisory Council on the Penal System, Interim Report, The Length of Prison Sentences (1977), para. 10.
[4] (1980), 71 Cr. App. Rep. 102; the Advisory Council's Interim Report, The Length of Prison Sentences, may well have been influential in promoting this view: see p. 173, *infra*.
[5] See *Sargeant*, p. 143, *infra*.

shown to be manifold and often insuperable.[1] So far as the threat of punishment is concerned, a survey of young men carried out by Willcock and Stokes in 1968[2] suggested that most people overrate their chances of detection and rank fear of what others will think above fear of punishment as a deterrent. Very naturally, however, the judges continue to pin their faith on the deterrent effect of punishment as an example to those contemplating crime and, very properly, they will no doubt continue to do so until there is an overwhelming body of evidence to the contrary. The very probably apocryphal statement of the judge who told the convict that he was not being hanged because he had stolen a sheep but in order to stop others stealing a sheep is founded on a common assumption which would take a lot of displacing. It must be conceded, however, that the deterrent effect of either the threat or the example of punishment probably varies considerably from crime to crime.

The judicial confidence in the deterrent effect of the example of punishment in the case of acquisitive crime may be illustrated by *Daher*,[3] where the Court of Appeal upheld a sentence of three years imprisonment on a Lebanese student of nineteen for the illegal importation of cannabis. Daher, previously of good character, had been induced to become the "runner" of some Lebanese drug exporters by the promise of money and a short holiday in England in addition to the payment of his air fare; his employers had also promised assistance to his impoverished family. On his arrival in England Daher was found to have £3,500 worth of cannabis in his suitcase. The following is an extract from the judgment of the Court of Appeal delivered by SALMON, L.J.

> "If a young man such as the appellant is given a six months suspended sentence, back he goes from whence he came and the news spreads like wildfire amongst all students. 'Well, this is not a bad way of trying to get money because if it comes off you have made a nice profit and had a good holiday, and if it does not come off you will just be sent home again.' On the other hand, if it is known among potential offenders in the Lebanon and elsewhere that, if they are caught attempting to smuggle drugs into this country, they will be severely dealt with, there may be a remarkable lack of enthusiasm for enterprises of this kind and great difficulties put in the way of people who run this filthy trade."

Similar confidence in the general deterrent effect of more severe sentencing was shown by the Court of Appeal in *Motley*.[4] In this

---

[1] D. Beyleveld, "Deterrence Research as a Basis for Deterrence Policies" (1979)[18]. Howard Jo. 135; *cf.* Nigel Walker, "The Efficacy and Morality of Deterrents" [1979] Crim. L.R. 129.

[2] H. D. Willcock and J. Stokes *Deterrents to Crime among Youths of 15 to 21* (Government Social Survey Report No. SS 356).

[3] (1969), 53 Cr. App. Rep. 490.

[4] (1978), 66 Cr. App. Rep. 274; see also *Bruce* (1977), 65 Cr. App. Rep. 148.

case Motley pleaded guilty to two counts of assault occasioning actual bodily harm and two counts of criminal damage, having thrown a beer can and part of a brick through the windscreens of two cars whilst travelling in a coach back from a football match. Upholding a Borstal sentence, LAWTON, L.J., said:

> "It is manifest now that that kind of sentence [i.e. non-custodial sentences] has not deterred the hooligans who go to football matches intent on causing disorder. Something has got to be done in order to ensure as far as possible that this kind of conduct comes to an end . . . We have no hesitation in saying that hooligans of the kind which the appellant has shown himself to be, who are 17 years and older, should expect to lose their liberty if they are convicted of offences of violence which cause injury to other people or criminal damage which ordinary sensible folk can fairly and justly call vandalism.
>
> The sooner football supporters appreciate when they get into their coaches or trains to go away to football matches if they use violence to other people the probabilities are that they will not be returning to their homes for some time [sic]. We are confident that if the courts impose a policy of this kind for the rest of this football season, there may be an improvement next year."

The deterrent effect of the example of punishment may well be greater in the case of a small community, such as that of Lebanese students with which *Daher* was concerned. Whether the optimistic views of LAWTON, L.J., in *Motley* were borne out by any diminution in the number of "football hooliganism" offences which might otherwise have taken place is one of the many questions on deterrence which simply cannot be answered. Such research as has been conducted into the general deterrent effect of really severe sentences (such as the sentence of 20 years detention imposed on a youth of 16 in *Storey*[1] at the height of public concern about offences of "mugging") gives no grounds at all for optimism about their efficacy.[2] The justifications for imposing a sentence aimed at general deterrence which exceeds the retributively appropriate sentence must therefore always be closely scrutinised.

(*c*) *Long term deterrence—denunciation or education.*[3] The deterrent theories considered so far may be said to be theories of short term deterrence in the sense that the threat or example of punishment is supposed to operate immediately on those contemplating crime. Such a person is supposed to say to himself "I had better not do it

---

[1] (1973), 57 Cr. App. Rep. 840.

[2] Baxter and Nuttall, New Society, 2nd January 1975; *cf.* also Beyleveld, p. 37, n. 1, *supra*, and the "attitude of scepticism" towards exemplary sentences adopted by the Advisory Council on the Penal System, Sentences of Imprisonment: A Review of Maximum Penalties, para. 203.

[3] *Cf.* Walker, "Punishing, Denouncing or Reducing Crime?" in Glazebrook (ed.), *Reshaping the Criminal Law*, p. 391.

because, if I am caught, I will get what I got before or worse": or "I had better not do it because, if I am caught, I will get what old—got." The theory now under consideration, the "denunciatory" or "educative" theory, may be described as one of long term deterrence. It is justification of punishment on the ground that it helps to maintain people's standards. The fact that people are punished for crime is believed to build up an abhorrence of it over the years and thus to reduce the number of those who would even remotely contemplate it. It is difficult to see how penological assumptions of this nature can ever be proved to be either right or wrong. The theory was very clearly stated by Sir James Stephen:[1]

> "If in all cases criminal law were regarded only as a direct appeal to the fears of persons likely to commit crimes, it would be deprived of a large part of its efficacy, for it operates, not only on the fears of criminals, but upon the habitual sentiments of those who are not criminals. A great part of the general detestation of crime which happily prevails among the decent part of the community in all civilised countries arises from the fact that the commission of offences is associated in all such communities with the solemn and deliberate infliction of punishment wherever crime is proved."

Unfortunately Stephen transferred the hatred from the crime to the criminal in a later passage which smacks of barbarism.

> "I think it highly desirable that criminals should be hated, that the punishments inflicted upon them should be so contrived as to give expression to that hatred, and to justify it so far as the public provision of means for expressing and gratifying a healthy natural sentiment can justify and encourage it."

It may be a counsel of perfection to say "hate the crime but not the criminal", but it is worth attempting.

The theory is stated in a more civilised way by Dr. A. C. Ewing in *The Morality of Punishment* published in 1929. He argues that the practice of punishment may be justified as an attempt at the moral education of the offender as well as others.

> "Now the existence of a penal law is an impressive condemnation of the practice prohibited by it. But surely this solemn, public condemnation on behalf of the community will have some effect not only on those actually punished but on others also. If it may help the offender to realise the badness of his action, may it not help others to realise this badness before they have committed the kind of act in question at all? This must not be confused with a purely deterrent effect. A man who abstains from crime just because he is deterred abstains through fear of suffering and not because he thinks it wicked; a man who abstains because the condemnation of the crime by society and the state has brought its wickedness home

---

[1] *History of Criminal Law*, vol. II, p. 79.

to him abstains from moral motives and not merely from fear of unpleasant consequences to himself."[1]

The negative version of the theory, i.e. that failure to punish a crime adequately will depreciate its seriousness,[2] is probably uppermost in the minds of the judges when they make remarks such as those cited from *Williams*[3] and *Llewellyn Jones*.[4] Whether it is being considered in its positive or negative form, the theory is regarded by some as retributive rather than utilitarian.

> "Retribution in punishment is an expression of the community's disapproval of crime, and if this retribution is not given recognition, then the disapproval may also disappear."[5]

In relation to general deterrence in both its short and long term forms, a question which may be raised is what justifies the use of the criminal as a means to the good of others, especially when that use consists of the infliction of pain? Sydney Smith gave the wrong answer to this question:

> "When a man has been proved to have committed a crime it is expedient that society should make use of that man for the diminution of crime. He belongs to them for that purpose."[6]

The right answer is that the criminal is not being used merely as a means. He is being given his just deserts although, in the view taken in this book, there is no reason why he should receive them at the hands of an earthly power if crime is not reduced thereby.

iii. *Reform.* Two aspects of the reformative theory of punishment must be distinguished, the idea that reform can come through the punishment itself and the idea of reform as a concomitant of punishment. On the first view, the pain of punishment is considered to have reformative merits of its own. This view is so unfashionable that nothing need be said about it beyond observing that solitary confinement is an example from former times, the theory being that suffering the loss of liberty in solitude would induce remorse, repentance and reform. The idea of reform as a concomitant of punishment is, by contrast, still fashionable. In the case of probation the reformative element is so much to the fore that probation is not regarded in law as punishment at all; although it is recognised that punitive elements are present in a Borstal sentence, Borstal sentences are still sometimes imposed and upheld as rehabilitative

---

[1] *The Morality of Punishment*, p. 96.
[2] See the extract from the American Law Institute's Model Penal Code, p. 22, *supra*.
[3] P. 129, *supra*.
[4] P. 129, *supra*.
[5] Goodhart, *The English Law and the Moral Law*, p. 93. Cf. *Sargeant*, p. 143, *infra*.
[6] Cited in *The Modern Approach to Criminal Law*, p. 40.

measures.[1] There is now little belief in the reformative (as opposed to the individual deterrent) effect of a short term of imprisonment; and longer terms of imprisonment, such as those served in so-called "training prisons", also place serious limitations on any process of rehabilitation, as the Advisory Council on the Penal System acknowledged:

> "Prolonged and repeated imprisonment is destructive of family relationships and, by encouraging the prisoner's identification with the attitudes of the prison community, increases his alienation from normal society. In addition, long-term institutionalisation is all too likely to destroy a prisoner's capacity for individual responsibility and to increase the problems he must face when he returns to society."[2]

It can therefore rarely be proper to impose a sentence of imprisonment primarily for reformative purposes.

Since reform is usually best secured through a non-custodial sentence, it is inevitable that the Courts will be confronted with conflicts between general deterrence and reform and between retribution and reform. The tendency of the Courts has been to resolve the conflict by letting reform go to the wall. Judges rightly recognise that the maxim "punish the offender rather than the offence" is only sound up to a point, for there are many situations in which the rights of the offender or the protection of the public require that the sentence should be concentrated on the offence.

The conflict between retribution and reform is illustrated by the problem of whether the availability of treatment facilities in prison should be allowed to *increase* the length of a prison sentence. The solution appears to depend on the gravity of the offence. We saw earlier that the Court of Appeal allows remission and parole to be taken into consideration when fixing the length of a sentence of imprisonment which is aimed at "reform or mental treatment",[3] but those were cases of crimes justifying a substantial prison sentence in any event. Where the crime is what may be termed a "run-of-the-mill" offence, however, it appears that a prison sentence should not be increased so as to allow a full programme of treatment.[4] The point is illustrated by the decisions in *Ford*[5] and *Moylan*.[6]

Ford had been sentenced to 27 months imprisonment for housebreaking and larceny, although his co-accused had only been given twelve months. The difference was largely due to the fact that Ford

---

[1] See *Coleman*, p. 82, *supra*.
[2] *The Length of Prison Sentences*, para. 10.
[3] *Turner*, discussed *supra*, p. 99.
[4] *Sheen*, [1979] Crim. L.R.189 ("relatively trivial examples of burglary").
[5] [1969] 3 All E.R. 782n.
[6] [1970] 1 Q.B. 142; [1969] 3 All E.R. 783.

was an alcoholic and it was felt that the additional time in prison was necessary for the completion of his cure. Nevertheless the Court of Appeal reduced Ford's sentence to twelve months.

> "In relation to offences of dishonesty, sentences of imprisonment, except where there is an element of protection of the public, are normally intended to be the correct sentence for the particular crime and not to include a curative element. This Court wishes to make it clear that what it is now saying has nothing to do with special cases such as those of possessing dangerous drugs or cases where protection of the public is involved."

Moylan had been given an eighteen months suspended sentence for larceny. He was subsequently convicted of causing malicious damage and being drunk and disorderly and was given three months immediate imprisonment. The judge who imposed this sentence brought the suspended sentence fully into operation, partly in the hope of curing Moylan of his alcoholism. The Court of Appeal held that this was wrong and activated the suspended sentence for six months only.

> "In our judgement, in cases of dishonesty where there is, as it were, a background of alcoholism in respect of the accused, the Court must first determine what are the limits of a proper sentence in respect of the offences charged. Within these limits it may be perfectly proper to increase the sentence in order to enable a cure to be undertaken whilst the accused is in prison. But, on the authority of *Ford*, it is clear that it is not correct to increase above that within the appropriate range of the offence itself merely in order to provide an opportunity of cure."

There might be something to be said for the compulsory cure of alcoholics and drug addicts,[1] but it certainly ought not to be introduced by the side-wind of long prison sentences for "run-of-the-mill" offences.

More frequent is the conflict between general deterrence and reform. The Court of Appeal frequently has to deal with cases in which an intrinsically serious crime has been committed by an offender who is young and of previous good character, and who therefore has a strong claim to a reformative rather than a punitive sentence. The decisions show that where the crime is thought to be serious or prevalent, a substantial tariff sentence will be upheld. Thus in *Newbury and Jones*[2] a sentence of three years detention was thought appropriate for a youth of 15 who pushed part of a paving stone off the parapet of a bridge, causing the death of a guard travelling in a train which passed beneath; and in *Elvin*[3] a sentence

---

[1] See p. 160, *infra*.
[2] (1976), 62 Cr. App. Rep. 291; there was an appeal to the House of Lords on another point.
[3] [1976] Crim. L.R. 204.

of four years imprisonment upon a youth of 17 with no previous convictions who had set fire to school buildings was upheld, as a general deterrent to discourage others from committing what was a particularly rife type of crime; and in *Smith and Wolard*[1] it was even said that general deterrence should be placed before reform when sentencing offenders for burglary of houses.

C. THE JUDGMENT IN *SARGEANT*

No statute contains a general statement of the aims which sentencers should seek to achieve, but the judges have from time to time, as we have seen in the preceding pages, discussed the relationship of principles of punishment to particular classes of case. One case in which several of the aims of sentencing were discussed is *Sargeant*.[2] The appellant was employed as a doorman at a discotheque. He observed a customer making a nuisance of himself, went over to the customer and butted him. From this a general affray resulted, although the appellant (who had received a painful blow in return) took no further part. He appealed against the sentence of two years imprisonment, and LAWTON, L.J., delivering the judgment of the Court of Appeal, stated:

> "What ought the proper penalty to be? We have thought it necessary not only to analyse the facts, but to apply to those facts the classical principles of sentencing. Those classical principles are summed up in four words: retribution, deterrence, prevention and rehabilitation. Any judge who comes to sentence ought always to have those four classical principles in mind and to apply them to the facts of the case to see which of them has the greatest importance in the case with which he is dealing.
>
> I will start with retribution. The Old Testament concept of an eye for an eye and tooth for tooth no longer plays any part in our criminal law. There is, however, another aspect of retribution which is frequently overlooked: it is that society, through the courts, must show its abhorrence of particular types of crime, and the only way in which the courts can show this is by the sentences they pass. The courts do not have to reflect public opinion. On the other hand courts must not disregard it. Perhaps the main duty of the court is to lead public opinion. Anyone who surveys the criminal scene at the present time must be alive to the appalling problem of violence. Society, we are satisfied, expects the courts to deal with violence. The weapons which the courts have at their disposal for doing so are few. We are satisfied that in most cases fines are not sufficient punishment for senseless violence. The time has come, in the opinion of this Court, when those who indulge in the kind of violence with which we are concerned in this case must expect custodial sentences.
>
> But we are also satisfied that, although society expects the courts to impose punishment for violence which really hurts, it does not expect the courts to go on hurting for a long time, which is what this sentence is likely to do. We agree with the trial judge that the kind of violence which

---

[1] (1978), 67 Cr. App. Rep. 211.
[2] (1974), 60 Cr. App. Rep. 74.

occurred in this case called for a custodial sentence. This young man has had a custodial sentence. Despite his good character, despite the excellent background from which he comes, very deservedly he has had the humiliation of hearing prison gates closing behind him. We take the view that for men of good character the very fact that prison gates have closed is the main punishment. It does not necessarily follow that they should remain closed for a long time.

I turn now to the element of deterrence, because it seems to us the trial judge probably passed this sentence as a deterrent one. There are two aspects of deterrence: deterrence of the offender and deterrence of likely offenders. Experience has shown over the years that deterrence of the offender is not a very useful approach, because those who have their wits about them usually find the closing of prison gates an experience which they do not want again. If they do not learn that lesson, there is likely to be a high degree of recidivism anyway. So far as deterrence of others is concerned, it is the experience of the courts that deterrent sentences are of little value in respect of offences which are committed on the spur of the moment, either in hot blood or in drink or both. Deterrent sentences may very well be of considerable value where crime is premeditated. Burglars, robbers and users of firearms and weapons may very well be put off by deterrent sentences. We think it unlikely that deterrence would be of any value in this case.

We come now to the element of prevention. Unfortunately it is one of the facts of life that there are some offenders for whom neither deterrence nor rehabilitation works. They will go on committing crimes as long as they are able to do so. In those cases the only protection which the public has is that such persons should be locked up for a long period. This case does not call for a preventive sentence.

Finally, there is the principle of rehabilitation. Some 20 to 25 years ago there was a view abroad, held by many people in executive authority, that short sentences were of little value, because there was not enough time to give in prison the benefit of training. That view is no longer held as firmly as it was. This young man does not want prison training. It is not going to do him any good. It is his memory of the clanging of prison gates which is likely to keep him from crime in the future."

This passage may be used to draw together a number of the considerations mentioned in Part B above.

In stating that the courts must have regard to public opinion when considering an offender's just deserts, LAWTON, L.J., draws attention to the denunciatory aspect of punishment. He treats it as a form of retribution, as did Sir James Stephen when he wrote that the common crimes are punished

> "for the sake of gratifying the feeling of hatred,—call it revenge, resentment, or what you will—which the contemplation of such conduct excites in healthily constituted minds."[1]

Although there clearly is a link between retribution and reprobait was argued above[2] that the denunciatory justification for punish-

---

[1] *Liberty, Equality and Fraternity* (London, 1874), pp. 161–2.
[2] P. 138, *supra*.

punishment may better be seen as a kind of long-term deterrence. In this sense, to keep an approximate correspondence between the degree of popular abhorrence for certain kinds of crime and the level of the tariff is important in order to reinforce public attitudes towards those offences.

Although LAWTON, L.J., places little faith in individual deterrence as a reason for making a particular sentence more severe than it might be on retributive grounds, he argues that general deterrence may be justifiable in certain kinds of case. His argument is less about theoretical justifications than about the practical utility of trying to deter certain kinds of conduct. Thus it is more practical to aim at deterring planned crimes than sudden and impulsive crimes. Whilst it may be true that those who commit planned and premeditated crimes may consider the likely punishment before they offend—although in some cases the probability of detection might be equally important to them—one could perhaps contend that a system which imposed high penalties for all offending, planned or impulsive, might be more effective in reducing crime than one which reserved the higher penalties for planned crimes. Even if this were true, however, the extra amount of crime-reduction obtained by punishing impulsive crimes as severely as planned crimes might not persuade the utilitarian that the extra suffering imposed on impulsive offenders was worthwhile, and would certainly not persuade the retributivist that the extra suffering was justified since impulsive crimes are generally regarded as less wicked than premeditated offences.

The view that a retributively appropriate sentence should not be increased in order to give time for rehabilitation has been explained above,[1] and is endorsed by LAWTON, L.J. As Professor Norval Morris has declared, "Power over a criminal's life should not be taken in excess of that which would be taken were his reform not considered as one of our purposes."[2] In this case, then, the sentence of two years was held to be "much too long", and it was reduced, in effect, to a sentence of eight months. Clearly LAWTON, L.J., thought this to be a sufficient individual deterrent for someone who had not previously been to prison, and it was also considered retributively appropriate in view of the impulsive nature of the violence.

Section 3.—**Theories of punishment in practical cases**

The object of this section is to consider some apparently simple but really very difficult general sentencing questions in the light of the

---

[1] P. 142, *supra*.
[2] 33 University of Chicago L Rev 638.

above discussion of the theories of punishment. The questions are difficult because they concern matters which sentencers, and indeed all those interested in the criminal law, tend to take for granted. In some instances it will be found that no theory of punishment provides a satisfactory answer; in others the only answer the theories do provide is in terms of what Bentham described as "vindicative satisfaction";[1] and, in almost every case, the dependence of our sentencing practice on retributive considerations is very marked. What follows is intended to be thought provoking rather than informative; the problems selected for discussion may be said to illustrate the relationship between the general principles of criminal liability and the aims of sentencing.

A. INTENTION, KNOWLEDGE AND RECKLESSNESS

Should a person who commits an offence with full knowledge of the prohibited circumstances be punished more than one whose offence is committed merely with recklessness as to those circumstances? Should a person who intends to cause the prohibited consequences be punished more than one who is merely reckless as to those consequences? The answer to these questions is relevant to sentencing for most serious offences, and is particularly important where the legislature grades offences and provides differing maximum penalties—as with wounding "with intent" under s. 18 of the Offences against the Person Act 1861 and malicious wounding under s. 20 of that Act, and as with the Criminal Law Revision Committee's recommended offences of "causing serious injury with intent to cause serious injury" and "causing serious injury recklessly".[2]

To answer the questions it is necessary to distinguish briefly between the various mental states. The discussion will concentrate on advertence to consequences, but the distinctions may equally be applied to advertence to circumstances.

Direct intention is where a person does an act desiring to produce the proscribed consequence. As JAMES, L.J., said in *Mohan*,[3] it consists of "a decision to bring about, so far as it lies within the accused's power, the commission of the offence". He not only chooses but aims to produce the consequence; if he did not produce it, he would regard himself as having failed in his enterprise.[4]

Foresight of certainty occurs where a person does an act believing that the proscribed consequence is practically certain to result from

---

[1] P. 129, *supra*.
[2] Fourteenth Report, Offences against the Person (Cmnd. 7844, 1980), para. 152.
[3] [1976] Q.B. 1 at p. 11.
[4] Cf. R. A. Duff, [1980] Crim. L.R. 147 at p. 150.

his conduct, although it is not his aim to produce that consequence. In such cases the defendant chooses to produce the consequence, but since it is not part of his aim he would not regard himself as having failed if by some chance it did not result.

Recklessness towards a consequence occurs when the defendant realises the risk that it may result from his conduct and unjustifiably takes that risk. He neither chooses nor aims to produce it, but he knowingly and unjustifiably chooses to risk producing it. Since the degree of known risk may vary, one may speak of degrees of recklessness.

Although it is important that the criminal law should adopt clear and, if possible, consistent meanings for its key terms, this has proved difficult. Bentham used a concept of "oblique intention" to include not only cases of foresight of certainty but also cases where the actor knew that the consequence was *likely* to result from his acts, and there is powerful judicial support for thus extending "intention" to cases of foresight of probability.[1] However, the Law Commission would treat cases where the consequence was foreseen as less than practically certain as cases of recklessness, not intention;[2] and the Criminal Law Revision Committee, in their recent review of the law on offences against the person, preferred that view.[3]

From this brief explanation we return to the question whether the distinctions between these mental states should be reflected by different sentences. The Criminal Law Revision Committee, in recommending separate offences of causing serious injury "with intent" and recklessly, were in no doubt:

> "There is, in our opinion, a definite moral and psychological difference between the two offences which it is appropriate for the criminal law to reflect."[4]

The relevance of this difference to sentencing is shown by their recommendation of a maximum penalty of life imprisonment for the offence "with intent", compared with a maximum of five years imprisonment for the reckless offence.

It is perhaps best to begin by exploring the difference between direct intention and recklessness. Two differences are particularly relevant to the present discussion. The first is that directly intentional acts are both more wicked and more socially dangerous than reckless acts, and therefore warrant higher punishment on both retributive and utilitarian grounds. The person who acts with direct

---

[1] E. g. Lord DIPLOCK in *Hyam* v. *Director of Public Prosecutions*, [1974] 2 All E.R. 41 at p. 59, and in *Lemon*, [1979] 1 All E.R. 898 at p. 905.
[2] The Mental Element in Crime, Law Com. no. 89, para. 43.
[3] Fourteenth Report, Part II.
[4] Fourteenth Report, para. 152.

intent is more wicked inasmuch as he "more unequivocally puts his own interests above the interests of society",[1] by deciding to try to produce the prohibited consequence as distinct from merely choosing to risk producing it (as the reckless actor does). He is more dangerous because, since the production of the consequence is (part of) his aim, he is more likely to try until he succeeds; the reckless actor, by contrast, will not regard himself as having failed if the consequence does not ensue and therefore will not on that ground try again. This greater social danger indicates that the directly intentional actor should receive a more severe sentence on both individual deterrent and general deterrent grounds. The utilitarian might add that punishing reckless actors less severely might also encourage them to take greater precautions against causing harm.[2]

The second difference between direct intention and recklessness stems from a separate axis of gravity, which may be termed "social justification". The point may be illustrated by contrasting the case of a man who intentionally kills his suffering wife in response to her pleas, with the case of a man who sets off a bomb in a railway station after giving some kind of warning, knowing of the risk that someone may be killed. The bomber will be regarded as having caused death recklessly, and in defining his act as reckless the law not only finds that he was aware of the risk but also finds that there was inadequate social justification for taking the risk which he believed he was taking. Now as the Criminal Law Revision Committee observed, the practical importance of the requirement of social justification must not be overstated:

> "In the vast majority of instances of offences against the person the risk taken is so obviously unjustifiable that the question is not raised and presents no problem, but there are borderline cases of which a definition must take account. Even where the person acting knows that there is a high probability that his act will cause death, it is not necessarily an unlawful act. He may be a surgeon acting in circumstances which make it reasonable to take even this grave risk. On the other hand, the risk may be an unreasonable one to take even though the possibility of the harmful result is only slight. At the other extreme from the surgeon, the 'Russian roulette' player who knowingly takes even a very slight risk of causing somebody else's death might well be held to do so unreasonably and therefore unlawfully."[3]

Every finding of recklessness involves a judgment of social justification, but in most crimes of violence it is a formality. The point relevant here is that a finding of direct intention involves no judgment of social justification at all, since it is not part of the definition

---

[1] D. J. Galligan, "Responsibility for Recklessness" (1978) 31 C.L.P. 55 at p. 75.
[2] R. Cross, "The Mental Element in Crime" (1967) 83 L.Q.R. 215 at p. 217.
[3] Fourteenth Report, para. 8.

of direct intent. In most crimes against the person the point would hardly be worth arguing. But the mercy killing example shows that in some cases of directly intentional harm we might still wish to reduce the punishment, believing that the defendant's action had some colour of social justification which differentiated it from most other offences from which that factor was absent. His offence manifested less wickedness and was less socially dangerous than the general run of intentional acts; indeed, on this ground his offence may be regarded as less wicked and less socially dangerous than most reckless offences, since most reckless acts have no colour of social justification at all.

Very few cases of directly intentional harmdoing fall within the argument of the last paragraph. In most cases the directly intentional act may be regarded as more wicked and more socially dangerous than the reckless act. Where, then, does foresight of certainty fit into the scheme? In analytical terms it is most accurately seen as a variety of recklessness. Recklessness may be represented as a plane of mental states of risk-taking, with the degree of risk varying from practical certainty down to remote possibility. Cases of foresight of certainty are in reality cases where the risk which the accused knows to attach to his conduct is so great as to amount almost to practical certainty:[1] they are not cases of intention, since the accused does not aim to produce the consequence. On the other hand, both the Law Commission[2] and the Criminal Law Revision Committee[3] would classify cases of foresight of certainty as cases of intention rather than recklessness. The reasoning is that where the accused has "no substantial doubt" that the consequence will result from his conduct (Law Commission) or "knows that in the ordinary course of things it will do so" (C.L.R.C.), the wickedness and social danger of his conduct lie closer to the directly intentional actor than to the reckless actor. He is virtually certain to cause the prohibited harm, whereas the truly reckless actor merely creates some degree of risk and therefore leaves the chance that no harm may result. On the other hand, the sentencer may argue that, whatever the legal classification, cases of foresight of certainty may properly be punished less severely than cases of direct intent because the production of the consequence is not actually part of the defendant's aim and because the social danger of his conduct is less, inasmuch as he is less likely to try again if the consequence does not result.

---

[1] Galligan, *op. cit.*
[2] Law Com. no. 89, The Mental Element in Crime, p. 56; but they now agree that the intent required for attempted crimes should be limited to "direct intentional", as explained by James, L.J., in *Mohan*: Law Com. no. 102, para. 2.17.
[3] Fourteenth Report, para. 10.

We may conclude, then, that in general, and on both retributive and utilitarian grounds, cases of direct intention should be punished more severely than cases of foresight of certainty, and cases of foresight of certainty more severely than cases of recklessness. But other factors may lead the sentencer to take a different view in a particular case. The issue of social justification was discussed above; and one might also maintain that a planned piece of unjustifiable risk-taking is more wicked and more dangerous than an intentional but impulsive offence.

B. NEGLIGENCE

Why punish negligent wrongdoing less severely than intentional or reckless wrongdoing?

It was suggested above[1] that negligence may properly be seen as a species of fault, but the degree of fault is generally lower in cases of negligence since there is no requirement that the defendant himself should have adverted to the risk which objectively was inherent in his conduct. The intentional or reckless wrongdoer must be found to have been aware of the risk created by his conduct and to have chosen to run the risk; the fault of the negligent wrongdoer is generally less—he failed to advert to the risk, although the reasonable man in his position would have done. Although its abolition has been proposed,[2] the present law of manslaughter is an example of the punishment of negligent wrongdoing. Why then should manslaughter by gross negligence be punished less severely than murder?

The most obvious and, it is submitted, the only satisfactory answer to this question is: Because the person who commits involuntary manslaughter by gross negligence is less wicked than the person who intentionally commits murder. On this basis, the only justification for the differentiation in terms of the theories of punishment is retributive—the quantity of punishment must be proportionate to the offender's deserts. If the harm is the same the negligent wrongdoer deserves less punishment because he is less wicked than the intentional wrongdoer. It is sometimes suggested, however, that the distinction can be justified on utilitarian grounds by reference to the greater social alarm caused by intentional wrongdoing. The fallacy underlying this suggestion can be demonstrated by reference to two hypothetical cases.

i. A, with callous premeditation, poisons his mother in order to inherit her money.

---

[1] P. 126, *supra*.
[2] Fourteenth Report of the C.L.R.C., para. 121.

ii. B, a grossly negligent motorist, who persistently drives while disqualified, runs down and kills a pedestrian.

It is possible to muster a mass of utilitarian arguments in favour of punishing B more severely than A. There is a greater chance of the recurrence of the homicide pointing to a longer term of imprisonment in the names of prevention and individual deterrence; there is the fact that B is the greater social menace because the number of his potential victims is far larger, and this calls for heavier punishment in the name of general deterrence; the fact that B is more likely to drive negligently in the future than A is to resort to poison makes him the cause of greater social alarm. None the less the retributive argument in favour of punishing A more heavily because he is the more wicked of the two is supported by one overwhelming consideration, whether it be called retributive or utilitarian. A society in which the deliberate poisoner was treated with the same degree of tolerance as the negligent motorist is treated by our society would be a most unpleasant society. It is in fact a very good thing that our sentencing system should be governed by retributive considerations at certain points, especially when those considerations relate to the apportionment of punishment to desert, rather than the appeasement of vindicative satisfaction.

C. ATTEMPTS AND OTHER INCHOATE CRIMES

Why punish an attempt less severely than the crime attempted would have been punished if it had been consummated?[1]

A few English statutes, particularly those relating to sexual offences,[2] provide a lower maximum penalty for the attempt, but the only provision of general application is s. 18(2) of the Powers of Criminal Courts Act 1973. This provides that, where the maximum penalty for an offence is laid down by statute, an attempter shall not be sentenced to a longer term of imprisonment or a larger fine than those to which he could have been sentenced for the completed offence.[3] The Law Commission has recently considered the matter and has endorsed the view that the maximum punishment for an attempt should generally be the same as that for the completed offence.[4] That, however, leaves the sentencer with the problem whether an attempt ought in fact to be punished as severely as the completed offence, and the following remarks of HUMPHREYS, J.

---

[1] We are heavily indebted to the discussion of this question in Hart, *Punishment and Responsibility*, pp. 129 *et seq.*

[2] Cf. Sexual Offences Act 1956, Sch. 2, as amended.

[3] Confirming the decision in *Verrier v. Director of Public Prosecutions*, [1967] 2 A.C. 195; *cf.* for summary trials, s. 28(1)(c) of Criminal Law Act 1977.

[4] Law Com. no. 102, Attempt, and Impossibility in relation to Attempt, Conspiracy and Incitement, paras. 2.107–2.110.

when sentencing a man to six years penal servitude for throwing corrosive fluid at a girl with intent to burn would probably not be regarded as untypical of the contemporary judicial approach to the punishment of attempts:

"There are in my opinion no mitigating circumstances in this case. You did it deliberately; you wrote a letter to her threatening her that unless she did what you wanted you would do this thing and that you had bought the vitriol for the purpose. After you had thrown the bottle of vitriol at her and had been arrested your only statement to the police officer was one of regret that you had not done all you had intended to do. In search of mitigating circumstances the only thing I can find is something which in truth does not redound to your credit and that is that in fact you did her no harm . . . But I do take it into consideration and I substantially lessen your sentence on account of that fact because it does, in my view, reduce your crime rather to the category of attempts than the category of completed crimes and you are entitled, fortunately for yourself, to have it remembered that you really only attempted to burn and disfigure this poor girl.[1]

It is impossible to prove affirmatively by reference to the criminal statistics that people are punished less for the attempt than for the consummated crime, but a small piece of research conducted some years ago by Mr. David Steer, now of the the Police College, shows that, for the three years 1965–67, significantly more non-custodial sentences were given for attempted breakings than for housebreaking and other breakings contrary to s. 26 of the Larceny Act 1916 and for breaking and entering with intent contrary to s. 27. There were also significantly more non-custodial sentences for the offences against s. 27 than for those against s. 26.[2] Of course these facts may be accounted for by considerations, such as the inefficiency of offenders guilty of attempts, other than the difference between attempts and consummated crimes. But the view that attempted crimes are generally punished less severely than completed crimes gains further support from a recent study of sentencing for sexual offences,[3] and it is therefore worth persevering with the inquiry why attempts should be treated more leniently.

Partial answers to this question are readily provided both by utilitarian and by retributive theory, but they only apply to certain types of case. The utilitarian answer was provided by Bentham:

"If the punishment of a preliminary offence or of an offence begun but not finished were the same as that of the principal or complete offence without

---

[1] *Carmichael* (1930), 22 Cr. App. Rep. 142. The sentence was reduced to 18 months by the Court of Criminal Appeal on the ground that the judge had not made enough allowance for provocation and other mitigating circumstances.

[2] See Tables X and XI. We are grateful to Mr. Steer for preparing these Tables.

[3] Home Office Research Study No 54, *Sexual Offences, Consent and Sentencing*, by R. Walmsley and K. White, at pp. 22 and 26.

allowing anything for the possibility of repentance or a prudent stopping short, the delinquent, perceiving that he had already incurred the whole danger by the single attempt, would feel himself to be at liberty to consummate the offence without incurring any further risk."[1]

This argument only applies to the rare case of the calm, reflective criminal whose initial failure has been undetected. In theory, punishing attempted murder less severely than murder could mean that someone who had shot at and missed his intended victim would not try again; but Bentham's argument does not apply to the case of the man who is apprehended before he could fire a second shot.

Blackstone provided a retributive answer based on the need to punish in proportion to the offender's wickedness, but it is even more restricted in its application than is that of Bentham.

"And yet, generally, a design to transgress is not so flagrant an enormity, as the actual completion of that design. For evil, the nearer we approach it, is the more disagreeable and shocking, so that it requires more obstinacy in wickedness to perpetrate an unlawful action, than barely to entertain the thought of it. And it is an encouragement to repentance, and remorse, even till the last stage of any crime, that it never is too late to retract; and that if a man stops even here it is better for him than if he had proceeded, for which reasons an attempt to rob, to ravish, or to kill is far less penal than the actual robbery, rape or murder."[2]

But what if the robbery was frustrated by detection, the rape because the victim succeeded in avoiding penetration after a desperate struggle, and the murder because the victim is cured by exceptional medical skill?

Two examples may be given of one of the situations in which it is most difficult to justify punishing an attempt less severely than the crime attempted. Suppose that A fakes a burglary in his house and posts a false claim for indemnity to his insurance company. After making investigations, the company's representatives post a cheque to A, but the letter is misdirected and the cheque is returned in due course to the company by which time the attempted fraud has been discovered. Suppose too that the facts are the same in the case of B except that he receives and cashes the cheque although the money is recovered after his apprehension. Why should A be punished less for attempting to obtain property by deception than B is punished for the full offence?

If utilitarian theories are applied, that of prevention suggests that A and B should be punished alike; the public needs just as much protection against the one as the other. Individual deterrence also demands equal punishment for each of the deceivers requires the

---

[1] *Theory of Legislation*, p. 427.
[2] *Commentaries* (1813 Edn.), Book IV, p. 14.

same amount of punishment to discourage him from trying again. Had the money not been recovered from B, greater punishment might have been called for in the name of both individual deterrence and retribution in his case. Where an offender keeps for himself the fruits of his crime he is both more wicked than the offender who returns his ill-gotten gains and in need of greater individual deterrence.

General deterrence would also appear to favour identity of punishment, but, at this point, allowance must be made for a somewhat sophisticated argument. It is sometimes suggested that general deterrence requires less punishment for an attempt because it is the threat of punishment appropriate to the main crime and the spectacle of people being punished for that crime which operates as a general deterrent. Intending criminals set out to succeed, no one aims at merely being guilty of a criminal attempt. Therefore a lighter punishment for an attempt would not augment the number of people who try to commit the main crime in the future. It is said that the weakness of this argument is that it assumes that everyone who sets out to commit the main crime is confident of success; but allowance must be made for those who say to themselves "We will try, because, if we succeed, the gain will be large enough to justify the risk of heavier punishment for the main crime, if we fail we will only suffer the lighter punishment for the attempt". This is of course a highly sophisticated argument too, but sophisticated arguments call for sophisticated replies and, in any event, the original argument is a weak one in the case of A and B. Even on a conviction for the main crime the general deterrent effect of the law's threat would not be reduced by a certain amount of leniency when the loot has been recovered before sentence.

If retributive theories are applied to the cases under consideration, there seems to be as little or as much legitimate demand for vindicative satisfaction on behalf of the insurance company in each instance. Another argument, combining the theory of fairness to the law-abiding with the utilitarian denunciatory or educative theory, is that less punishment is necessary for the attempt than for the completed crime in order to satisfy the demands of fairness to those who have obeyed the law and to show that crime does not pay.

The upshot of the above discussion is that the question whether an attempt should be punished less severely than the completed crime is largely dependent on the reason why the attempt failed. If it failed because the attempter voluntarily abandoned the attempt, he should be punished less because he is less wicked or needs less deterring. If it failed because of his incompetence, either in executing his design clumsily or in choosing a method which, owing to his failure to appreciate the true facts, proved to be impossible, he may be punished less on the ground that he represents less of a social danger than successful criminals.[1] If it failed because of someone's intervention before he had done all he set out to do, he may be treated more leniently than the successful criminal: his wickedness may be less, since (as Blackstone said) it takes more wickedness to carry through a plan than to conceive it, and it may be desirable (on a utilitarian view) to mark each stage of an attempt by a portion of punishment in order to deter the attempter from pursuing his criminal design to its conclusion. There remain difficulties, however, with cases such as that of A and B, where the attempter has done all the acts he intended and has failed to produce the planned result. Where the successful criminal keeps for himself a profit from the offence he may be viewed as more wicked than the attempter, and so may be punished more severely on retributive grounds. The utilitarian might argue, more generally, that a portion of punishment should always be withheld in order to deter the unsuccessful attempter from trying again. And if vindication is stressed, the sentence should be less because there is less vindicative satisfaction to be provided, for the simple reason that the attempt caused little or no actual harm. This may well be the view which influences sentencing practice. On principle, however, there is no distinction in point of either wickedness or social danger between the successful criminal and the unsuccessful attempter in this last class. Chance may well be the only explanation of why one attempt succeeded and the other failed, and a sound sentencing policy should take little notice of a factor which lies outside the offender's control.[2] He should be judged on the basis of what he intended to do, believed he was doing or knowingly risked.

More remote from the completed crime lie the preparatory offences, such as possession of an offensive weapon, going equipped for stealing and loitering with intent. Although the relevant principles are similar to those for punishing attempts, the fact that preparatory crimes are generally further removed from the completed crime means that there is usually more opportunity for abandoning any plan to use a weapon or instrument, and so in general a preparatory offence should attract less punishment than the attempt. However, a preparatory offence may be charged in a serious case where the offender has behaved recklessly but has not actually committed an attempt. Thus in *Pennifold and Naylor*[3] a group of men drove through

---

[1] Cf. Law Com. no. 102, para. 2.96 (on impossibility).

[2] *Cf.* the inclusion of attempts and other inchoate offences in the notion of dangerousness employed by the Butler Committee, Mentally Abnormal Offenders, para. 4.41, and by the Advisory Council on the Penal System, Sentences of Imprisonment: a Review of Maximum Penalties, para. 198.

[3] [1974] Crim. L.R. 130.

a residential area firing rifle shots into the lighted rooms of houses. No one was injured. One offender was sentenced to ten years imprisonment for the possession of firearms and ammunition and for criminal damage. In reducing the sentence to three years, the Court of Appeal remarked that if someone had been killed a sentence approaching ten years might have had to be considered. The difference between three and ten years is surely carrying vindicative satisfaction too far.[1]

The sentence for conspiracy contrary to s. 1 of the Criminal Law Act 1977 is limited, by s. 3 of that Act, to the maximum sentence for the crime which the offenders conspired to commit. As an inchoate crime, conspiracy should in general be punished on the same principles as attempts. The reason why the conspiracy failed to result in the commission of the completed offence should be examined, and even if it is found that the conspiracy manifested as much wickedness as the completed crime, reasons of vindicative satisfaction may indicate a lower punishment where the intended victim has suffered less, or not at all.

Conspiracies might, however, be regarded as more serious crimes than attempts. Indeed, at common law it was held in *Verrier* v. *Director of Public Prosecutions*[2] that some conspiracies might call for a greater punishment than could be imposed for the completed offence. Although s. 3 of the Criminal Law Act now prohibits courts from exceeding the statutory maximum for the completed offence in conspiracy cases, a court might still wish to visit conspirators with more severe punishment than it would mete out to an individual committing the completed offence, whilst keeping within the statutory maximum. The argument is that the nature of the offence is exceptionally changed by the co-operation of large numbers in its commission, because of the greater chance of the occasioning of alarm and of the use of force. In fraud cases, the co-operation of different people in different places may facilitate both the execution and the concealment of the design. These considerations go to show that any offence, whether inchoate or completed, which is committed by a number of people acting in concert may be viewed as presenting a greater social danger than the same offence committed by an individual. On general deterrent grounds the sentence for "group" offences may therefore be longer. Sentences for rape by gangs are on this account higher than those for rape by an individual.[3] The House of Lords in *Verrier* were therefore right in

---

[1] See *infra*, "Causing Harm which was Not Contemplated".
[2] [1967] 2 A.C. 195.
[3] E.g. *Hume*, [1973] Crim. L.R. 320.

regarding the fact that the offence was committed by a group as an aggravating factor, although they were surely wrong to hold that the punishment for conspiracy to commit an offence either could or should exceed the maximum sentence for the completed offence committed by a group. A conspiracy may also be regarded as more serious than an attempt and, indeed, than a single completed offence where it consists of an agreement to commit a series of offences.[1] Whereas the sentences for a series of completed offences might be consecutive and might therefore exceed the maximum for a single offence, the sentence for a single conspiracy to commit a series of offences would be limited by that maximum.

D. CAUSING HARM WHICH WAS NOT CONTEMPLATED

Why punish someone more severely if he causes more harm than he contemplated?

Our investigation of the punishment of attempts led to the general conclusion that the infliction of less punishment where less harm was caused than the offender intended could only be justified on the grounds either that there is less vindicative satisfaction to provide or that crime should not pay. Is there any consideration, other than the fact that there is more vindicative desire to gratify, to justify the infliction of a heavier punishment when the offender did more harm than he intended?

The crime of involuntary manslaughter may be used as an example.

> "A man is guilty of involuntary manslaughter when he intends an unlawful act and one likely to do harm to the person and death results which was neither foreseen nor intended. It is the accident of death resulting which makes him guilty of manslaughter as opposed to some lesser offence such as assault, in the present case abortion. This can no doubt be said to be illogical since the culpability is the same, but nevertheless it is an illogicality which runs throughout the whole of our law, both the common law and the statute law. A comparatively recent example is clearly that of dangerous driving and causing death by dangerous driving."[2]

In the case of involuntary manslaughter, the propriety of increasing punishment on account of the "accident of death" was the subject of debate at least as far back as 1900. In that year the Queen's Bench Judges prepared a Memorandum on sentencing.[3]

---

[1] See I. H. Dennis, "The Rationale of Criminal Conspiracy" (1977) 93 L.Q.R. 39 at pp. 60–3.
[2] Lord PARKER, C.J. in *Creamer*, [1966] 1 Q.B. 72.
[3] Jackson, *Enforcing the Law*, Appendix 5.

The majority favoured punishing as for assault in cases of involuntary manslaughter caused by an assault, but BRUCE, J. dissented on the ground that loss of life is always an element to be taken into consideration in awarding punishment. Anyone who has witnessed the anguish of the deceased's wife at a trial for causing death by reckless driving after the judge has merely fined the accused £50 and disqualified him for driving for a year or two, must feel a certain sympathy with BRUCE, J.; but is it ever justifiable to allow someone's natural resentment to increase another person's punishment beyond his deserts? The Court of Appeal remains undecided on the point: in O'Neill,[1] where a single punch caused the victim to fall, his head struck a kerb and he died, the Court held that sentence should be based on the assault intended and not on the death which accidentally resulted; whilst in Mallett,[2] on similar facts, the Court approved the principle of a sentence which took account of the accidental death.

In their Fourteenth Report, the Criminal Law Revision Committee recommend the abolition of the offences of involuntary manslaughter and causing death by reckless driving, on the ground that "the offender's fault falls too far short of the unlucky result".[3] Even if these reforms are implemented, however, the problem of sentencing will remain. A court passing sentence for assault or for reckless driving, for example, would have to consider whether to increase the sentence where the offender had caused harm which he did not contemplate. Dr. Hood's research into the sentencing of motoring offenders by magistrates suggests that unintended harm does often lead to an increase in sentence.[4] There will be greater resentment from the victim and his family where greater harm results, but it is doubtful whether this is sufficient reason for punishing an offender more severely on account of harm which he did not contemplate. In principle the punishment should, as the Model Penal Code suggests,[5] be limited to the harm which the offender intended or knowingly risked.

E. INTOXICATION

The law provides a number of offences in which intoxication itself is a requirement, such as drunken driving, drunk and disorderly and drunk in charge of a loaded firearm. But where an intoxicated

---

[1] (1967), 51 Cr. App. Rep. 241; to similar effect, Shelton (1979), 1 Cr. App. Rep. (S) 202.
[2] [1972] Crim. L.R. 260; cf. Pennifold and Naylor, discussed supra, p. 155.
[3] Cmnd. 7844 of 1980, para. 120.
[4] Sentencing the Motoring Offender (1972), pp. 130–5.
[5] S. 7.01(2), discussed supra, p. 22.

person causes harm, should he be liable to punishment for the offence of which he caused the *actus reus*? If the intoxication was involuntary, as where someone "laced" the defendant's drink or where a doctor failed to warn his patient about the effect of combining alcohol with a prescribed medication, the intoxicated harmdoer should not be criminally liable. Where the intoxication can be described as voluntary, however, three situations must be considered.

First, the intoxication may have been so acute that at the time of the offence the defendant did not realise what he was doing and therefore lacked the *mens rea* for the crime. At present English law allows such intoxication as a complete defence to crimes of "specific intent" but not as a defence to crimes of "basic intent".[1] The Criminal Law Revision Committee propose to allow acute intoxication as a defence to crimes of intention but not to crimes for which recklessness is sufficient.[2] But should a person who is so intoxicated as to lack *mens rea* be punished for the harm he caused? Bentham regarded cases of acute intoxication as "unmeet for punishment", since the threat of punishment could not be expected to influence the intoxicated harmdoer at the time of his act,[3] but that is to take an unduly restrictive view of both the reasons for and the potentialities of punishment. One reason for punishment is that the harmdoer was at fault. Now it is true, as the retributivist would concede, that his fault is generally less than that of the sober and knowing criminal, and indeed that the degree of fault is not necessarily reflected by the nature of the harm he causes whilst intoxicated. His real fault lies in allowing himself to become uncontrollably intoxicated and thereby creating a risk that harm may be caused. Why then, it may be asked, does the law only allow severe penalties where an intoxicated person causes harm, and not simply (as a kind of preparatory crime, like drunken driving) whenever a person becomes intoxicated? The answer may lie in a combination of the utilitarian principle of economy of threats with popular views on liberty: to provide substantial punishment for intoxication itself would be regarded as an undue curtailment of liberty for a relatively small chance that harm would result, and would entail a style of law enforcement which would be unpleasant; by reserving substantial punishment for cases where harm does result, the risk has at least materialised and punishment in those cases may have a general effect. Bentham's view that cases of acute intoxication are unmeet for punishment neglected the possibility, recognised in punishing

---

[1] *Director of Public Prosecutions* v. *Majewski*, [1977] A.C. 443.
[2] Fourteenth Report, Part VI: *cf.* Ashworth, [1980] Crim. L.R. 556.
[3] *Principles of Morals and Legislation*, Ch. 13, para. 9.

negligence, that some punishment may deter both the offender and others from becoming uncontrollably intoxicated in the future. On what basis should the punishment of the intoxicated harmdoer be calculated? It would be wrong to punish him to the same extent as the sober and knowing criminal, for if he was acutely intoxicated he *ex hypothesi* did not contemplate the harm done. If he knew from previous experience that he was likely to behave in that way when intoxicated, the case may be treated as one of gross negligence. If he had no such knowledge, then the Butler Committee recommended that one year's imprisonment would be a realistic maximum for a first intoxicated offence.[1] In cases where serious harm is caused, however, many sentencers might follow the Criminal Law Revision Committee[2] in giving way to the intuitively strong call for vindicative satisfaction.

Cases of acute intoxication are rare. More frequent is the second kind of case, where there is partial intoxication which loosens the inhibitions and leads a person to do things he would not do if sober. The Court of Appeal appears not to regard the intoxication as a mitigating factor in these circumstances, and will uphold a sentence which reflects the gravity of the harm caused.[3] This approach is probably based on the assumption that the offender knew what he was doing and ought to have stopped himself. But is the partially intoxicated offender so wicked as the sober harmdoer? If the court is satisfied that the offence resulted from the intoxication rather than from a preconceived plan, then the offence is *ceteris paribus* less serious than the same offence by a sober person. Similarly, where the offence is an isolated incident which is out of character for the defendant, he should have the benefit of some mitigation. In general, however, there is strong utilitarian argument for maintaining a realistic level in the sentencing of partially intoxicated offenders in order to deter both the defendant and others from indulging themselves to the detriment of the public.

Thirdly, cases where the offender is a drug addict or alcoholic present a different sentencing problem. On one view, punishment is unjustified because the state of addiction is almost as blameless as mental disorder. We saw earlier that it is doubtful whether courts should lengthen a custodial sentence in order to allow time for a treatment programme;[4] in recent years the Court of Appeal has held non-custodial curative sentences to be appropriate for

---

[1] Cmnd. 6244, para. 18.58.
[2] 14th Report, Cmnd. 7844, para. 261.
[3] *Thomas*, p. 209.
[4] P. 141, *supra*.

addicts.[1] Another view is that the addict bears some responsibility
for his condition and should be punished for that. As Lord PARKER,
C.J., put it in 1967:[2]

> "A man in the position of the appellant is not sentenced because he is an
> addict; everybody is extremely sorry for him. What he is being sentenced
> for is commencing the taking of this drug."

Punishment may therefore be justified on retributive grounds and on
general deterrent grounds, and there is a body of scientific evidence
to the effect that individual prevention may be brought about by
a punitive regime for addicts as efficaciously as by curative
treatment.[3]

F. PROVOCATION

Should a person who commits an offence as a result of provocation
be punished less severely? English law recognises the mitigating
effect of provocation by allowing it to reduce a crime of murder to
one of manslaughter, and the judgment in *Sargeant*[4] is evidence that
provoked offences are generally treated as less serious than unpro-
voked crimes.

The retributivist can justify lower sentences for provoked offences
on the simple ground that they evince less wickedness. They are
usually committed suddenly; since the incident typically arises from
something done to the offender, his conduct and character lie closer
to victims than to deliberate criminals; and there is some element of
partial justification in his conduct, in the sense that the provoker's
behaviour towards him was wrongful.[5] The utilitarian might begin
by arguing that if the defendant was provoked into such an intense
rage that the threat of punishment could not have influenced his
behaviour he should not be punished at all; but punishment in such
cases might well have a long-term deterrent effect.[6] If the defendant was less intensely affected by the provocation, the utilitarian
might increase rather than reduce his punishment, arguing that
greater punishment is necessary to counteract the strength of the
provocation. Bentham sought to avoid this conclusion by reasoning
that in provocation cases the offender is likely to be less depraved in

---

[1] E.g. *Heather* (1979), 1 Cr. App. Rep. (S) 139, substituting a probation order with a
condition of residence in a special hostel, for a "well justified" sentence of five years
imprisonment.
[2] *Fraser*, [1967] 3 All E.R. 544.
[3] Cf. Fingarette, "Addiction and Criminal Responsibility" (1975) 84 Yale L.J. 413.
[4] P. 143, above.
[5] *Cf.* Ashworth, [1976] C.L.J. 292.
[6] See *supra*, pp. 138–140.

character—since he did not initiate the offence—and therefore less likely to re-offend, and so he requires less punishment.[1]

What is the provoked offender being punished *for*? The answer, surely, is that he is punished for failing to control his emotions. His reaction to the provocation may be understandable, but the law nevertheless provides neither justification nor excuse for people who give vent to their feelings in a way which contravenes its prohibitions. The mitigating effect will be greatest where the provocation is grave, and where the retaliation is either sudden or the result of an accumulation of emotional stress. The mitigation will be less where the provocation is less serious or where there is some evidence of prepared retaliation.[2]

G. MENTAL DISORDER

Why not punish the mentally disordered? Even the briefest consideration of this crude question calls for a good deal of sub-division.

i. *Mental disorder at the time of the offence*

(a) *McNaghten insanity.* Only two or three persons each year are acquitted on the ground of insanity. There is strictly no sentencing problem because the Court must direct detention at the Queen's pleasure. On the assumptions made in this book with regard to the general objects of State punishment, it is not at all difficult to justify the acquittal of those who come within the McNaghten Rules. If the aim of the penal system is to reduce crime by making as many people as possible want to obey the criminal law, the punishment of someone who was insane in the McNaghten sense at the time of the act or omission constituting the offence is excluded simply because it is not deserved, and the spectacle of the infliction of undeserved punishment is not calculated to promote respect for the law.

> "The execution of an offender is for example, but so it is not when a madman is executed; but should be a miserable spectacle, both against law, and of extreme inhumanity and cruelty, and can be no example to others."[3]

There is therefore ample retributive and deterrent justification for not punishing the mentally disordered. Where a plea of insanity succeeds, the Court must direct detention in a mental hospital at the Queen's pleasure. The Butler Committee, which recommended a new form of the special verdict, also recommended that the Court should have a discretion to make any non-punitive order when the special verdict is returned.[4] An appropriate social or medical

---

[1] *Theory of Legislation*, p. 262.
[2] *Cf.* Ashworth, "Sentencing in Provocation Cases" [1975] Crim. L.R. 553.
[3] 3 Co. Inst. 6.
[4] Cmnd. 6244, paras. 18.42 to 18.45.

disposal could then be made, and the mandatory and indefinite commitment to mental hospital of, for example, a shoplifter who is found insane (as occurred in one 1978 case) would rightly be avoided.

(*b*) *Diminished responsibility.* Section 2 of the Homicide Act 1957 enables a jury to return a verdict of manslaughter on a murder charge if the accused was suffering from "such abnormality of mind . . . as substantially impaired his mental responsibility for his acts and omissions in doing or being a party to the killing". The object of the section is to give the Courts completely flexible powers in the matter of sentence, and enables a Court to make a hospital order in an appropriate case and even a probation order where the accused is unlikely to be dangerous to the public.

Are sentences of imprisonment proper in s. 2 cases? A life sentence intended for the protection of the public might be proper; although a hospital order with restrictions would be preferable in these cases, the medical evidence required by s. 60 of the Mental Health Act 1959 may not always be forthcoming, and an adequately secure mental hospital may not always be available. But, as Table XII shows, the Courts have in recent years passed as many determinate as indeterminate sentences of imprisonment in diminished responsibility cases. Some of these may undoubtedly be explained by the practice of "stretching" s. 2 so as to provide a defence to murder for those whose conduct attracts sympathy but whose case cannot otherwise be reduced to manslaughter (e.g. mercy-killing, or provocation falling outside the legal doctrine). The Criminal Law Revision Committee recommend that diminished responsibility be retained as a fairly flexible defence,[1] and so this particular phenomenon will remain. But some sentences of imprisonment under s. 2 are clearly imposed as punitive sentences for persons who are admittedly suffering from a degree of mental disorder. A retributive argument in favour of this practice may be put in the following terms:

(1) One way of justifying the total absence of punishment for those who were insane at the time of the offence is to say that they ought not to be punished because they could not help committing the criminal act.[2]

(2) In s. 2 of the Act of 1957 the accused's "mental responsibility" means his capacity to control himself.

(3) It is justifiable to punish, though the punishment should be less severe than would otherwise be the case, where the accused had

---

[1] Fourteenth Report, para. 93.
[2] One of the main criticisms of the McNaghten Rules is that they fail to make allowance for want of control due to mental illness.

some capacity to control his actions although that capacity was substantially decreased by mental illness.

If Professor Walker is right when he says "Experience suggests that some people conform without seriously thinking of doing otherwise, others try to conform and succeed, others try again without succeeding, and some do not try at all",[1] those in the last category may properly be punished for not trying at all, and those in the last category but one for not trying hard enough. Thus, even though the Court has found that his responsibility was "substantially impaired" by mental abnormality, there may remain a portion of responsibility for which punishment is appropriate.[2] It is doubtful, however, whether a judge can fairly estimate the difficulties of self-control experienced by a mentally disordered individual. By comparison with provocation cases, where there are established benchmarks of gravity, it must be hard in diminished responsibility cases to fix the length of a prison sentence appropriate to the failure of self-control. It is submitted that the judge should be guided by the medical evidence and (in contested cases) by the jury's verdict: occasionally the medical evidence may indicate that treatment in prison is preferable to treatment in hospital, as with some forms of personality disorder and psychopathy,[3] but more frequently a medical disposal will be indicated. There will, however, remain the problems of ensuring the offender's admission to hospital and of whether such orders should invariably be indeterminate, to which attention was drawn earlier.[4]

(c) *Other mental disorder.* There are also cases where the evidence shows that the defendant, although not mentally disordered within the meaning of the Mental Health Act, should not be sentenced as a mentally sound and fully responsible adult. It may appear that his intelligence was below average and that he had to cope with extreme family difficulties,[5] or that his low I.Q. was combined with other physical handicaps which placed him in unusual difficulties.[6] It is proper on retributive grounds that the humane practice of mitigating sentence in such cases should be continued.

ii. *Mental disorder at the time of sentence.* Each year some twenty or thirty people are found unfit to plead. Under the present law the Court must confine them to hospital indefinitely and, although they could be put up for trial if and when cured, they are in fact very

---

[1] *Crime and Insanity in England*, p. 162.
[2] *Morris*, [1961] 2 Q.B. 237.
[3] Ashworth and Shapland, "Psychopaths in the Criminal Process" [1980] Crim. L.R. 628.
[4] P. 73, *supra.*
[5] *Smith* (1967), 51 Cr. App. Rep. 376.
[6] *Stone*, [1977] 2 All E.R. 341.

rarely tried in these circumstances. The Butler Committee recommended, however, that mandatory commitment should be replaced by a discretion in the Court to make any non-punitive disposal, including probation orders with a condition of psychiatric treatment and hospital orders.[1]

Most people who are significantly mentally disordered at the time of sentence may well have been mentally disordered at the time of the offence and, provided there is evidence to this effect, it is submitted that the courses canvassed in the previous paragraphs should be followed. What should be done when there is evidence warranting a hospital or guardianship order but no evidence of abnormality at the time of the offence? Why should the accused not be punished in such a case? It is submitted that there are two reasons for not punishing him. In the first place, the evidence warranting a hospital order may lead to a strong suspicion of mental disorder at the time of the offence; secondly, the punishment of someone suffering from one of the types of disorder mentioned in s. 60 of the Mental Health Act 1959 partakes of cruelty. On the other hand, the Kantian might argue that someone who was responsible at the time of the offence must be given his deserts even though he has since become mentally disordered. Alternatively, it may be claimed that after he has been cured he must undergo some punishment so that it may act as an individual deterrent. Yet many people abhor the punishent of those who suffer from mental disorder, and punishing the mentally disordered surely does not increase the deterrent effect of the law.

---

[1] Cmnd. 6244, paras. 10.27 to 10.30.

IV

FIXING THE LENGTH OF A
PRISON SENTENCE

Someone has been convicted on indictment of an offence punishable
with imprisonment and the permitted maximum is substantial, say
ten or fourteen years, or life; the judge has decided that there is no
alternative to imprisonment, how is the length of sentence to be
determined? We now take this question up where it was left in
Chapter II. We will assume that there has been no request for other
offences to be taken into consideration and that the offender has only
been convicted of one offence, so that no problem arises with regard
to concurrent or consecutive sentences. We will also assume that
there is no question of the offender's undergoing some kind of cure
during his sentence, so the judge may not take into account the
possibilities of remission and parole. We know that the judge will be
influenced by the permitted maximum, but we also know that this
may not be very helpful to him because the permitted maximum is
so rarely imposed for any offence. To what extent is it possible to go
further in the way of generalisation concerning matters which will
influence the judge?

It is clear that judges think in terms of a range of sentence
appropriate to the offence in the particular circumstances in which it
was committed, although the precise nature of this range may be
rather less clear. The notion of the normal range of sentence is
analysed in section 1. The ranges vary according to the gravity of
the offence; this is a hydra-headed notion depending in part on the
offence itself as contrasted with other offences (robbery as contrasted
with theft, for example) and in part on the circumstances of the
offence (armed robbery from a bank, for example, as contrasted with
the snatching of a handbag accomplished with comparatively little
violence). An attempt is made to analyse the notion of gravity in
section 2 where it will become plain that the "circumstances of the

166

offence" must be taken to include such matters as its prevalence, the social position of the offender and even his record, for these matters undoubtedly affect the Court's views about gravity. The judge will also be influenced by circumstances peculiar to the case which cannot be brought under the head of gravity. These include the offender's contrition, his cooperation or want of cooperation with the police, and the treatment meted out by the Court to a co-defendant. The relevance of these matters is the bearing which they have on the overriding requirement that justice must not only be done but also be seen to be done. They are discussed in section 3.

This is not an exhaustive account of the matters affecting the length of sentence. Reference has already been made to a number of others such as the offender's age and mental disorder; it would be possible to enumerate a mass of further details which might properly influence the judge. Obvious instances are the length of previous sentences served by the offender for, on the whole, the Courts deplore a very substantial jump from a fairly short sentence to a long one; the offender's sex and family situation, for the Courts do all they can to avoid a prolonged separation of a mother from her children; and the fact that the offender was a foreigner unused to the habits of this country. Shortage of space and the difficulty of making useful generalisations preclude a detailed discussion of these further matters; but they ought not to be left out of account by anyone who wishes to have a comprehensive picture of our sentencing system.

Section 1.—**The ranges of prison sentences—"the tariff system"**

A. THE NOTION OF A TARIFF

Is it right to speak of a "tariff of prison sentences"? The Report of the Streatfeild Committee on the Business of the Courts published in 1961 said "Yes", para. 257 of the Report stating that:

> "Sentencing used to be a comparatively simple matter. The primary objective was to fix a sentence proportionate to the offender's culpability, and the system has been loosely described as 'the tariff system'. The facts of the offence and the offender's record were the main pieces of information needed by the Court, and the defence could bring to notice any mitigating circumstances. The information was about past events which could normally be reliably described; and it was readily available."

Even as a description of earlier practice, however, that statement gives an unduly narrow impression of the tariff system by using the expression with exclusive reference to the offender's culpability. The tariff is based on "gravity", and gravity includes matters other than culpability such as the danger caused to society by the offence and the alarm occasioned to the public. This was evident in the latter part of the nineteenth century,[1] and clearly emerges from the Alverstone Memorandum of 1901—a Memorandum drawn up by Lord ALVERSTONE (the then Lord Chief Justice) as a result of deliberations by the judges, following public and parliamentary disquiet about alleged disparities in sentencing. In practical terms the Memorandum seems to have had little effect: it was sent to the Home Office and no further action was taken upon it. But it does show that it is possible to speak of a "tariff", or at least a normal range of sentences:

> "The Judges of the King's Bench Division are agreed that it would be convenient and of public advantage in regard to certain classes of crime to come to an agreement, or, at least, to an approximate agreement, as to what may be called a 'normal' standard of punishment: a standard of punishment, that is to say, which should be assumed to be properly applicable, unless the particular case under consideration presented some special features of aggravation or extenuation."[2]

In respect of most offences it was not found possible to do more than recommend "a range of punishments within certain limits" and throughout the Memorandum speaks of periods such as three to five years penal servitude as the "correct range". When dealing with rape, for instance, the Memorandum mentions five to seven years penal servitude as giving:

> "a reasonable range of punishment to be increased if there are accompanying circumstances of aggravation, such, for example, as rape by a gang or by a parent or master, or with brutal violence, and to be reduced if there are extenuating circumstances."

So far as the latter are concerned MATTHEW, J. thought that, where there was temptation, or no great violence, eighteen months imprisonment or three years penal servitude would be appropriate. It was agreed, however, that rape is an offence which "covers varying degrees of wickedness, and the just punishment for which requires varying degrees of severity". This, however, could be said of several offences, and the Memorandum makes a similar point in relation to offences of burglary. Although some of the ranges of punishment specified in the Memorandum appear very wide, they at least serve to set "certain limits" and to give some notion of the comparative gravity of types of offence.

---

[1] For fascinating accounts of the development of sentencing principles in the nineteenth century, see D. A. Thomas, *Constraints on Judgment* (1979), and Sir Leon Radzinowicz and Roger Hood, "Judicial Discretion and Sentencing Standards: Victorian Attempts to Solve a Perennial Problem" (1979) 127 U. Pa. L. Rev. 1288.

[2] The full Memorandum is set out in Appendix E to the report of the Advisory Council on the Penal System, Sentences of Imprisonment: A Review of Maximum Penalties (1978), at p. 191.

Many modern judicial statements support the view that what is generally called "the tariff" is a matter of ranges of sentences rather than fixed terms. To mention one that has already been quoted, in *Moylan*, WIDGERY, J., speaking for the Criminal Division of the Court of Appeal said:

> "The Court must first determine what are the *limits* of a proper sentence in respect of the offences charged. Within those *limits* it may be perfectly proper to increase the sentence in order to enable a cure to be undertaken whilst the accused is in prison but . . . it is clear that it is not correct to increase the sentence above that within the appropriate *range* of the offence itself merely in order to provide an opportunity for a cure."[1]

It is commonplace for the Court of Appeal, when allowing an appeal against sentence, to speak of the judge's sentence as being "beyond the normal range" etc. And it is understood that, on the hearing of such appeals, it is not uncommon for the appellant's counsel to be asked what is the range of sentence which he considers would have been appropriate. Nevertheless, the word "tariff" is anathema to some judges, and their objection to it is, to quote one of them,

> "because it suggests that the sentence is governed by a simple and singular idea rather than by a combination of often complex factors, and it gives the impression of an automatic and inhuman approach."

These objections have great force for at least three reasons. In the first place, the gravity of the offence is only one, though often the most important one, of the factors affecting the length of a prison sentence; secondly, gravity is itself a complex concept and the statement that no two cases are alike is none the less true for being a truism; finally, any suggestion that the length of a prison sentence can be determined without reference to the conglomeration of circumstances which passes under the name of the "human factor" would be unacceptable to a large, though by no means all inclusive, number of people concerned with sentencing practice. But the judges who object to the use of the word "tariff" in this context recognise the importance of some degree of uniformity in sentencing practice. At some stage in their thought process, they compare the sentence they have in mind for the particular case, not only with previous sentences of their own, but also with the sentences which other judges are giving for the type of offence under consideration. It cannot be said that they exclude altogether the notion of the appropriate range of sentence, although it may well play its part in determining the final sentence at a later stage in their case than in that of some other judges.

---

[1] P. 142, *supra*; italics supplied.

B. THE NORMAL RANGES OF SENTENCE

Is it possible to be more specific about the nature of these ranges of sentence which appear to play some part in the mental processes of any judge when fixing the length of a sentence? The answer to this question has been sought in the Criminal Statistics and in the judgments of the Court of Appeal.

i. *Use of a statistical norm.* In the course of a lecture in 1969, McKENNA, J., after considering the views that punishment is a deterrent or alternatively a requital for wickedness, said that:

> "In practice the judge escapes these perplexities by pursuing the ideal of equal punishment. If he has no certainty about the right sentence to deter or to punish, he can at least try to give the kind of sentence recently given by others for the offence in question, irrespective of his own view of its likely deterrent effect or of the duty, if he recognises it, of punishing the wicked. These recent sentences are taken by him as a standard. In his exercise of trying to give the same sentence as others have given he has the help of the Criminal Statistics."[1]

McKENNA, J. then sets out the statistics with regard to the length of prison sentences for rape in 1967[2] and concludes:

> "About half of the offenders receive sentences of over two and up to four years, which may perhaps be considered as the range of the normal sentence for rape in 1967".

It is not for one moment suggested that McKENNA, J. claimed to be using a phrase of precise statistical significance—the expression was obviously a convenient one for the purpose of his lecture; but, in the context of the present discussion, the reference to the Criminal Statistics was unfortunate for two reasons. In the first place, any other range could have been selected as the normal range on the same basis. It is true that 66 of the 142 prison sentences of 1967 were for over two and up to four years, but it is equally true that 70 sentences were for over six months and up to three years; why should not this be considered to have been the normal range of sentences for rape in 1967? The second reason why the reference to

---

[1] 32 M.L.R. 601 at p. 610.
[2]

Year	Length of Imprisonment										total
	6 mos. & under	Over 6 mos. & up to 1 year	Over 1 year & up to 2 years	Over 2 years & up to 3 years	Over 3 years & up to 4 years	Over 4 years & up to 5 years	Over 5 years & up to 7 years	Over 7 years & up to 10 years	Over 10 years determinate	Life	
1967	2	8	20	42	24	14	16	8	—	8	142

the Criminal Statistics was unfortunate in the context of the present discussion is that they are useless for the purpose in hand, which is an attempt to explain judicial thinking with regard to the ranges of sentences. The sentences recorded in the Criminal Statistics were pronounced after all relevant circumstances of aggravation and mitigation had been taken into account. The Criminal Statistics cannot be used as a basis of arriving at a range of sentence appropriate to an average case which is to form the starting point of a line of thought beginning before those circumstances have been taken into consideration. This, as we shall see in Chapter V, is one blemish on the scheme of "normal maximum" penalties recommended by the Advisory Council on the Penal System, which also has its basis in the Criminal Statistics.

ii. *Use of appellate decisions.* Great use is made of the concept of the normal range of sentences by Mr. D. A. Thomas, the leading English academic legal authority on sentencing. He argues that

> "the central idea is that within the scope of any legal definition a variety of typical factual situations will recur; with each of these typical factual situations there are associated upper and lower limits within which the sentence should normally fall, in the absence of exceptional circumstances in the offence and without regard to mitigating factors peculiar to the offender himself. The difference between the upper and lower limits applicable to a particular typical situation constitutes the 'range', 'bracket', 'normal level' or 'pattern of sentence' for that variation of the offence."[1]

The normal range appropriate for each typical variation of an offence "must be identified in the decisions of the Court of Appeal in dealing with cases within the general category concerned".[2] The deduction of normal ranges from Court of Appeal decisions has two obvious drawbacks: first, and most important, the Court tends mainly to hear appeals against sentences which are alleged to be too severe, and therefore has far more opportunity to consider the propriety of high rather than low sentences, which means that there may be few decisions on non-serious variations of some offences; secondly, the Court will only reduce a sentence if it is wrong in principle, with the result that a sentence which is allowed to stand may in fact be rather higher or (in those cases where the Court describes a sentence as "not a day too long") rather lower than the Court itself would have imposed if the original discretion had been theirs and not that of the trial judge. However, in the last ten or fifteen years the sentencing decisions of the Court of Appeal have undoubtedly become more sophisticated in their style, and in some cases the Court has travelled beyond the particular facts in order to

---

[1] *Principles of Sentencing* (2nd Edn., 1979), p. 33.
[2] *Op. cit.*, p. 32.

suggest ranges of sentence for other manifestations of the same offence.[1] Inasmuch as the *obiter dicta* in these decisions are treated as authoritative, then the Court of Appeal has the means to shape the normal ranges of sentence for the less serious manifestations of offences, which do not generally come before them.

We have seen that sentences for rape were the subject of particular attention in the Alverstone Memorandum and in the lecture by McKenna, J. Whereas in his earlier work Mr. Thomas asserted that the "effective range" for rape sentences was "between about ten years' imprisonment and two to three years imprisonment",[2] an assertion which was open to the charge of attaching undue weight to sentences in the higher echelons, the latest edition of his work describes three normal ranges of sentence for rape, according to the characteristics of the offence in question: two to three years for mitigated cases (such as minimal injury or the victim's consent to some degree of familiarity), five to eight years for aggravated cases (involving gang rape or considerable violence), and three to five years for cases without aggravating or mitigating features.[3] A glance at the relevant statistics (see Tables XIIIA and B) shows that some 50 per cent of rape sentences were for between two and four years imprisonment, but this, of course, is not necessarily inconsistent with the normal ranges described by Mr. Thomas—it may merely suggest that there are more "mitigated" and "average" rapes than "aggravated" rapes. However, the quantitative information given by the statistics can play a valuable corrective role to the qualitative holdings of the Court of Appeal in some spheres. For example, the statistics in Table XVI show that a very small proportion of sentences for burglary—a mere 14 per cent of those sentenced to imprisonment in the Crown Court, let alone those given non-custodial sentences and dealt with by magistrates—are for three years or over. This makes it highly improbable that a sentence of three years imprisonment is in any sense "normal" for a single domestic burglary, particularly since many of the sentences in the statistics will be inflated by other offences taken into consideration. Yet Mr. Thomas has shown that it can be inferred from Court of Appeal decisions that "a sentence of three years will not necessarily be considered excessive on the facts for a single burglary, at least of a private home".[4] This, then, is one sphere in which the criminal statistics perform a valuable corrective function in the interpretation

---

[1] See heading iv, p. 174, *infra*.
[2] *Principles of Sentencing* (1st Edn., 1970), p. 109.
[3] *Principles of Sentencing* (2nd Edn., 1979), pp. 113–17; the three normal ranges are presented as part of a "scale" running from two to twelve years.
[4] *Op. cit.*, p. 150.

of the Court of Appeal's decisions—as, indeed, Mr. Thomas acknowledges in his commentary on the recent decision in *McCann*.[1] From the fact that the Court has upheld sentences of three years for a single burglary (usually, be it noticed, in the case of an offender with a previous record of burglary) it does not necessarily follow that it is right to regard three years imprisonment as part of the normal range of sentences for a single domestic burglary.[2]

iii. *Communication of "normal ranges"*. It is unlikely that many judges have resort to the Criminal Statistics for the purpose of forming views about current sentencing practice.[3] Judges who have been consulted say that they are primarily influenced by conversations with other judges, consideration of reports of cases on sentencing and attendance at sentencing conferences. In the case of the Queen's Bench Judges, there is the further important source of information concerning the practice of other judges in the vast number of papers perused by them annually on applications for leave to appeal to the Court of Appeal against sentence. Many of the judges who sit in the Crown Court, such as Recorders and Circuit Judges, do not have the benefit of this experience, however. They must rely on the printed word, notably Mr. Thomas' book and reports of Court of Appeal decisions, and on informal and formal discussions with other sentencers at sentencing conferences and elsewhere. With the recent appointment of a Judicial Studies Board, it is likely that in future most of those who are empowered to pass sentence in the Crown Court will have attended at least an introductory course on sentencing.

iv. *Modification of "normal ranges"*. There have been attempts to modify the normal ranges of sentence for various kinds of offence and thereby to lower the tariff. In 1977 the Advisory Council on the Penal System published an interim report on The Length of Prison Sentences, the central argument of which was this:

"Research findings up till now indicate that shorter sentences are no less effective than longer ones. Unless and until there is evidence to the contrary, it will be logical and economical to reduce the length of sentences in the middle and lower ranges. A general lowering of sentence lengths need not disturb the relativity of individual sentences; existing distinctions between different offenders and different offences could still be successfully maintained. Although in our final report we hope to make recommendations for a new system of maximum penalties, at this juncture we wish merely to pose a few simple questions. Are there not cases of two years imprisonment where 18 months, or 15 or even less, might safely be passed, and sentences of twelve months when six months would do just

---

[1] [1980] Crim. L.R. 734.
[2] See the discussion on *Harrison* (p. 54, *supra*.)
[3] For an exception see *Thomas* (1973), 57 Cr. App. Rep. 496.

as well? And for the offender going to prison for the first time, should not even a shorter sentence suffice?"[1]

In fact the report did more than pose a few simple questions: it "advocated" that courts should "stop at the point where a sentence has been decided upon and consider whether a shorter one would not do just as well".[2] The Home Office ensured that a copy of the report was sent to every judge and every bench of magistrates in the country. The Advisory Council's recommendations were aimed at so-called "run-of-the-mill" offences, without further specification, and this rather vague approach was followed by Lord LANE, C.J., when in Upton[3] he declared that courts should use imprisonment sparingly and make sentences "as short as possible" for "non-violent petty offenders". However in Bibi[4] a specially constituted Court of Appeal, consisting of Lord LANE, C.J., LAWTON and SHAW, L.JJ., made a powerful and much more clearly focussed attempt to reduce the normal ranges of sentence for certain types of crime. After stating that a court must first be satisfied that an immediate custodial sentence is necessary, Lord LANE declared that the sentence should be as short as possible, and went on:

"Many offenders can be dealt with equally justly and effectively by a sentence of six or nine months' imprisonment as by one of 18 months or three years. We have in mind not only the obvious case of the first offender for whom any prison sentence however short may be an adequate punishment and deterrent, but other types of case as well.

The less serious types of factory or shopbreaking; the minor cases of sexual indecency; the more petty frauds where small amounts of money are involved: the fringe participant in more serious crime: all these are examples of cases where the shorter sentence would be appropriate.

There are, on the other hand, some offences for which, generally speaking, only the medium or longer sentences will be appropriate. For example, most robberies; most offences involving serious violence; use of a weapon to wound; burglary of private dwelling-houses; planned crime for wholesale profit; active large scale trafficking in dangerous drugs. These are only examples. It would be impossible to set out a catalogue of those offences which do and those which do not merit more severe treatment. So much will, obviously, depend upon the circumstances of each individual offender and each individual offence.

What the court can and should do is to ask itself whether there is any compelling reason why a short sentence should not be passed. We are not aiming at uniformity of sentence; that would be impossible. We are aiming at uniformity of approach."

This judgment of the Lord Chief Justice may prove to be of great significance. It goes some distance towards the clear specification of

[1] Para. 14.
[2] Para. 12.
[3] (1980), 71 Cr. App. Rep. 102.
[4] (1980) 71 Cr. App. Rep. 360.

offences for which sentences might be reduced. On the same day, the same Court of Appeal delivered judgments on ten further appeals against sentence for such crimes as burglary, indecent assault, wounding and deception.[1] If there is to be an attempt to alter the tariff, then this approach of seeking to lower the normal range of penalties for particular kinds of offence is surely more likely to succeed than general exhortations to impose lower sentences for "run-of-the-mill" offences. It may also be thought more likely to succeed since the instructions emanate from the Lord Chief Justice and two senior Lords Justices rather than from the Advisory Council, whose function was to advise the Home Secretary. Whether it does succeed will be an interesting test of the structure of judicial authority in matters of sentencing.

C. DETERMINING THE SENTENCE

Once the sentencer has located the normal range of sentences for the offence, he must go through two further stages of reasoning in order to determine the sentence appropriate to this offender for this crime. He must place the particular offence within the normal range according to its relative gravity: if it is a serious form of the offence it should be placed towards the top of the range, whereas if it is a fairly trivial manifestation of the offence it should be placed at the foot of the range. When the sentencer has thus arrived at the sentence proportionate to the gravity of the particular crime, that becomes, according to Mr. Thomas, the "ceiling" for the sentence in the case:

> "The governing principle is that the gravity of the particular incident in the abstract—the relationship of the facts to the established scale of ranges—determines the upper limit of permissible sentences in that case."[2]

The final stage in fixing the length of sentence is, according to Mr. Thomas, "to make allowance for mitigation, reducing the sentence from the level indicated by the facts of the offence by an amount appropriate to reflect such mitigating factors as may be present".[3] If there are no mitigating factors in the case—indeed, if the offender has a long criminal record—this does not in theory justify the court in going above the sentence appropriate to the gravity of the case: hence the use of the term "ceiling". In practice, however, there are a number of decisions in which the Court of Appeal appears to have approved a sentence above the ceiling.[4]

---

[1] The decisions are reported at [1980] Crim. L.R. 734–40, with commentaries by Mr. Thomas.
[2] *Principles of Sentencing* (2nd Edn, 1979), p. 35.
[3] *Op. cit.*, p. 46.
[4] *Cf. Harrison* (p. 54, *supra*).

It was mentioned above that one of the drawbacks of treating the decisions of the Court of Appeal as the basis for constructing normal ranges of sentence is that the cases which reach that Court are often far from normal. There is no prosecution appeal against sentence in England, and so all the appeals coming before the Court have been initiated by defendants who believe their sentences to be too severe. Few cases therefore call into question the propriety of low sentences or the proper approach to less serious kinds of lawbreaking, and this means that Court of Appeal decisions provide only patchy guidance to the factors relevant to the placement of offences in the lower echelons of the ranges. Occasional attempts to remedy this deficiency have been made by the Court of Appeal in recent years, especially when LAWTON, L.J., has been presiding. One example of a "guideline judgment" which essays a general description of the factors governing the placement of offences within the normal range is to be found in *Taylor, Simons and Roberts*, a case of unlawful sexual intercourse with a girl under the age of 16. The style of the "guideline" approach is conveyed by the following passage from the judgment of LAWTON, L.J.:[1]

"It is clear from what the learned trial judge said that there is doubt amongst many at the present time, as to what is the proper way of dealing with these cases. What does not seem to have been appreciated by the public is the wide spectrum of guilt which is covered by the offence known as having unlawful sexual intercourse with a girl under the age of 16. At one end of that spectrum is the youth who stands in the dock, maybe 16, 17 or 18 years of age, who has had what started off as a virtuous friendship with a girl under the age of 16. That virtuous friendship has ended with their having sexual intercourse with one another. At the other end of the spectrum is the man in a supervisory capacity, a schoolmaster or social worker, who sets out deliberately to seduce a girl under the age of 16 who is in his charge. The penalties appropriate for the two types of case to which I have just referred are very different indeed. Nowadays, most judges would take the view, and rightly take the view, that when there is a virtuous friendship which ends in unlawful sexual intercourse, it is inappropriate to pass sentences of a punitive nature. What is required is a warning to the youth to mend his ways. At the other end, a man in a supervisory capacity who abuses his position of trust for his sexual gratification, ought to get a sentence somewhere near the maximum allowed by law, which is two years' imprisonment. In between there come many degrees of guilt. A common type of offender is the youth who picks up a girl of loose morals at a dance, takes her out into the local park and, behind the bushes, has sexual intercourse with her. That is the kind of offence which normally is dealt with by a fine. When an older man in his twenties, or older, goes off to a dance and picks up a young girl, he can expect to get a much stiffer fine, and if the girl is under 15 he can expect to go to prison for a short time. A young man who deliberately sets out to

---

[1] [1977] 3 All E.R. 527 at p. 529.

seduce a girl under the age of 16 can expect to go to detention. The older man who deliberately so sets out can expect to go to prison. Such is the wide variety of penalties which can be applied in this class of case."

Strictly speaking, remarks of this kind are merely *obiter dicta*; their effect on sentencing practice remains to be seen, but this style of judgment (in combination with that in *Bibi*) offers one method of structuring English sentencing practice without resort to statute.

This discussion of the three stages in fixing the length of a prison sentence—locating the applicable normal range of sentences, placing the offence within that range according to its relative gravity, and then reducing the sentence if there are mitigating factors—must be read in the context of sentencing practice. As Table I shows, less than half of the adult male offenders sentenced at Crown Court receive a custodial sentence. The concept of a normal range is therefore properly extended to cover non-custodial penalties as well, as the reference to fines in the above quotation from LAWTON, L.J., reminds us. On the other hand, a discussion of the *normal* range of prison sentences should not be taken to raise doubts about the propriety of sentences outside those ranges for crimes which fall outside the normal categories. In upholding a sentence of 12 years imprisonment for rape and buggery in *Jones*,[1] the Court of Appeal criticised counsel for referring them to other decided cases on rape and declared that "it is wrong in rape cases to think in terms of a pattern or tariff". If the concepts of tariff and normal range are properly used, however, they can surely be helpful in determining the appropriate sentence for all kinds of crime, rape included.

D. THE QUESTION OF PUBLICATION

Should a list of the ranges of sentences for the average cases of the most usual offences be published? There is quite a lot to be said on both sides. Three points in favour of publication are first, the slight appearance of mystique presented by the current state of affairs; a tendentious critic could in fact say that the English law of sentencing is like the Roman law was before the publication of the Twelve Tables, except that the procedure is a judicial and not a sacerdotal mystery; secondly, some judges, while speaking of a tariff system, hint that it is not always as easy to find out what the tariff is as it has been made to appear in the previous paragraphs; thirdly, publication might have merits from the point of view of general deterrence, although the likelihood of a thorough consideration of the tariff and its implications among those contemplating crime may legitimately be the subject of considerable scepticism.

---

[1] [1976] Crim. L.R. 203.

Three points that may be made against publication are first, that there is nothing mysterious or difficult to know about the present ranges; second, that the present system is far too vague and far too variously applied by different judges to admit of publication; third, publication might impede change, for there is little doubt that the normal ranges of sentences do vary over the years (although a perusal of the Memorandum of 1901 may be thought to suggest that the variation is not as great as is sometimes supposed).

The first two points made in the last paragraph are not of course mutually consistent, and the third point might be countered by suggesting that listing and publication would make it easier for the Court of Appeal to accomplish what it set out to do in *Bibi*. However, in view of the fact that some judges seem to attach far greater significance to the ranges of sentences than others, publication may perhaps not be thought worthwhile, although at least one Queen's Bench Judge is in favour of it and the pros and cons are very evenly balanced.

Section 2.—**Gravity**

A. GRADING OF OFFENCES

The grading of offences according to gravity is primarily the work of the Legislature in fixing the maxima and, as we have seen, the fixing of the maxima has not been systematic; but, in the case of the more common offences, it is possible with the aid of judicial comments and judicial sentencing practice, to detect five things which are considered to affect the gravity of an offence. They are social danger, alarm, social disapproval, harm and wickedness. An attempt will be made to illustrate these matters affecting gravity by means of a series of questions relating to the more common type of crime; this will be followed by a discussion of proportionality in general.

i. *Social danger.* Why is handling stolen goods subject to a higher maximum than theft? The answer lies in the greater social danger of handlers. As CANTLEY, J., explained:[1]

"It is often said, and rightly said, that there would not be so many thieves if there were no receivers. Professional thieves do not steal goods merely for their own consumption; they steal them for disposal and it is essential to the success of the criminality that there should be receivers, big receivers and small receivers, like this appellant, who will dispose of their goods unobtrusively in various markets:"

In terms of the theories of punishment, we have here a conflict

---

[1] *Battams* (1979), 1 Cr. App. Rep. (S) 15 at p. 16.

between retribution and general deterrence, and general deterrence wins. If punishment always had to be proportionate to wickedness, theft would, more often than not, have to be punished more severely than receiving; but it is not difficult to see that a case can be made out for the view that it is more important to deter professional receivers than to deter professional thieves, hence the higher maximum. It must not be supposed that general deterrence always prevails in conflicts with retribution, even in the case of offences against property. The blackmailer is arguably less of a social menace than the thief, but he is certainly regarded as more wicked and this was the consideration which led the Criminal Law Revision Committee to recommend a maximum of fourteen years (the same as that for handling) as contrasted with the ten year maximum for theft; these recommendations are adopted in the Theft Act. Judging by the low maxima for many types of blackmail in the past, the blackmailer has not always been considered as wicked as the thief, but the Committee stressed the much greater detestation with which the offence is now commonly regarded.[1]

Tables XIV, XV and XVI are of some interest when the practical effects of the matters mentioned in the last paragraph come to be considered. It would be unwise to reach firm conclusions on the basis of the criminal statistics because they do not reveal such relevant information concerning the offenders covered by their tables as previous convictions and the amount of property involved; but it certainly seems that, although there is a greater chance that a convicted blackmailer will be sent to prison than a convicted thief, the chances of a handler being sent to prison are less than those of a thief whether they are convicted in the Crown Court or before Magistrates. On the other hand it seems that, if it is decided to send them to prison, a convicted handler is likely to be subjected to a longer sentence than a convicted thief, a difference which may reflect the more severe view taken of professional receivers of stolen goods. A convicted blackmailer runs a greater risk of a longer sentence than either of the other two. The difference between a statutory maximum of fourteen and ten years may therefore operate in practice to affect the length of prison sentences, but the fact that only one sentence of ten years or over was imposed for handling during the decade 1969–78 gives pause for thought on the question whether this particular differential is necessary. Indeed, some 90 per cent of prison sentences for theft and for handling in the years 1976–78 were for two years or under (see Table XVI).[2]

---

[1] Eighth Report, para. 124.
[2] The Advisory Council on the Penal System, however, suggested a "normal maximum" of three years. See p. 204, *infra*.

ii. *Alarm.* Why is burglary subject to a higher maximum and generally treated more seriously than theft?[1] The answer seems to be that the offence tends to cause more alarm. Before the Theft Act 1968 came into force, burglary could only be committed in respect of dwelling houses at night, and one of the factors which caused the common law to treat the crime as a very serious one was the alarm it occasioned to the inhabitants of the dwelling houses. To do by day or in buildings other than dwelling houses what would, if done in a dwelling house by night, have been burglary, was housebreaking before the Theft Act came into force.

> "With better street lighting in most places night is no longer so much more favourable than day to criminals, nor so much more frightening to householders than it was in the days when the distinction between burglary proper and housebreaking was drawn. Moreover in some places housebreakers choose a time in the morning when the housewife has to go out and leave the house empty; and it is sometimes quite as upsetting and even frightening for a woman to find on her return that the house has been ransacked during her absence as it is to have her house burgled at night."[2]

The justification given by the Criminal Law Revision Committee of the separate offence of aggravated burglary where the accused had with him firearms or explosives included the fact that it must be extremely frightening to those in the building.[3] It must be said, however, that all these justifications apply far more to domestic burglaries than to burglaries of shops, warehouses etc.

In terms of the theories of punishment, the distinction between domestic burglary and theft can, like that between handling and theft, be explained on the basis of the predominance of general deterrence over retribution. Tables XIV, XV and XVI show that burglars are generally punished more severely than thieves or handlers in both the Crown Court and Magistrates' Courts. The domestic burglar may not deserve any more punishment than the thief, but he runs the risk of getting more because his conduct is more alarming; but, unlike the distinction between handling and theft, that between burglary and theft can be justified on retributive grounds. If it is, in general, more alarming to be the victim of a burglary than to be the victim of theft, heavier punishment can be justified on the

---

[1] Under the Theft Act 1968 the maximum for burglary is 14 years while the maximum for theft is 10 years. See Tables XIV and XVI; sentences in excess of 10 years are occasionally imposed for burglary even when it is not aggravated.

[2] Eighth Report of the Criminal Law Revision Committee, para. 74; for a study of the alarm caused by domestic burglary, see M. Maguire in (1980) 20 Brit. Jo. Criminol. 261.

[3] *Ibid.*, para. 81. The maximum punishment for aggravated burglary is imprisonment for life.

ground of what Bentham called "vindicative satisfaction"; there is more dissatisfaction or resentment to be appeased.

iii. *Social disapproval.* Why are homosexual offences generally subject to higher maximum penalties than heterosexual offences? The reason appears to be that, at the time when the statutory maxima were set, it was supposed that society as a whole dispproved of them more strongly. This is not the place for a discussion of the question whether the mere fact that certain conduct excites intolerance, indignation and disgust in most members of society can ever alone justify its punishment because, since the Sexual Offences Act 1967, in the case of most homosexual offences, there are other elements such as the lack of consent or youth of the victim. But the magnitude of the difference between the maxima for homosexual and heterosexual offences is striking. Under s. 14 of the Sexual Offences Act 1956, an indecent assault upon a woman is punishable with a maximum of two years imprisonment, whereas indecent assault upon a male is punishable with ten years under s. 15; as a result of increases in the maxima by the Sexual Offences Act 1967, consensual homosexual offences by adults against youths (including those between the ages of sixteen and twenty-one) are subject to high maxima as contrasted with the two years maximum for unlawful intercourse with girls between the ages of thirteen and sixteen.

It is doubtful whether, even on a version of the retributive theory which regarded social disapproval as a sufficient determinant of the degree of punishment, such a wide difference is justified. In fact the courts do not treat homosexual offences as significantly more serious than heterosexual offences in their sentencing practice, although it remains true that a homosexual offence which is reported to the police is more likely than a heterosexual offence to result in prosecution.[1]

iv. *Harm.* Why is assault causing actual bodily harm punishable with five years imprisonment under s. 47 of the Offences against the Person Act 1861, while common assault is only punishable with imprisonment for a year? The answer, and it is one that could be given to a number of similar questions, is that the amount of harm done is considered to increase the gravity of the offence. This view is justifiable on more or less any theory of punishment when the greater harm was foreseen, but, as we saw in Chapter III, it is a view which it is exceedingly difficult to justify in terms of the theories of punishment when the harm was not foreseen. For this reason the Criminal Law Revision Committee have recommended the abolition

---

[1] Home Office Research Study No. 54, *Sexual Offences, Consent and Sentencing*, by R. Walmsley and K. White, Ch. 4.

of a number of offences which specify the occurrence of harm beyond that which was intended or knowingly risked.[1]

v. *Wickedness*. What justifies the distinction between s. 18 and s. 20 of the offences against the Person Act 1861? Under s. 18 causing grievous bodily harm with intent to do so is punishable with imprisonment for life as a maximum, under s. 20 the malicious causing of such harm is only punishable with five years imprisonment. Under s. 20 mere foresight of the possibility of bodily harm appears to suffice to found liability,[2] whereas, in order to secure a conviction under s. 18, the prosecution must show that the accused acted with the intention of inflicting grievous bodily harm on his victim. One answer to the question is that the conduct covered by s. 18 is more wicked than that covered by s. 20, inasmuch as intentional wrongdoing is generally more serious than reckless wrongdoing. It is also possible to argue that heavier punishment is demanded for the offence under s. 18 on utilitarian grounds because its perpetrator is a greater social menace, and it is not possible to refute this argument as a corresponding argument was refuted when the distinction between negligent and intentional wrongdoing was considered in terms of the theories of punishment.[3] The point made at that stage was simply that a persistently negligent motorist may be a greater social menace than a far more wicked murderer who is unlikely to repeat his offence. If the argument is confined to isolated instances in which the *actus reus* is the same, the intentional wrongdoer must always be regarded as a greater social menace, or the cause of greater alarm, than one who is merely reckless in the sense that he disregards a single foreseen risk (which is the position with regard to someone guilty of an offence against s. 20 of the Offences against the Person Act), or the merely negligent wrongdoer.

We have already seen an instance, in the case of offences against property, in which greater wickedness seems to be the sole justification for the heavier punishment of the crime, *viz.* the fact that the blackmailer is, in theory and practice, subject to greater punishment than the thief.[4]

vi. *Proportionality in general*. Whilst such matters as social danger, alarm, social disapproval, harm and wickedness may influence the views of the legislature and the courts on the relative seriousness of offences, the courts must also pay regard to questions of proportionality within the whole sentencing structure. If murder is taken to be the gravest crime, then sentences for other crimes must

---

[1] See p. 158, *supra*.
[2] *Mowatt*, [1968] 1 Q.B. 421.
[3] P. 150 *supra*.
[4] See Tables XIV and XVI.

not exceed the sentence for murder. The abolition of the death penalty for murder and the rise in terrorism and organised crime has thrown this difficult issue into sharp relief, and it was confronted by the Court of Appeal in *Turner*.[1] Part of the difficulty is that murders themselves vary in gravity, but the Court boldly started from the assumption that very few murderers are kept in custody beyond 15 years, and then asked itself:

> "If a man is convicted of murder, and has a reasonable chance of being let out before the expiration of 15 years, what is the appropriate sentence for someone who has been convicted of a lesser offence than murder? Ought it to be any more than the sentence which is likely to be served by someone convicted of murder? It is that aspect of this problem which has concerned this Court very much when dealing with these 17 appeals, because it seems to us that it is not in the public interest that even for grave crimes, sentences should be passed which do not correlate sensibly and fairly with the time in prison which is likely to be served by somebody who has committed murder in circumstances in which there were no mitigating circumstances."[2]

LAWTON, L.J., went on to suggest that the courts should draw a distinction between two categories of serious crime. In the first category are offences which are "wholly abnormal", inasmuch as they are either "horrifying" or dangerous to the State, and as examples he mentioned "bad cases of espionage", "cases of horrid violence" such as torture, bomb outrages and political terrorism. Crimes in this first category might well attract sentences approaching the effective sentence for murder without mitigating circumstances (i.e. sentences of around 20 years imprisonment, from which one third remission would be deducted). Such a case was *Termine*,[3] where a sentence of 21 years was upheld for offences of attempted robbery, possession of firearms and false imprisonment arising out of the "Spaghetti House siege" in London, when hostages were taken and political demands made. Into the second category fall "crimes which are very grave and all too frequent", including serious cases of robbery in which firearms are carried, such as *Turner* itself. The Court indicated that "the starting point" for this kind of offence was a sentence of 15 years (which, less one third remission, would amount to 10 years in prison). If more than one crime in this category had been committed, the Court said that "the maximum total sentence should not normally be more than eighteen years", thereby preserving the distinction from "first category" crimes and from murder.

---

[1] (1975), 61 Cr. App. Rep. 67.
[2] At pp. 90–1.
[3] (1977), 64 Cr. App. Rep. 299.

The guidance given in *Turner* must of course be viewed in the light of the facts of the case. Other forms of armed robbery may be less serious, such as the petrol station and betting shop robberies in *Jenner* which, being less lucrative and not being committed by experienced organised criminals, resulted in sentences of nine years.[1] Some robberies, even though not involving firearms, may be regarded as more serious, such as the sophisticated and stealthy raid on bank deposit boxes in *Wilde*.[2] The degree of organisation, the corruption of a bank employee and particularly the fact that valuables worth more than one million pounds remained unrecovered led the Court in that case to remark that *Turner* was not intended "to fix a ceiling which has to be slavishly followed" and to arrive at 20 years as the appropriate sentence. The principle of proportionality put forward in *Turner* nevertheless remains important if the structure of sentences for serious offences is to develop satisfactorily.[3]

B. THE CIRCUMSTANCES OF THE OFFENCE

Social danger, alarm, social disapproval, harm and wickedness are also factors which are held to affect the gravity of the circumstances of a particular offence as contrasted with the gravity of one offence compared with another.

The fact that the pedlar of hard drugs is a greater social menace than the consumer is reflected in the differences in the sentences they receive for being in unlawful possession of dangerous drugs.

Eighteen months might, at first sight, be considered to be on the high side as a sentence for riotous and unlawful assembly on youthful offenders demonstrating against a dinner, the object of which was to encourage the inhabitants of Cambridge to spend their holidays in Greece, but the great alarm occasioned to those participating in the dinner was held to justify the treatment of the offences as of a serious nature.[4]

One of the reasons why men of thirty and over tend to receive sentences near or approaching the maximum of two years for unlawful intercourse with willing girls between the ages of thirteen and sixteen is probably the general social disapproval of such conduct on the part of an older man rather than his greater wickedness. The Court of Appeal has made it clear that, even where the girl acted as temptress and instigator, older men who commit the offence must expect to go to prison.[5] It seems that nothing but the fulfilment by

---

[1] [1977] Crim. L.R. 623.
[2] (1978), 67 Cr. App. Rep. 339.
[3] It was apparently followed in *Davies*, [1980] Crim. L.R. 598.
[4] *Caird* (1970), 54 Cr. App. Rep. 499.
[5] *Taylor*, [1977] 3 All E.R. 527, p. 176, *supra*; *O'Grady* (1978), 66 Cr. App. Rep. 279.

the judges of their role of denunciators of breaches of the law which arouse the particular hostility of decent people can account for the upholding by the Court of Appeal of a sentence of eighteen months imprisonment for consensual buggery with a nineteen-year-old married woman.[1]

Matters requiring special consideration in relation to the notion of the gravity of the circumstances of an offence are its prevalence, the extent to which it is part of organised criminal activity, the social or professional position of the offender and the offender's record. It will be convenient to illustrate these matters by a further series of questions.

i. *The prevalence of the offence.* Does the fact that a particular offence is more than ordinarily prevalent either generally, throughout the country, or in a particular locality ever lead to an offender receiving a higher sentence than he deserved? The answer is: Yes, within limits because desert is a moral concept and gravity, the notion to which our sentencing system is so largely geared, is, though in part a moral concept, something more. This point was put very clearly in para. 280 of the Streatfeild Report.

> "To some extent it is one of the objectives of practically every sentence to fix a penalty which will deter others from committing a like offence or will at any rate not have an anti-deterrent effect. In general the Courts proceed on the assumption that this will be achieved by fixing a sentence proportionate to the offender's culpability, but occasionally the need to deter others is regarded as so pressing that it becomes the dominant consideration and the court passes a sentence which is especially designed to be exemplary. It may be, for instance, that a sentence of three years' imprisonment would normally be the appropriate sentence for a particular assault, but assaults of that type have recently been prevalent in the area, and the court imposes a sentence of five years with the specific aim of reducing the number of such assaults or of arresting the increase."

A sentence aimed primarily at discouraging a prevalent offence is sometimes spoken of as "an exemplary sentence" as in the above quotation, and sometimes simply as "a deterrent sentence". Some judges even speak of there being three types of sentence, the ordinary "tariff" sentence, the individualised sentence (probation or discharge at the one extreme, a life sentence at the other) and an exemplary sentence. Most judges appear to consider that prevalence adds to the gravity of an offence, and occasionally feel justified in sentencing up to, and even a little beyond, what they consider to be the sentence appropriate to the offence itself. However, a court which today reasoned as the Streatfeild Committee did would probably find the sentence reduced on appeal since, as Thomas states,

---

[1] *Harris* (1970), 55 Cr. App. Rep. 290.

"In so far as the term 'exemplary sentence' forms part of the Court [of Appeal] 's vocabulary, it refers to a sentence which, to serve the purpose of general deterrence, relates strictly to the facts of the offence and makes no allowance for any mitigating factors."[1]

A court which wishes to pass a sentence based on general deterrence must therefore keep within the ceiling fixed by the gravity of the offence but, in order to achieve the deterrent effect, may leave out of account factors which would normally result in mitigation. Unless one maintains that an offender has no shadow of right to have mitigating factors taken into account, this practice requires justification.

One justification for thus basing a sentence on general deterrence[2] might be its superior effectiveness. Examples are cited from time to time to support this claim, but it always seems to be possible to explain the fact that the offence ceased to be quite so prevalent on some other hypothesis. It is this possibility that makes a scientific appraisal of certain aspects of our sentencing system so difficult. It may be said that further research is necessary, but precisely how the research is to be conducted and with what prospects of success is another matter. The Streatfeild Committee suggested that a start should be made by gathering systematic information on the deterrent effect of sentences generally from representative samples of relevant opinion. Such a study, it was thought, might throw up material and hypotheses which could then be used in a survey of the reactions to particular sentences; eventually, with the participation of the Courts, it was suggested that the reactions to sentences which were specifically intended to be exemplary should be surveyed. Unfortunately the Report does not make it clear what opinion is to be considered relevant, whose reactions are to be surveyed, and how such a survey could answer such questions as: Did those sentences account for the lessening of the prevalence of that offence? or: Would that offence which remained prevalent have become more prevalent if those sentences had not been passed?

The most celebrated examples of exemplary sentences in recent times are those of four years passed by SALMON, J., on nine youths, six of whom were seventeen, for wounding with intent and assaults. The crimes were committed in the Notting Hill area in 1958 and the following words spoken by SALMON, J. when passing sentence speak eloquently of the foul racist conduct of the accused.

"You stand convicted on your own confessions of a series of extremely grave and brutal crimes. On the night of August 24 you nine men formed

---

[1] *Principles of Sentencing* (2nd Edn), p. 36.
[2] See the discussion of the conflict between retribution and general deterrence *supra*, p. 141.

yourselves into a gang and set out on a cruel and vicious man hunt. You armed yourselves with iron bars and other weapons. Your quarry was any man, providing there were not more than two of them together, whose skin happened to be a different colour from your own. Your object was to instil stark terror and inflict as much pain and grievous injury as you could.

During that night you savagely attacked five peaceful, law-abiding citizens without any shadow of an excuse. None of them had done you any harm. None of them had given you the slightest provocation. Indeed, you knew nothing about them, except that their skin happened to be of a colour of which you apparently did not approve. Two of them were lucky enough to escape before you were able to inflict other than comparatively minor injuries. The other three you left bleeding and senseless on the pavement.

It was you men who started the whole of this violence in Notting Hill. You are a minute and insignificant section of the population who have brought shame upon the district in which you lived, and have filled the whole nation with horror, indignation, and disgust.

Everyone, irrespective of the colour of his skin, is entitled to walk through our streets in peace, with his head erect, and free from fear. That is a right which these courts will always unfailingly uphold.

As far as the law is concerned you are entitled to think what you like, however foul your thoughts; to feel what you like, however brutal and debased your emotions; to say what you like providing you do not infringe the rights of others or imperil the Queen's peace, but once you translate your dark thoughts and brutal feelings into savage acts such as these the law will be swift to punish you, the guilty, and to protect your victims.

I bear in mind what has been said on your behalf: you are young and have no previous convictions. Your victims, though grievously injured, after two or three weeks in hospital have sufficiently recovered to be allowed to return home and it is unlikely that they will suffer any permanent physical ill effects from your savage attacks. But for those facts I would have imposed much longer sentences. As it is I am determined that you and anyone anywhere who may be tempted to follow your example shall clearly understand that crimes such as this will not be tolerated in this country, but will inevitably meet in these courts with the stern punishment which they so justly deserve."[1]

One of the points made when the sentences were under appeal was that the judge had been mistaken in supposing that the conduct of the accused caused race riots to flare up elsewhere, but the sentences were confirmed by the Court of Criminal Appeal who spoke of SALMON, J.'s words as "wise, just and necessary".

"It was said that the Judge at the trial had the impression that this was the start of the racial troubles, but this Court disregarded such matters altogether. Let it be assumed that there had been serious trouble previously, the time had certainly come for the Courts to put down offences such as these with a heavy hand."[2]

---

[1] [1958] Crim. L.R. 709. For the view that the sentences were not strictly exemplary, see Thomas, *Principles of Sentencing* (1st Edn), p. 36.
[2] *Hunt, The Times*, 26th November 1958.

The sentences were imposed and confirmed in 1958. They were followed by a cessation of behaviour like that of the accused, although there was a recrudescence of racial trouble in 1961, but the cessation may have been due to such factors as public disgust about the behaviour of the accused, increased policing of the area or the actual removal from circulation of the prime instigators.[1]

An instance of an exemplary sentence passed on account of the prevalence of an offence in a particular locality is provided by *Elvin*.[2] A youth of 17 with another youth set fire to a school and was sent to prison for four years. The offence was common in the locality and the sentence was expressed to be exemplary. The Court of Appeal upheld the sentence as

> "entirely appropriate to the gravity of the crime that they committed, quite apart from the fact that this is the classic situation in which an exemplary sentence to discourage other people from . . . committing a particular form of offence which is at the time rife in the locality is justified."

Once again it would be interesting, to the extent that it might be possible, to discover whether the sentence had the desired effect.

ii. *Organised crime.* Does the fact that an offence results from organised criminal activity lead to a higher sentence? The answer seems to be in the affirmative,[3] and two justifications are that such offences are clearly and fully intentional, and that they involve the co-operation of a number of persons and therefore present a greater danger to society than offences by individuals.[4] Over and above these considerations, however, it may be said that organised criminal activity constitutes the most deliberate form of defiance of the law, that meticulous precautions may be taken to avoid detection, that the scale of operation is often wide, and that the pressure exerted on each member by the others may make it difficult to withdraw and may therefore tend to perpetuate the organisation. The long sentences approved in this kind of case, such as the highly organised robberies in *Turner* and *Wilde*[5] and "the worst drug conspiracy that has yet fallen to be dealt with in our courts" (*Kemp*),[6] may therefore be justified partly on the ground that the offenders are

---

[1] Wootton, *Crime and the Criminal Law*, p. 100; Jackson, *Enforcing the Law*, p. 208; Walker *Sentencing in a Rational Society*, p. 93.

[2] [1976] Crim. L.R. 204; Thomas, *Principles of Sentencing* (2nd Edn.), p. 36; *cf.* also *Campbell* (1979), 1 Cr. App. Rep. (S) 12.

[3] *Cf.* Thomas, *Principles of Sentencing* (2nd Edn.), pp. 151–2, discussing the hijacking of lorries and their loads, and *cf. Roscoe* (1979), 1 Cr. App. Rep. (S) 24.

[4] See the discussion of conspiracy *supra*, p. 156.

[5] P. 183, *supra*.

[6] (1979), 69 Cr. App. Rep. 330 at p. 352; the case went to the House of Lords on the question of forfeiture: *Cuthbertson*, [1980] 2 All E.R. 401, p. 68, *supra*.

more wicked because they plan their depredations calmly and calcu-
latingly, and perhaps more strongly on the ground that such activities present a particularly great danger to the normal functioning of
society.

iii. *The position of the offender*

(a) *Professional or fiduciary position.* Does the fact that the offence
was in some sense a breach of trust affect its gravity? To this the
answer is most emphatically "Yes". In many cases the emphasis is
on general deterrence at the expense of individual deterrence and
retribution. Thus in *Coleman*,[1] Lord PARKER, C.J., speaking for the
Court of Appeal in affirming a sentence of four years for larceny by a
servant and falsification of accounts said:

> "If it was a question of preventing the appellant from doing anything like
> this again, it would not be necessary to pass any substantial sentence, but,
> as has been pointed out, nearly always when these cases occur with bank
> clerks and accountants, the man or woman concerned is a person of the
> highest character, otherwise he or she of course would not have been put
> in the position of trust. But Courts have always taken a serious view of
> such cases as this of a gross breach of trust extending over, in this case,
> perhaps five years or six years or so."

The utilitarian might support this approach by arguing that the
amount of punishment must be substantial to counteract the degree
of temptation: even if the person tempted needs less punishment on
grounds of individual deterrence since he is unlikely to be placed in
such a position again, the existence of a permanent temptation to
persons in positions of trust justifies substantial sentences on
grounds of general deterrence. There are also retributive and denunciatory elements in the sentencing of persons in breach of trust,[2]
and these come to the fore where there is no financial gain, as where
a father, guardian or schoolteacher[3] commits offences against young
children in his care.

(b) *Social position.* Does the fact that the offender is in a high social
position affect the gravity of his offence? It seems that often it does,
and some reasons for this were given in *Cargill*,[4] where a prominent
citizen of Hull was convicted of unlawful intercourse with a girl of
fifteen. He was sentenced to nine months imprisonment and, on
appeal, it was argued that account should be taken of the fact that he
was a ruined man who had lost many appointments in consequence

---

[1] (1967), 51 Cr. App. Rep. 244.
[2] See p. 129, *supra*.
[3] *Cf. Usher*, [1980] Crim. L.R. 601 (schoolteacher convicted of unlawful intercourse
with, and abduction of, girl pupil).
[4] [1913] 2 K.B. 271; *cf. Bottomley* (1922), 16 Cr. App. Rep. 184 at p. 193, and *Fell*,
[1963] Crim. L.R. 207.

of the conviction. The retort of the Court was:

> "It is very desirable, if possible, to pass a sentence on a man in a good position exactly the same as on a man in a different position. It is true that the sentence is harder, but the offence is correspondingly greater; the man ought to know better, and the way of meeting that is to give exactly the same sentence. The sentence is worse, but by reason of the offender's position the offence is worse."

To describe the sentence as worse is to take account of its side-effects, which the courts have often shown unwilling to do in other respects. To describe the offence as worse is to impute greater wickedness to the offender because, in view of the social position he holds, he "ought to know better". But, in the absence of any breach of trust by the offender, this argument should not be used to impose a greater sentence or to ignore mitigating factors such as good character: the sentence, as the Court said, should be the same as on a man in a different social position.

iv. *The offender's record.* Can the offender's record increase the gravity of an offence and, if so, how? The answer to the first half of this question was given by Lord DONOVAN at the beginning of his speech in *Director of Public Prosecutions* v. *Ottewell.*[1] It would be a mistake to suppose that the accused's record is only relevant to the quantity of sentence when the circumstances are such as to warrant an extended sentence for the protection of the public. A man must not be punished twice for his past offences, but this record may justify a severer sentence for the current offence. Lord DONOVAN said:

> "As ASHWORTH, J. indicated in his judgement, judges have always (and I think rightly) felt themselves entitled to deal with a persistent offender by increasing the sentence which they would have passed if he were not. This is not to punish the offender again for his past crimes. Nor is it always primarily for the protection of the public. It may simply be because in the judge's view the sentences passed for previous offences have proved to be an insufficient deterrent and that the effect of a longer sentence must be tried, perhaps in the offender's own interest; or, it may be that the repetition of the offence has itself increased the gravity of the offence."

The first possibility has already been mentioned and nothing more need be said about it;[2] but how can past offences affect the gravity of a current crime?

The clearest answer is that they remove an offender's claim to the mitigation he would receive if he was of previous good character or if the offence was an isolated lapse. On the retributive theory,

---

[1] [1970] A.C. 642 at p. 650; [1968] 3 All E.R. 153 at p. 158.
[2] P. 53, *supra.*

repeated floutings of the law may be said to call for higher punishment on each occasion on which they occur simply because the flouting is more gross: the offender has had a clear warning, in the form of conviction and sentence on a previous occasion, and yet has offended again. But this reasoning must not be allowed to lead to sentences beyond what is appropriate to the gravity of the crime: the principle in *Clarke*[1] surely has this wider application.

Section 3.—**The avoidance of a sense of injustice and the exercise of mercy**

The assumption that the object of the sentencing system is to promote the reduction of crime by making as many people as possible want to obey the criminal law requires, not only that there should be punishment according to desert (a result achieved with a fair degree of success by the system of punishment according to gravity), but also that the system should be administered with as little appearance of injustice and as mercifully as possible. So far as the criminal himself is concerned, punishment has less chance of benefiting him if he labours under a sense of injustice; so far as the public is concerned, respect for the criminal law will diminish if it is thought to be unjustly or mercilessly administered.

Instances of the influence of the Courts' desire to avoid even the appearance of injustice on the length of their sentences are provided by cases dealing with co-defendants, occurrences at the trial, the giving of credit for going straight, the offender's contrition and the offender's cooperation with the police. When these matters have been considered a few words will be added about the judicial exercise of mercy.

A. CO-DEFENDANTS

The principle of justice that like cases should be treated alike is fundamental, and someone who has received a sentence of imprisonment when his co-accused was fined, or a much heavier prison sentence than that received by his co-accused, is not likely to be readily perceptive of reasons justifying the differences. Accordingly:

"The Court, on many occasions, has reduced a sentence to bring it more in line with a sentence imposed on a co-accused; it is something which this Court tries to do in the general run of cases on the basis that only thereby can a sense of grievance be averted. But there is no principle of law that sentences must strictly compare."[2]

---

[1] P. 135, *supra*; see also the "ceiling" principle which restricts the use of exemplary sentences, p. 186, above.

[2] *Coe*, [1969] 1 All E.R. 65; *Ball* (1951), 35 Cr. App. Rep. 164; *Pitson* (1972), 56 Cr. App Rep. 391.

The Court of Appeal did not vary the appellant's sentence in the case in which these observations were made. A case in which the Court of Appeal did vary a sentence on the ground under consideration is *Street*.[1] Two men were separately convicted of handling stolen television sets, which they acquired from the same third party. Despite the similarity of the circumstances and of their criminal records, the first man was given a suspended sentence of 12 months whilst Street, dealt with a month later, was sentenced to 12 months immediate imprisonment. The Court clearly thought that Street's sentence was correct in principle and "could not understand" why the first man had been treated with such leniency. Yet the Court, acknowledging that Street was "suffering from a real sense of grievance", suspended his sentence. This case is a further illustration of circumstances in which retribution may be made to give way to expediency. A purist might argue that the right course would have been to increase the first man's sentence; but he did not appeal and, as we saw earlier,[2] there is neither a power in the Court to increase an appellant's sentence nor a right of prosecution appeal against an allegedly inadequate sentence.[3]

B. OCCURRENCES AT THE TRIAL

In *Aston*,[4] the accused was sentenced to two years imprisonment after pleading guilty to housebreaking. On leaving the Court he said to the Recorder "And you call that British justice, you—". Later on in the day the Recorder caused Aston to be brought up from the cells and addressed him as follows:

> "After the sentence of the Court had been passed upon you, you expressed grave doubt as to my parentage. The sentence for the offence to which you pleaded guilty I vary to one of four years penal servitude."

The Recorder indicated to the Court of Criminal Appeal that he had decided that the offence merited more than two years imprisonment, but the Court restored that sentence on the ground that justice must be seen to be done. It is open to question whether justice can ever be seen to be done when a sentence is increased as it was in *Aston*, whatever the cause of increase may be; but there is no doubt of the sentencing judge's power to vary sentence as long as he does so within the prescribed time.[5]

---

[1] [1974] Crim. L.R. 264.
[2] P. 113, *supra*.
[3] For further discussion of the complexities to which the sentencing of co-defendants can give rise, see *Hair and Singh*, [1978] Crim. L.R. 698 and commentary by Mr. D. A. Thomas.
[4] [1948] W.N. 252. See also *Reeves*, p. 24, *supra*.
[5] See now Courts Act 1971, s. 11; *Menocal*, [1979] 2 All E.R. 510; and P. Mirfield, "Alteration of Sentences and Orders in the Crown Court" [1980] Crim. L.R. 17.

A stronger case than *Aston* is *Hargreaves*.[1] Hargreaves was given three years concurrent on four counts of receiving. The Judge had said that one of the most terrible aspects of the case was that the accused had called his fifteen year old son to give false evidence. In fact, Hargreaves had only agreed to his son being called under pressure from his legal advisers. The Court of Criminal Appeal reduced the sentence to two years because, although the sentence was not wrong in principle, the accused would suffer from a sense of injustice if it were allowed to stand for it took into account a matter for which he was not to blame. The case is stronger than *Aston* because both Courts clearly thought that the sentence was right in principle, and the Court of Criminal Appeal only varied it because of expediency. This behaviour cannot be explained on the basis of any theory of punishment; but it is none the less desirable for that.

C. CREDIT FOR GOING STRAIGHT

A frequent ground for reducing a sentence on appeal is that inadequate credit was given to an accused with a record for keeping out of trouble for a substantial period of time. It used to be a ground for reducing a period of preventive detention to a lesser period of imprisonment and even for putting the appellant on probation. Thus in *Brighton*[2] the Court of Criminal Appeal reduced a sentence of three years for receiving to two years although the judge had said that he took the fact that the accused had gone straight for twelve years into account in not awarding preventive detention. In reducing the sentence further, the Court said that greater credit was due to him for the efforts he had made.

The reduction of punishment in such a case is based on the assumption that the conviction-free period is not merely the outcome of lucky non-detection but shows that the offender is not a persistent or professional criminal. It could be justified on the utilitarian ground that the offender needs less punishment to deter or reform him than a more hardened criminal; but the simple idea that the Courts give credit for what they take to be honest endeavour so as to make their sentencing practice reflect the ordinary notion that it is desirable to reward people for trying to be good is rather more convincing.

D. CONTRITION

There are cases in which a sentence has been reduced on appeal because the judge made insufficient allowance for the accused's

---

[1] [1964] Crim. L.R. 236.
[2] [1963] Crim. L.R. 64.

contrition. A very strong example is *Davies*.[1] A schoolmaster had pleaded guilty to seven indecent assaults on male pupils aged from ten to eleven. He had one previous conviction for indecent exposure, and he was sentenced to six years imprisonment in all for the assaults. The Court of Criminal Appeal reduced the sentence to four years because, though the accused had to be punished severely to mark the disapproval of society and to deter others, he was not a constitutional homosexual requiring to be kept out of circulation; moreover, he had shown real repentance.

> "This is above all a case where the prisoner has shown a real degree of repentance. . . . He pleaded guilty despite the offer of considerable sums of money from friends to conduct his defence. . . . He recognised that he had to be punished and felt that he wanted the punishment. . . . The fact that he has shown this degree of repentance makes this Court come to the conclusion that it would be right to interfere in this case."

If contrition is genuine, it can be argued that the offender has already had and will, independently of anything the judge does, continue to have part of his punishment in the feelings of remorse. It is also arguable that the contrite offender requires less punishment to reform him because he has already reformed. There is no doubt that it is in accordance with popular notions of what is proper for credit to be given for contrition and *vice versa*; but it is difficult to see how a Court can ever be really satisfied about the genuineness and probable degree of permanence of the contrition. It is easier where there is tangible evidence in the form of some kind of voluntary restitution, or where the offender voluntarily owns up *before* he is detected;[2] but a mere plea of guilty is probably accounted for, more often than not, by the hope of a lighter sentence rather than by real contrition.[3]

E. COOPERATION WITH THE POLICE

The informer has been detested throughout history, but it has none the less been found necessary for the State to rely on informers of one sort or another. One form that reliance can take is the granting of a reduced sentence to an offender who cooperates with the police. In rare cases this may be a sign of contrition, but, more often than not, the transaction is one of sheer expediency although the sense of justice of an accused whose cooperation with the police was not suitably rewarded would no doubt be shocked. In *James and*

---

[1] [1965] Crim. L.R. 56. The quotation from the judgment is taken from Mr. D.A. Thomas's article in 20 Alabama L Rev at p. 201.

[2] *Wigley*, [1978] Crim. L.R. 635; *Whybrew*, [1979] Crim. L.R. 599.

[3] See p. 117; *supra*.

Sharman[1] the two accused had received sentences of seven and ten years penal servitude for burglary; but James's sentence was reduced to three years by the Court of Criminal Appeal because he had informed on his co-accused. DARLING, J. made the following observations in justification of this decision:

> "It is expedient that they should be persuaded not to trust one another, that there should not be 'honour among thieves'. He is now rewarded for informing against his accomplices, especially for denouncing Stephen Sharman and for refusing a bribe not to give evidence."

In more recent times the Courts have had to deal with a number of participants in large-scale crime who have then informed on their fellow criminals. In *Lowe*[2] a sentence of $11\frac{1}{2}$ years imprisonment was imposed for "a massive number of very serious offences", taking account of Lowe's assistance to the police. By the time the case came before the Court of Appeal, information given by Lowe had led to the recovery of nearly half a million pounds worth of stolen property and to the implication of some 50 or more persons in other offences. ROSKILL, L.J., stated:

> "It must therefore be in the public interest that persons who have become involved in gang activities of this kind should be encouraged to give information to the police in order that others may be brought to justice and that, when such information is given and can be acted upon and, as here, has already been in part successfully acted upon, substantial credit should be given upon pleas of guilty especially in cases where there is no other evidence against the accused than the accused's own confession. Unless credit is given in such cases there is no encouragement for others to come forward and give information of invaluable assistance to society and the police which enables these criminals—and these crimes are all too prevalent, not only in East London but throughout the country—to be brought to book."

Thus, despite the fact that Lowe admitted committing some 90 offences including several armed robberies, and that "crimes of this gravity must receive proper punishment", the Court reduced his sentence to five years. This large and further discount took account of his immense assistance to the police, and also of the fact that both in prison and on release he would need close and inevitably restrictive protection against those upon whom he had informed.

F. MERCY

Although it is right that justice should be tempered with mercy, relatively little room is left for mercy in sentencing if "justice" is

---

[1] (1913), 9 Cr. App. Rep. 142.
[2] (1977), 66 Cr. App. Rep 122; *cf.* also *Davies and Gorman* (1978), 68 Cr. App. Rep. 319.

broadly construed and all appearance of condonation of the offence is to be avoided. No doubt the word "mercy" is occasionally used when allowance is made for some of the matters so far discussed in this section, but it is justice, or at least the avoidance of an appearance of injustice, that requires such allowance to be made. There are other cases in which mercy is excluded because the reduction of a just sentence would amount to a partial condonation of an offence in relation to which the interests of potential victims of subsequent offenders require that there should be no relaxation of the general deterrent effect of the sentence. Thus it has been held that offences against the Official Secrets Acts must be seen to be punished even though there is psychiatric evidence that the offender will deteriorate during her thirty months imprisonment.[1]

Subject to the above points, "mercy" in the sense of the non imposition or reduction of a just sentence on the ground of benevolence is no doubt a comparatively frequent characteristic of judicial action. Although, in cases in which an occasional offender who might justly have been given a prison sentence is discharged or put on probation, statute requires the court to have come to the conclusion that punishment is "inexpedient", the judge, the public and the offender regard the act as one of mercy. Further instances of such acts are provided by cases in which allowance is made for the offender's family circumstances such as the desirability of his being released in time for the birth of his child or even in time for Christmas at home. It is by no means unknown for the Court of Appeal to reduce a sentence as an act of mercy because it has already had the desirable effect of making the offender realise how much trouble he has caused,[2] or when, in a case which caused much public concern, "matters have cooled down a little" between the imposition of sentence and the hearing of the appeal.[3]

Section 4.—**A further illustration and conclusions**

The chapter concludes with a further illustration of some of the matters which have been discussed above by a reference to some of the justifications given by the Court of Criminal Appeal for the long sentences imposed by EDMUND DAVIES, J., in the great train robbery case of *Wilson and others.*[4]

---

[1] *Bingham*, [1973] Q.B. 870; [1973] 2 All E.R. 89; 57 Cr. App. Rep. 439.
[2] *Pritchard* (1973), 57 Cr. App. Rep. 492.
[3] *Jones* (1971), 56 Cr. App. Rep. 212.
[4] [1965] 1 Q.B. 402; [1964] 3 All E.R. 269. The quotations given in the text are from the judgment of FENTON ATKINSON, J., dismissing Wilson's appeal against sentence (at pp. 409–10).

A. THE CASE OF *WILSON*

In the small hours of August 8th, 1963, the Glasgow to London mail train which contained a vast quantity of notes en route to London banks for cancellation, was held up. The robbers got away with about £2,600,000 of which only some £280,000 was recovered. After trials lasting more than ten weeks, six of the major participants, including Wilson, were found guilty of conspiracy to rob and robbery with aggravation.[1] They were sentenced to twenty-five years imprisonment for the conspiracy and thirty years imprisonment for the robbery, the sentences to run concurrently. The quotations from the judgment of FENTON ATKINSON, J. dismissing their appeals to the Court of Criminal Appeal listed three important points, the predominance, in serious cases involving a "gang" element, of considerations of general deterrence and the protection of the public over retribution and individualisation, the importance attached to cooperation with the police and the plea of guilty, and the importance attached to depriving professional criminals of the opportunity of enjoying the fruits of their crimes.

i. *Deterrence and protection of the public against gangs.* The crime was described as:

> "an act of organised banditry directed at a vital public service and it had the character of warfare against the community, touching new depths of lawlessness for which the type of sentence normally imposed for armed robbery is, in our view, inadequate."

(This remark was directed against the point made in argument that even very serious robberies tended only to attract sentences of ten to fifteen years.)

> "In our judgment, severely deterrent sentences were necessary, not only to protect the community against these men for a very long time, but also to demonstrate as clearly as possible to others tempted to follow them into lawlessness on this vast scale that, if they are brought to trial and convicted, commensurate punishment will follow; and that being so, for the reasons given recently in this Court in *R. v. Curbishley*[2] minor differences in age and record between these men become, in our view, irrelevant."

Curbishley was a case of robbery in which deterrent sentences of fifteen years on several offenders were upheld against an argument that the sentence was inordinately long for a younger member of the gang. The Court said that the sentences were passed to deter others and to show that crime did not pay. In the case of a deterrent sentence there was said to be no ground for distinguishing between the defendants on the score of either age or record.

---

[1] Other participants were convicted and received lesser sentences.
[2] [1964] Crim. L.R. 555, C.A.

"The maximum sentence on count two was imprisonment for life, and such a sentence might well have been imposed. In our view sentences approximating to the maximum were fully justified, not because those who rob a mail train are necessarily worse men than others who commit certain types of crime for which lesser penalties are laid down, but because of the grave threat which such crimes as this present to the public as a whole."

The first sentence of this last quotation is rather paradoxical; it is one of the few modern instances in which a life sentence is spoken of as meaning something like what it says; yet, had they been given a choice, it is virtually certain that all six appellants would have opted for life rather than thirty years, and it is most improbable that any of them would, as lifers, have served anything like the twenty years which will be the minimum they will all serve unless released on licence. The subsequent prison escapes by some of these men show that one of the drawbacks of very long sentences is their tendency to induce an utterly uncooperative state of mind in the prisoner with few thoughts other than that of escape.

ii. *Want of cooperation etc.*

"Certainly there was no one of them who could claim favourable consideration for assisting the course of justice or restoring any of the proceeds of the crime which, if we accept some of the submissions made to us, they will be free to enjoy in some ten years from now."

One of the other participants who pleaded guilty to the conspiracy charge, having previously given information to the police which facilitated the recovery of £800,000, was sentenced to twenty years imprisonment instead of the twenty-five years imposed on the major participants; his sentence was further reduced by the Court of Criminal Appeal because his role in the conspiracy had probably not been a major one.

iii. *Deprivation of fruits.* The concluding portion of the last quotation was of course a reference to the importance of preventing criminals from enjoying the fruits of their crimes. There is something absurd about arguing for a reduced sentence in the case of people who may be presumed to be likely to have access to enormous sums of money on their release. This point had been put very clearly by EDMUND DAVIES, J. when sentencing Wilson:

"It would be an affront to the public weal that any of you should be at liberty in anything like the near future to enjoy any of those ill-gotten gains. Accordingly, it is in no spirit of mere retribution that I propose to secure that such an opportunity will be denied all of you for an extremely long time."[1]

---

[1] Taken from a transcript kindly supplied by Lord EDMUND-DAVIES.

At the sentencing level, the most interesting problem raised by the case of "The Great Train Robbery" is what would have happened if all six of the major participants had been told by EDMUND DAVIES, J. that their sentences would be thirty years but that the sentences would be reduced to twenty years if half or approximately half the money were restored, and to ten years if the whole or approximately the whole of the money were returned. With such vast sums of money and so many years of sentence to play with, it would be possible to ring the changes on the above question to suit more or less anybody's taste.

B. CONCLUSION

If there were such a thing as the scientific control of crime by means of the imposition of prison sentences of various lengths, the system explained in this chapter would, to say the least, leave a great deal to be desired. The scientific control of crime through the imposition of prison sentences would entail the use of such empirically verified generalisations as that a year is always more efficacious than six months, that two years is more efficacious for offenders over thirty than for those under that age who generally do better with a year, or that three years is more efficacious in the case of theft than it is in the case of assault for which a year is generally the best length of sentence. By contrast the system which has just been described is based on a number of different impress- ionistic ranges of sentences for the different offences based on a notion of gravity which turns out, on analysis, to be popular moral- ity with a strong admixture of expediency; anything less scientific would be difficult to imagine. However, there is at present no such thing as the scientific control of crime through the imposition of prison sentences of varying lengths because there are no empirically verified generalisations such as those which have just been mentioned. If there ever is to be such a thing as the scientific control of crime by the means we are considering, there will have to be a great deal of random experimentation. The Courts would have to sentence offenders who appeared to them to have identical relevant characteristics to terms of imprisonment of different lengths, and it is very doubtful whether any Court could ever be persuaded to carry out its sentencing on a random basis. In default we shall have to be content with second best, rather long term and not very reliable research; but the unscientific nature of the present sentencing sys- tem must be borne in mind when proposals for reforming the sen- tencing system are being considered.

V

SOME FURTHER QUESTIONS

By way of conclusion, a few further questions may be raised with regard to retribution and sentencing reform.

A. RETRIBUTION

Is the present English sentencing system too retributive? The answer suggested by this book is "Yes and no"; but, before enlarging on it, reference may be made to the two extreme views that it is altogether insufficiently retributive and that it is altogether too much so.

i. *Insufficient retribution.* The answer that the system is not retributive enough is provided by Kantians and "Blimps".

It is doubtful whether there are any purely Kantian penal theorists in contemporary England; but, if there is anyone who holds the view that crime must be punished as a kind of enforced atonement, he would be bound to say that our system is not retributive enough. There is, from such a point of view, far too much non-punishment on the ground of expediency, examples being provided by probation and discharge. On the view that the object is atonement, there is also too much under-punishment in the sense that convicted criminals get less than their just deserts; one among many instances is the lengths to which Courts are sometimes prepared to go in endeavouring to secure equality of punishment among co-defendants.

The "Blimps" consider that the present system is altogether too soft. They contend that prison conditions are not hard enough, that prison sentences are too short, and that not enough convicted criminals are sent to prison. The first of these contentions can hardly be true of the conditions under which the majority of prisoners have to serve their sentences: as Lord LANE, C.J., recently remarked, "overcrowding in many of the penal establishments in this country is such that a prison sentence, however short, is a very unpleasant experience indeed for the inmates".[1] So far as the second and third contentions are concerned, one may dissent from them as generalisations without denying the existence of instances of unduly short sentences or of cases in which fines were imposed when imprisonment would have been proper; indeed, a striking example of the latter is provided by *Riddle and Stevens*.[2] Judicial complaints about the excessive leniency of some sentences are more often based on deterrent than on retributive considerations, and there is a lack of large scale evidence that our sentencing system is insufficiently retributive because too soft.

ii. *Excessive retribution.* The view that our sentencing system is altogether too retributive stems from the argument is that it is unscientific to draw the numerous distinctions which are undoubtedly drawn today on the basis of proportionality to wickedness; but it is questionable whether a system which ignored the retributive notions prevailing in the society in which it operates might not, in the long run, lead to a diminution of respect for the criminal law. It may, however, fairly be asked whether these notions are as prevalent as is sometimes supposed. The position of the judges is certainly a little ambivalent, for they claim to be the mouthpiece of the public and yet there are instances in which their views are probably more moralistic than those of a considerable sector, if not a preponderance, of the public. For example, it is difficult to reconcile some judicial pronouncements with the widespread opinion that a large number of people tends not to think it immoral to steal from a supermarket, to "pilfer" from an employer or even to rifle a gas meter. If this is too gloomy a picture of the present state of affairs, there can be little doubt that the conduct which has just been mentioned differs from many people's conception of theft. Yet the following remarks of WINN, L.J. are probably typical of the judges:

> "The old idea that one can take by way of gain from the Army, Navy or other institution without being guilty of theft is an all too prevalent, and one must say utterly unmeritorious distinction of conscience these days, and possibly is responsible for quite a lot of dishonesty. It really is to be hoped that sooner or later the public will manage to see the lack of distinction more clearly."[3]

Is there a complete lack of distinction? To what extent do the public share the retributive views expressed by the judges in some of their utterances about sentences? The first of these questions might appear to be entirely philosophical, whereas the answer to the

---

[1] *Upton* (1980), 71 Cr. App. Rep. 102 at p. 104.
[2] P. 134, *supra*.
[3] *Nelson*, [1967] 1 All E.R. 358, n.; 51 Cr. App. Rep. 98.

second can plainly only be found by painstaking and none too easy empirical research. Yet the answer to the first question is not wholly independent of empirical considerations. To what extent are super-markets and employers insured against pilfering? To what extent is the public's failure to perceive the lack of the distinction mentioned by WINN, L.J. due to its view (correct or erroneous) about insurance? Has the absence of an identifiable individual victim anything to do with the matter? The prevalence of retributive notions in contemporary society and the impact on such notions of the corporation and insurance company cry out for empirical re-search.

iii. *The position adopted in this book.* To revert to the answer sug-gested in this book to the question whether the present English sentencing system is too retributive, the answer is "Yes" if a "re-tributive system" is one which can, at points, only be justified on the ground that it exists to provide what Bentham termed "vindicative satisfaction" for the victims of crime; instances are provided by the punishment as distinct from the compulsory treatment of the men-tally disordered[1] and the treatment of involuntary manslaughter as something different from the assault or other unlawful act which caused death.[2] If, on the other hand, a "retributive system" means one under which punishment frequently has to be justified on the sole ground that it is a method of giving wrongdoers their deserts, it is submitted that the present English sentencing system is not too retributive because the meting out of deserts is an adequate justifica-tion of punishment in its own right, provided it reduces crime, which to some extent it obviously does.

The first half of the above answer must not be taken as in any sense a denial of the utility of attending to the natural resentment of the victim and other members of the public when giving reasons for sentence, any more than the second part of the answer should be taken as a denial of the importance of other considerations than the assessment of deserts. Someone who deserved imprisonment may sometimes justifiably be put on probation simply because that is thought to be the surest way of inducing him to turn over a new leaf and to afford protection to potential victims of the future, although it provides little vindicative satisfaction to the actual victim. Con-versely, it may sometimes be right to send an offender to prison in spite of the fact that it is thought that probation might be best for him, the justification for such an action being general deterrence in either its short-term form of an endeavour to influence those contem-

---

[1] Pp. 69 and 162, *supra.*
[2] P. 157, *supra.*

plating crime, or its long-term form of the maintenance of standards; in such a case the sentencer may properly use the occasion to stress the desirability of satisfying the just resentment of the victim. None of this is intended, however, to minimise the importance of doing everything possible to insure that the victim is compensated by the offender (although this can rarely be achieved) and, in appropriate cases, by the State (although discussion of the role of the Criminal Injuries Compensation Board lies outside the scope of this book).[1]

The position adopted in this book is therefore that the proper function of State punishment is to reduce crime by giving offenders their deserts. This does not rule out leniency in terms of putting on probation an offender whose case might merit imprisonment if it were not for personal or social factors revealed in the reports to the Court. It does, however, argue against the imposition of sentences going beyond the gravity of the offence. It may be said that in general the English sentencing system adopts a similar position, if one bears in mind the occasional departures from that position arising from sentences of life imprisonment[2] and from sentences lengthened for either curative[3] or general deterrent reasons,[4] and if the prevailing conception of "gravity" is accepted (see Chapter IV). It is also noteworthy that in the last ten years there has been a marked shift of opinion in the United States towards a position similar to that adopted in this book. Under the banner of "the Justice model", there has been a growing rejection of the primacy of the rehabilitative or reformative aim of sentencing and an increasing emphasis on the retributive principle of giving offenders their just deserts.[5] This movement has also been influential in England, both before[6] and since[7] the publication of the Home Office study of the effectiveness of sentencing which demonstrated the almost total absence of evidence that any particular form of sentence is more effective than any other sentence.[8] A number of the themes of this revival of what is, in effect, a form of "limiting retributivism" have already been propounded in Chapter III of this book.

---

[1] *Cf.* for a brief discussion, M. Wasik, "The Place of Compensation in the Penal System" [1978] Crim. L.R. 599; for a detailed analysis, D. Miers, *Responses to Victimisation* (1978).

[2] See p. 49 *supra* and p. 209, *infra*.

[3] P. 140, *supra*.

[4] P. 136, *supra*.

[5] See, for example, American Friends Service Committee, *Struggle for Justice* (1971); A. von Hirsch, *Doing Justice* (1976); Twentieth Century Fund Task Force on Criminal Sentencing, *Fair and Certain Punishment* (1976); and P. O'Donnell, M. Churgin and D. Curtis, *Towards a Just and Effective Sentencing System* (1977).

[6] R. Hood, *Tolerance and the Tariff* (1974).

[7] A. E. Bottoms and R. H. Preston, *The Coming Crisis in Penology* (1980).

[8] P. 96, above.

B. SENTENCING REFORM

References have been made throughout the book to the report of the Advisory Council on the Penal System on Sentences of Imprisonment: A Review of Maximum Penalties in 1978, and some brief comments may now be made on the proposals for sentencing reform contained in that report.[1] The Advisory Council were instructed, *inter alia*, "to consider the general structure and level of maximum sentences of imprisonment available to the courts [and] to assess how far they represent a valid guide to sentencing practice". Although there had long been concern that the existing statutory maxima afforded too little guidance to the courts on the appropriate level of sentences and on differentials between offences, the Advisory Council steered clear of the difficulties involved in drawing up a new scheme of maximum penalties which would fulfil those functions. Instead they recommended a two-tier structure of sentencing: first there would be "normal maximum sentences", set at a level consistent with existing sentencing practice and usually well below the existing statutory maxima; secondly there would be "exceptional sentences", allowing courts in certain circumstances to impose a sentence which is not only higher than the normal maxima but which might even go beyond the statutory maxima which exist at present.

i. *Normal maxima*: The reservations which the Advisory Council entertained about the traditional approach to maximum penalties, which is tied to the notion of the worst possible case, have already been discussed.[2] Drawing an inference from their precise terms of reference, quoted above, the Advisory Council set themselves the task of devising a structure of maximum penalties which would represent "a valid guide to sentencing practice". They felt that "on an issue so important as the relative seriousness of offences there should be some common scale to which both Parliament and the courts can adhere".[3] This scale was sought in the current practice of the courts. What the Advisory Council did was to examine the statistics for length of sentences of immediate imprisonment for each offence for the three years 1974, 1975 and 1976. The "normal maximum sentence" for each offence would generally be set at a level which would include 90 per cent of prison sentences for that crime in those years; the calculation could, of course, be carried out on more recent statistics. By this means the normal maxima would be closely tied to the actual practice of the courts. Moreover the

---

[1] Two most helpful critiques of the report are those by Radzinowicz and Hood, [1978] Crim. L.R. 713, and by D. A. Thomas, (1979) 42 M.L.R. 309.

[2] P. 39, above.

[3] Sentences of Imprisonment: A Review of Maximum Penalties (1978), para. 162. (All paragraph references below refer to this Report.)

normal maxima, being lower than the statutory maxima to which the judges have been accustomed, might influence courts to impose lower sentences for ordinary or "run-of-the-mill" offences in accordance with the Advisory Council's earlier recommendation.[1] Where the case was not ordinary but "exceptional" a court would be empowered, as is explained in section ii below, to exceed the normal maximum penalty.

A structure so squarely based on the practice of three chosen years might appear to offer insufficient scope for change and innovation. The Advisory Council attempted to introduce flexibility into the scheme by proposing that the normal maximum penalty for any new criminal offence should be determined according to the normal maxima for analogous offences; that the whole scheme should be subject to periodic review by the Home Secretary in consultation with a standing body such as the Advisory Council itself (it will be recalled that the Advisory Council was abolished in 1979); and that the scheme should not at first be embodied in legislation but that the judges be encouraged "to work for an experimental period to new maxima calculated as we have suggested".[2]

One underlying premise of the Advisory Council's recommendations, foreshadowed in their Interim Report on The Length of Prison Sentences, is that "for many ordinary offenders a shorter sentence than the one imposed would be just as effective as a longer one",[3] and this has recently been strengthened by the results of a Home Office study of the effects of taking offenders out of circulation. On the basis of calculations from criminal records, the authors argue that if the time which each incarcerated offender spent in prison were reduced by four months (i.e. his nominal sentence length reduced by six months), the total number of criminal convictions in a given year would increase by only 1·6 per cent.[4] If this finding, however, supports one premise of the Advisory Council's recommended scheme, there remains the question whether their conclusions offer the most appropriate path for sentencing reform in England.

In some respects the Advisory Council failed to carry through the logic of their own approach. Thus it is surprising, in view of their commitment to reducing the level of sentences for ordinary offences, that they resolved not to propose normal maxima of less than two years imprisonment or to set normal maxima at levels other than whole years. This latter point is important to the Advisory Council's

---

[1] The Length of Prison Sentences (1977).
[2] Para. 317.
[3] Para. 188; see p. 173, *supra*.
[4] Home Office Research Study No. 64, *Taking Offenders out of Circulation* (1980), pp. 14–18.

own example of burglary: 84 per cent of sentences of immediate imprisonment were for two years or less, and 96 per cent for three years or less, and three years was selected as the normal maximum penalty. If it could be established that 90 per cent of prison sentences for burglary were for two-and-a-half years or less, would it not be better to set the normal maximum at that level rather than at three years? Of course small fractions of a year should be avoided, but the point is of no mean significance in view of the large number of sentences for burglary and other property crimes, and "it is wrong that an offender should lose his liberty for a day longer than is absolutely necessary to satisfy the proper aims of penal policy".[1] If courts work to a normal maximum of three years rather than two-and-a-half years, that wrong is risked.

It must be questioned, however, whether it is proper to base a system of norms for sentencing upon figures from the criminal statistics. Some disadvantages of this were pointed out in Chapter IV,[2] and the Advisory Council's report shows little appreciation of the difficulties inherent in their approach. The 90 per cent of sentences which set the level of the normal maximum were pronounced after all relevant circumstances of aggravation and mitigation were taken into account. Thus on the one hand that level is inflated to an uncertain extent by cases in which consecutive sentences were passed or other offences taken into consideration, whilst on the other hand the level may be depressed by allowances made for mitigating factors. One might suppose that the former would have more effect on the 90 per cent level than the latter. The Advisory Council recommended that, if their system of normal maxima were introduced, there should be a rule that "sentences passed on the same occasion for a number of offences should not in total exceed the maximum that could have been imposed for the most serious of the offences", unless the criterion for passing an exceptional sentence (discussed below) were satisfied.[3] No less important, however, are the questions whether the levels chosen as normal maxima are artificially inflated by sentences imposed on multiple offenders, and exactly how the normal maxima would fit into the tariff approach described in Chapter IV. Since one of the declared aims of the Advisory Council was to bring maximum penalties closer to existing sentencing practice, it is both surprising and unfortunate that they chose to work from the gross sentencing statistics rather than attempting to identify normal ranges of sentence, and that they failed to explain how their proposed normal

---

[1] Para. 188.
[2] Pp. 170–171, *supra.*
[3] Para. 220.

maxima would relate to normal ranges of sentence and to other principles of sentencing.

This leads to the question of alternative approaches to sentencing reform. Two are to be found in the United States, although there are already several variations on each of them. One approach is for the legislature to lay down presumptive sentences, leaving the Court with little discretion in the matter of sentencing. Thus the Californian Determinate Sentencing Act 1976 states:

"The Legislature finds and declares that the purpose of imprisonment for crime is punishment. This purpose is best served by terms proportionate to the seriousness of the offence with provision for uniformity in the sentences of offenders committing the same offence under similar circumstances. The Legislature further finds and declares that the elimination of disparity and the provision of uniformity of sentences can best be achieved by determinate sentences fixed by statute in proportion to the seriousness of the offences as determined by the Legislature to be imposed by the trial court with specified discretion."

This approach therefore requires the legislature to divide each offence into a number of variants, to attach a presumptive sentence to each variant, and then to provide for an aggravated and a mitigated form of each presumptive sentence. Thus once the sentencer has identified the variant of the offence which he is dealing with, he has a choice of only three sentences—the presumptive, the aggravated and the mitigated. Quite apart from the formidable problems of drafting (and perhaps re-structuring of the criminal law) to which this approach gives rise, there are a number of other objections. The divisions of an offence may be either too crude (if only a few variants are distinguished) or too complicated (as where a statute distinguishes some 15 or 20 variants of a crime such as burglary or robbery); presumptive sentencing invests the prosecution with great power to influence sentence through its choice of charge and (where there is a guilty plea) through its presentation of the facts; and it might tend to ossify, or even to inflate, general levels of sentencing.[1] The proclaimed elimination of disparity may lead to the promotion of an arid, arithmetical consistency, and it may be said that presumptive sentencing purchases the control of judicial discretion and the legislative regulation of sentencing differentials at too high a price.

The second alternative is the "guidelines" approach, once again found in several variations in the United States.[2] The fundamental idea is that a study of the actual sentencing practice of the courts

---

[1] See generally D. A. Thomas, *Equity in Sentencing* (Albany, New York, 1977).
[2] *Cf.* L. T. Wilkins, [1980] Crim. L.R. 201, and M. H. Tonry and Norval Morris, "Sentencing Reform in America" in Glazebrook (ed.), *Reshaping the Criminal Law* (1978), p. 434.

should make it possible to produce a table which sets out along one axis variations in the gravity of offences, and along another axis variations in factors personal to the offender, and that the intersection of these axes should indicate to the sentencer an appropriate sentence for the particular case (say, 12 months imprisonment). The guidelines would allow for a margin of tolerance (say, 3 months shorter or longer) to enable the sentencer to give effect to any further factors which he believes relevant, but the important point is that the guidelines in no way prevent the court from passing a completely different sentence. The court is at liberty to impose a sentence outside the guidelines, provided that there is a statement of reasons. However, under the guidelines approach there would be constant monitoring of the sentences passed by the courts, and there would be periodic meetings of judges to discuss emergent trends and to deal with general issues raised by the reasons given for departing from the guidelines in particular cases. These meetings might lead to the periodic revision of some or all of the published guidelines; they might also lead to discussions with any judges whose sentences appeared to be more than usually outside the guidelines. Different kinds of guidelines approach offer different starting points: although it has been assumed here that the guidelines would in the first place reflect existing sentencing practice, they might alternatively be drawn up, as in some States, by an independent Sentencing Commission. Characteristic of the guidelines approach, however, is the discretion left to the judge in sentencing. The guidelines are for guidance and (unless the alternative of having an independent Sentencing Commission were adopted) the only pressure towards conformity would be the collegial pressure of the opinion of other judges. If the guidelines were framed initially so as to reflect existing practice and were reviewed by a committee of judges (with the assistance of information compiled for the purpose), most of the requirements laid down by the Advisory Council would be fulfilled. The Advisory Council said.[1]

> "The guidelines approach is of particular interest to us because it has roughly the same objective as our own recommendations, namely to give formal recognition to what the courts are already practising. Sentencing guidelines would have, of course, a more direct impact upon sentencing than our own proposals, and we doubt whether such a sophisticated formalisation of the 'tariff' would be acceptable in the English context. Nonetheless, we consider that the progress of this new concept in sentencing should continue to be watched."

Whether the Advisory Council were right to prefer their own approach of "normal maxima" to a guidelines approach is a matter

---

[1] Appendix C, para. 20.

for debate. Guidelines might appear more restrictive than the normal ranges of sentence which currently influence sentencing, but if that were seen by the judiciary as a disadvantage it might be counterbalanced by the advantage of allowing the judges to regulate the guidelines for themselves, as suggested by Wilkins.[1] What is surely more important, however, is to examine the assumptions behind our notions of "gravity". The Advisory Council's declaration that

> "the essential strength of the recommendations in this report is that they eschew all fresh and controversial value judgments, but rest squarely upon the contemporary practice of the courts"[2]

is unconvincing and unfortunate. If it is said that the existing "tariff" is uncontroversial this may well be because neither the public nor parliamentarians know enough about the value judgments implicit in it; indeed, it is curious that whenever there is a public outcry about a particular sentence or group of sentences, the official rebuttal often takes the form that the critics know too little of sentencing in general and of the particular circumstances of this case. Sentencing inevitably involves the making of value judgments, and if these were to be more clearly explained, the justifications for the complex notion of "gravity" which underlies English sentencing practice could be more meaningfully discussed. Hood has argued that "the only sure and just way" of re-assessing our sentencing system would be "by forcing judges to articulate the moral judgments on which their sentence is passed".[3] The Advisory Council's report contributed little to this articulation; a modest start to the task was attempted in Chapters III and IV, above.

ii. *Exceptional sentences.* The normal maximum sentences devised by the Advisory Council were intended to deal with ordinary offenders. When sentencing an exceptional offender, Courts should be empowered to exceed the normal maximum and to impose an exceptional sentence. Before discussing the problems of defining and of identifying exceptional offenders, we consider the Advisory Council's notion of what an exceptional sentence should involve.

Their recommendation was that a court which resolved to pass an exceptional sentence should not be bound by any maximum sentence. There would be some procedural safeguards—the judge must warn the offender and his advisers that he is minded to impose an exceptional sentence, so that they have a fair opportunity to prepare an argument against this course (although the Advisory

---

[1] [1980] Crim. L.R. 201.
[2] Para. 164.
[3] Roger Hood, *Tolerance and the Tariff* (1974), p. 8

Council pusillanimously declined to recommend that reasons should be given for imposing an exceptional sentence); and legal aid for an application for leave to appeal against an exceptional sentence would be an entitlement. However, the court would be able to exceed the normal maximum sentence for the offence by any amount. The Advisory Council appear to have been driven to this conclusion by their resolve not to review the statutory maximum penalty for each offence: bereft of a meaningful scale of statutory maximum sentences, the Advisory Council could only propose that the upper limit of exceptional sentences be left in the hands of the judges, as it is in Scotland.[1] After thus placing their trust in the judiciary, the Advisory Council promptly declared that "the possibility that a court might impose a sentence of quite inordinate length has to be faced".[2] The usual provision for parole eligibility after serving one-third of the sentence was thought insufficient to curb judicial enthusiasm, and so the Advisory Council recommended that an offender serving an exceptional sentence should be eligible for parole after one-third or after the normal maximum sentence for his offence, whichever is less.

Who, then, is the exceptional offender? The Advisory Council recommended that this question should be answered by a provision in the following form:[3]

"No court should pass a sentence of imprisonment exceeding the new maximum term unless, by reason of the nature of the offence and the character, conduct and antecedents of the offender, the court is of the opinion that a custodial sentence of exceptional length is necessary for the protection of the public against serious harm."

This is a broad provision, particularly in view of the recommendation that no maximum at all be set on exceptional sentences, and too much might be thought to rest on the words "serious harm". The Advisory Council were more specific in the body of their report, but decided to recommend the broad formula for fear that they might otherwise deprive the judges of the flexibility to deal adequately with unforeseen cases. In explaining what they understood by "serious harm", the Advisory Council described four categories of case:[4]

"We have no doubt that it includes serious physical injury; serious psychological effects of the kind which impair a person's enjoyment of life or capacity for functioning normally (for example, some sexual offences);

---

[1] Sentences of life imprisonment, however, would still be confined to a limited group of offences: see para. 233 and p. 49, *supra*.
[2] Para. 214.
[3] Para. 207.
[4] Para. 196.

exceptional personal hardship (for example, financial loss which markedly affects a person's way of life); and damage to the security of the State (for example, as a result of espionage), or to the general fabric of society."

They added that the categories should be taken to refer not only to cases where such harm had been inflicted but also to cases where there had been a threat, attempt or conspiracy to commit such harm or where the offence had purely by good fortune failed to result in the full harm intended, and this is surely right in principle.[1] However, the phrase "damage . . . to the general fabric of society" is alarmingly wide, and the extent of the third category is unclear (if hardship to the victim is of the essence, it should surely be established that the offender intended or knowingly risked this consequence).

Whilst it was not the Advisory Council's intention to restrict the exceptional sentence to violent or so-called "dangerous" offenders, there is little discussion in the report about other types of case to which they thought it might properly be applied. The normal maximum sentences recommended by the Advisory Council were to be set at the level of 90 per cent of sentences for the particular offence; yet it does not follow that the remaining 10 per cent would fall within the proposed categories of "serious harm", or indeed that those offenders (such as the top 10 per cent of sentenced thieves or deceivers) are exceptional in anything more than a statistical sense.

The statistical basis of the Advisory Council's proposals means that exceptional sentences would not necessarily be for a period longer than the offender might expect to receive under the present system. But the proposals were clearly intended to give courts the *power* to exceed what we might call the "proportionate" sentence for the offence, and so the question of justifying this excess must be confronted. It was argued in Chapter III that the retributivist notion of proportionality ought to operate so as to limit the duration of the State's control over an individual offender.[2] It is preferable that the limit should be fixed according to an "objective" and openly discussable notion such as the gravity of the offence, rather than according to the subjective predictions of a judge, psychiatrist, social worker, criminologist or penal agent. Proportionality as a limiting principle has often been invoked to criticise "exemplary" sentences imposed in the hope of achieving a general deterrent effect, to criticise proposals to allow greater executive control over the length of custodial sentences (such as those of the Advisory Council on

---

[1] See p. 151, *supra.*
[2] Pp. 131–142, *supra.*

Young Adult Offenders in 1974),[1] to criticise the proposal for a sentence which might be lengthened as well as shortened by the executive (such as the Butler Committee's proposed "reviewable sentence" for dangerously unstable offenders),[2] and to criticise the perpetuation of executive discretion as to the release of offender-patients in mental hospitals who are subject to restriction orders without limit of time.[3] The sentence of life imprisonment stands as an exception to the proportionality principle, and to that sentence (as to restriction orders and to the proposals just mentioned) there is the further objection that indeterminacy may have profound psychological effects upon the offender, as the Advisory Council acknowledged.[4] But even if the argument is restricted to determinate sentences, whose maximum duration is set by the court but on grounds which go beyond the gravity of the particular offence—and this is the essence of the Advisory Council's recommendation for exceptional sentences—there is a departure from the proportionality principle which calls for justification.

The main justification advanced by the Advisory Council resides in public protection, and is discussed below. But it should first be noticed that the Advisory Council contemplated the limited use of exceptional sentences for deterrent reasons. Whilst they professed an "attitude of scepticism" towards the justifications for sentences aimed at general deterrence, they did accept that exceptional sentences might be appropriate for "offenders convicted of extremely lucrative crimes, if there were reason to think that the gains from such crimes were being regarded as sufficient recompense for serving shorter sentences". That, as they conceded, would "in effect amount to the recognition of an exceptional category of robberies, frauds or similar offences".[5] The imposition of very long sentences for robberies and other forms of organised crime was discussed above.[6] If burglary and shoplifting committed by "professionals" were treated as "similar offences", for example, then the way would be open to a far greater use of exceptional sentences than the Advisory Council perhaps contemplated. Moreover, since the "reason to think that the gains" were "sufficient recompense for serving shorter sentences" might well come from the offender's criminal record, the Advisory Council's declared policy that the exceptional sentence is "not concerned, as was the extended

---

[1] P. 83, *supra*.
[2] Mentally Abnormal Offenders (Cmnd. 6424), Ch. 4.
[3] P. 74, *supra*.
[4] P. 50, *supra*.
[5] Para. 204.
[6] P. 183, *supra*.

sentence, with mere persistence in crime"[1] begins to appear less water-tight and little less convincing.

The principal purpose of the exceptional sentence, according to the Advisory Council, would be public protection. The formal reasoning behind this departure from the proportionality principle must presumably be that a combination of (a) the magnitude of the harm involved and (b) the magnitude of the risk of repetition justifies the State in placing the interests of society above the interests of the offender. Public protection is therefore paramount when dealing with this class of offender, and the Advisory Council emphasised that

"a protective sentence is not justified solely by the seriousness of the harm done, risked or intended at the time of the original offence. There must be good reason to believe that on release the offender is substantially more likely than other men or women of similar age and circumstances to do serious harm. For example, there might be evidence that his offence was not an isolated incident resulting from an unusual situation which is unlikely to occur, but is part of a recurring pattern; or that it was intended to achieve a declared objective to which he remains dedicated (such as unaccomplished revenge)."[2]

It is clear from this passage that the Advisory Council's exceptional sentence would in many cases rest on a prediction of dangerousness. Much has been written on the concepts of "dangerousness" and "the dangerous offender" in the United States and in England, and the report of a committee set up by the Howard League for Penal Reform (the Floud Committee) is expected in 1981. If there is to be a departure from the proportionality principle in this kind of case, two issues must be settled: How serious must the predicted harm be? How likely must it be to occur? In practice these issues are often intertwined, and on a theoretical level it might be argued that a lower degree of probability should be sufficient if the harm risked is particularly serious, and that where there is a very high probability of further offences the likely harm need not be so serious. However, the issues will be taken separately here.

How serious must the predicted harm be? We have seen that the Advisory Council decided to employ the broad phrase "necessary for the protection of the public against serious harm". They conceded that their formula "may not be considered sufficiently precise to become statute law".[3] Could one improve upon it? The Butler Committee attempted to list qualifying offences for their proposed "reviewable sentence" for dangerously unstable offenders.[4] That

---

[1] Para. 217.
[2] Para. 205.
[3] Para. 316.
[4] Mentally Abnormal Offenders, paras. 4.39–4.45 and Appendix 4.

sentence was to serve a rather more specific purpose, but the Butler Committee's approach bears examination here. They listed qualifying offences in two schedules. Schedule A contained a selection of offences which already carry a maximum of life imprisonment, and an offender convicted of any such offence would be liable to the "reviewable sentence"; Schedule B contained a number of offences involving grave harm or the risk of grave harm to others, but a person committing such an offence would only be liable to a "reviewable sentence" if he had previously been convicted of a schedule A offence. Now it might be said that one drawback of this approach is "the risk of excluding relevant cases by mischance".[1] On the other hand, it is arguable that a person should not be liable to be deprived of his liberty for a period disproportionate to his offence unless the legislature has so declared: in sentencing as, for example, in the crime of conspiracy, the possibility that the courts might have insufficient powers in a few unprecedented cases could be seen as "an inevitable and acceptable price to pay in order to avoid the creation of oppressive 'catch-all' provisions".[2] To draw up a suitable list is no simple task, but considerations of justice and fairness require that the effort be made.

How probable must it be that the harm will occur? Before attempting to answer this question, it is necessary to consider the kinds of evidence which should be accepted as a sufficiently reliable basis for taking the decision. There are some British statistics which suggest that a further offence of violence can be predicted from an offender's criminal record,[3] but the general tendency has been to rely on the predictions of those experts who have had the opportunity to observe the offender's behaviour. We saw earlier that the predictions of psychiatrists remain central to the decision whether or not to impose life imprisonment,[4] and when the Advisory Council refer, in connection with the exceptional sentence, to evidence that the offender is substantially more likely than others to do serious harm and evidence that his behaviour is "part of a recurring pattern",[5] it seems that they have this kind of expert evidence in mind. Yet the available research findings inspire little confidence in the accuracy of such predictions. Evidence from the United States indicates a tendency to detain more people for longer periods on the basis of such predictions, and suggests that if the detainees were suddenly released the rate of offending would be lower and less serious than

---

[1] Para. 206.
[2] Law Com. no. 76, Conspiracy and Criminal Law Reform (1976), para. 1.08.
[3] Walker, Hammond and Steer, "Repeated Violence" [1967] Crim. L.R. 465.
[4] P. 50, *supra*
[5] Para. 205, quoted *supra* at p. 213.

the predictions might have led one to expect.[1] A recent Home Office study in England reached similar conclusions. In a large sample of prisoners some 77 men were found whom prison staff and researchers rated as "dangerous". Some 52 of these were subsequently released and their criminal careers were followed for five years. It was found that 13 violent offences were committed by the 52 men in this period, and of these 9 were "dangerous" offences, although a further 9 "dangerous" offences were committed by other men in the sample of 700 who had not been identified originally as "dangerous". Thus

> "Had all the released dangerous prisoners been confined for at least another five years, only nine of them would have been prevented from committing further dangerous acts, while at least 39 would have been excessively punished for no good purpose. At the same time, an equal number of dangerous offences would have been perpetrated by people who could not easily have been identified as likely to do so."[2]

The last two observations are not particularly helpful. To say that "at least 39 would have been excessively punished for no good purpose" is inaccurate: they would have been detained for the purpose of preventing 9 "dangerous" offences, and that purpose may be "good" even if it is held not to be good enough in the circumstances. To point out that an equal number of dangerous offences would have been committed by others is beside the point: if one could predict with certainty that a small group of persons were responsible for half the offences, that might well be a reason for taking special measures against them even if one could not predict who would commit the other half of the offences.

The drift of the passage just quoted is that 9 "positive" cases out of 48 is an unacceptably low rate upon which to justify preventive confinement disproportionate to the offence committed. However, it must be said that some of the 77 men originally identified as dangerous had not been released or had been released too recently to be included in the research; since these were predominantly lifers, the true "dangerousness" rate in the sample might well have been higher. To return to the question of what degree of probability there must be that the harm will occur, it may not be satisfactory to make a straight comparison between persons who have already been convicted of serious offences and their possible innocent victims.

---

[1] Cf. the discussion of the evidence deriving from the "Baxstrom affair" by A E. Bottoms, "Reflections on the Renaissance of Dangerousness" (1977) 16 Howard Journal 70, and in Home Office Research Study No. 64, *Taking Offenders out of Circulation*, pp. 2–4.

[2] *Taking Offenders out of Circulation*, p. 29.

The Advisory Council stated:

> "We cannot accept, however, that such arithmetic is decisive. That would be so only if unnecessary detentions and mistaken releases were counted as equivalent; and of course the consequences are very different. The death or injury of a blameless victim cannot be put in the same moral scales as the further detention of a person who has culpably done, risked, attempted or threatened serious harm."[1]

This is not to maintain that a person who is labelled "dangerous" loses all his rights. But it would be far too simplistic to argue that we have here a conflict between the interests of the State in public protection and an individual's rights not to be detained for a period disproportionate to the gravity of his offence, and that it is wrong to sacrifice individual rights for the sake of increasing general social welfare. We are not dealing here with a simple "individual v. State" dichotomy.[2] Where "dangerous" offences are concerned—certainly offences in the first three of the Advisory Council's categories— any failure of public protection falls upon an individual victim. That is not usually true of espionage, but it is of cardinal importance when the disproportionate detention of seriously violent offenders is being considered. Bottoms concludes that

> "we should not be prepared to sanction an indeterminate preventive sentence except on one who has already committed an act of really extreme severity, such as murder or attempted murder, and who has therefore on retributive grounds subjected himself to the possibility of a very high degree of State intervention."[3]

Leaving aside the reference to indeterminacy, we might argue that a disproportionate sentence should not be passed unless (a) the person has committed a sufficiently serious offence (using lists similar to those proposed by the Butler Committee), and (b) the court hears evidence that it is more probable than not that the offender would, if released within the normal maximum period, commit a further offence within the lists. Predictions of that kind are difficult, and their fallibility has been acknowledged above, but it is doubtful whether we can forsake them. What must be attempted in this difficult area is to hold the balance between undue reliance on predictions, undue danger to innocent individuals, and undue derogation from the few remaining rights of a convicted offender.

Finally, it may be asked whether the approach to "dangerousness" should differ where the offender is mentally disordered. Section 65 of the Mental Health Act 1959 empowers courts to impose restriction orders without limit of time.[4] If disproportionate

---

[1] Para. 200.
[2] *Cf.* Ashworth, "Concepts of Criminal Justice" [1979] Crim. L.R. 412 at p. 418.
[3] 16 Howard Journal at pp. 80–1.
[4] P. 71, *supra.*

detention ought to be permissible for ordinary offenders only in certain circumscribed cases, is it right that it should be more widely available when dealing with mentally disordered offenders? The standard argument is that "there is often a very strong causal connection between an offender's mental disorder and his capacity to do serious harm", and that it is "rarely possible to feel confident that no such relationship exists".[1] These remarks imply a rather lower standard of proof than that applied to the dangerousness of non-disordered offenders. It is further argued that s. 65 is essential for the offender "whom the court considers much more dangerous than is implicit in the particular offence for which he has been brought to trial". The Advisory Council's proposals took account, as we have seen, of serious harm that was not caused but risked, attempted or threatened; this argument seems to go further and to suggest that preventive confinement might be proper where an objectively trivial offence is claimed by an expert witness to be a mere preliminary to some seriously harmful event. There may be a small number of cases where an expert can make this prediction with great confidence, on the basis of his knowledge of a particular offender-patient. The difficulty is that s. 65 extends far wider than that. The existence of these few extraordinary cases should not be used to avoid a rigorous examination of the reasons given for applying different standards to the detention of mentally disordered offenders. It must be said that in general the reasons advanced heretofore have not been persuasive.

---

[1] White Paper, Review of the Mental Health Act 1959 (Cmnd. 7320, 1978), Ch. 5.

APPENDICES

APPENDIX I

STATISTICAL TABLES

Table I (see introduction and Chapter 1, sections 1 and 2, *passim*)

Methods by which offenders of both sexes aged 21 years and over were dealt with by English Courts or Police in 1978

(*Source: The Criminal Statistics, England and Wales, Tables I & II*)

Method of dealing with the offender	indictable offences		non-indictable offences	
	Crown Courts[a]	Magistrates Courts	non-motoring	motoring
	%[b]	%[b]	%[b]	%[b]
absolute discharge	n	1	1	1
conditional discharge	4	11	3	n
recognizance	1[c]	1	1	n
probation	5	6	1	n
fine	16	63	91	98
community service	4	2	n	n
suspended sentence	22[d]	8	1	n
immediate imprisonment	47	7	1	n
hospital order	1	n	n	n
otherwise dealt with[e]	1	2[f]	1	n
total dealt with by the courts[g]	44,832[h]	178,140	309,563	927,767
cautioned by the police[g]	10,707[j]		17,389[j]	179,643[k]

a. This figure includes a small number of non-indictable offences (such as assault on a police officer) which are now triable in the Crown Court.

b. Since percentages are given as whole numbers, they do not always total 100 per cent.

c. Includes offenders bound over to come up for judgment if called upon.

d. Includes suspended sentence supervision orders.

e. Includes one day's imprisonment, and no penalty.

f. Nearly all committed to the Crown Court for sentence.

g. Since individuals may be deal with more than once in the same year, these figures represent occasions and not individuals.

h. Includes persons committed to the Crown Court for sentence.

j. Source: *Criminal Statistics, England and Wales 1978*, Ch. 5.

k. Source: *Return of Offences relating to Motor Vehicles for 1978*.

n. Negligible, i.e. less than 0·5 per cent.

Table II (see introduction and Chapter 1, sections 1 and 2, *passim*)

Methods by which offenders of both sexes aged 21 years and over were dealt with by English Courts or Police in 1973

(*Source: The Criminal Statistics, England and Wales, Tables I & II*)

Method of dealing with the offender	indictable offences		non-indictable offences	
	Crown Courts	Magistrates' Courts	non-motoring	motoring
	%[a]	%[a]	%[a]	%[a]
absolute discharge	n	1	1	1
conditional discharge	3	11	3	n
recognizance	1[b]	1	1	n
probation	7	8	1	n
fine	20	63	92	99
suspended sentence	22[c]	7	1	n
immediate imprisonment	44	6	1	n
extended sentence	n	—	—	—
hospital order	1	n	n	n
otherwise dealt with[d]	2	4[e]	n	n
total dealt with by the courts[f]	36,251[g]	142,681	324,155	1,045,077
cautioned by the police[f]	8,964[h]		19,236[h]	203,838[j]

a. Since percentages are given as whole numbers, they do not always total 100 per cent.

b. Includes offenders bound over to come up for judgment if called upon.
c. Includes suspended sentence supervision orders.
d. Includes community service orders; and deferred sentences if the offender was finally dealt with in 1973.
e. Nearly all committed to the Crown Court for sentence.
f. Since individuals may be dealt with more than once in the same year, these figures represent occasions and not individuals.
g. Includes persons committed to the Crown Court for sentence.
h. Source: *Criminal Statistics, England and Wales*, Ch. 4.
j. Source: *Return of Offences relating to Motor Vehicles for 1973*.
n. Negligible, i.e. less than 0·5 per cent.

Table III (see introduction and Chapter 1, sections 1 and 2, *passium*)

Methods by which offenders of both sexes aged 21 years or over were dealt with by English Courts or Police in 1969

(*Source: The Criminal Statistics, England and Wales, Tables I & II*)

Method of dealing with the offender	indictable offences		non-indictable offences	
	Assizes & Quarter Sessions	Magistrates' Courts	non-motoring	motoring
	%^{a}	%^{a}	%^{a}	%^{a}
absolute discharge	n	1	1	1
conditional discharge	3	11	3	n
recognizance	1^b	n	1	—
probation	9	8	1	n
fine	12	55	92	98
suspended sentence	20	13	1	n
immediate imprisonment	53	8	1	n
extended sentence	n	—	—	—
hospital order	1	n	n	n
otherwise dealt with	n	4^c	n	n
total dealt with by the courts	27,549^{de}	137,283^d	285,632^d	797,022^d
cautioned by the police	6,901^d		15,096^{df}	224,249^{dg}

a. Since percentages are given as whole numbers, they do not always total 100 per cent.

b. Includes offenders bound over to come up for judgment if called upon.

c. Nearly all committed to Quarter Sessions for sentence.

d. Since individuals may be dealt with more than once in the same year, these figures represent occasions and not individuals.

e. Including persons sentenced at higher courts after conviction at lower courts.

f. Includes women cautioned for loitering or soliciting for the purpose of prostitution.

g. Source: Return of Offences Relating to Motor Vehicles for 1969.

n. Negligible, i.e. less than 0·5 per cent.

Table IV (see p. 46)

Breakdown of 259 life sentence prisoners who, on 31st December 1978, had served nine years or more

(*Source: Fourteenth Report of the Criminal Law Revision Committee, Annex 3*)

Years detained	Murder	Manslaughter diminished responsibility	Manslaughter	Other offences	Total
26–27	1				1
21–22	4				4
19–20	2	1			3
18–19	1	1			2
17–18	3	1			4
16–17	4	1	1		6
15–16	7				7
14–15	6	3			9
13–14	17*	1	1	1	20
12–13	19	4		4	27
11–12	28*	5	1	9	43
10–11	43	3*		12	58
9–10	51	8	1	15	75
Total	186	28	4	41	259

* Includes one woman in each case.

Table V (see p. 48)

Life sentences with a minimum recommendation under section 1 of 1965 Act

(*Source: Fourteenth Report of the Criminal Law Revision Committee,* (*Cmnd. 7844, 1980*), *Annex 4*)

Number of recommendations up to 31 December 1978

1 recommendation for 10 years
7 recommendations for 12 years
1 recommendation for 14 years
29 recommendations for 15 years
3 recommendations for 17 years
2 recommendations for 18 years
33 recommendations for 20 years
9 recommendations for 25 years
14 recommendations for 30 years
1 recommendation for 35 years
Total 100

Table VI (see p. 48)

Life sentence prisoners (including H.M.P.): daily average population

(*Source: Prison Statistics, England and Wales, Table 1.2*)

	1968	1969	1970	1971	1972	1973	1974	1975	1976	1977	1978
M	551	613	715	818	857	916	995	1105	1190	1268	1343
F	10	13	15	16	14	17	26	32	33	41	44
Total	561	626	730	834	871	933	1021	1137	1223	1309	1387

Table VII (see p. 59)

*Persons aged 17 or over sentenced by Magistrates' Courts for indictable offences or sentenced by higher courts: use of different sentences or orders 1965–1971

Sentence or order	1965	1966	1967	1968	1969*	1970*	1971*
	%	%	%	%	%	%	%
Conditional discharge	8·6	8·1	9·2	9·7	9·6	8·8	9·5
Probation	13·2	12·6	13·2	11·1	10·7	9·9	10·2
Fine	53·0	53·7	54·0	47·4	49·6	50·5	51·2
Detention Centre	2·6	2·6	2·5	2·4	2·4	2·5	2·4
Borstal Training	2·4	2·7	2·6	2·4	2·4	2·6	2·5
Suspended sentence	—	—	—	12·4	11·0	10·8	9·7
Imprisonment (immediate)	17·7	18·0	16·2	12·3	12·0	12·7	12·1
Other sentence or order	2·5	2·3	2·3	2·3	2·3	2·2	2·4
Total	100·0	100·0	100·0	100·0	100·0	100·0	100·0
Number sentenced	156,698	172,095	182,088	194,906	232,716	249,940	254,631

* Owing to the Theft Act 1968, the figures for 1969, 1970 and 1971 are not exactly comparable with those for previous years.

Table VIII (see p. 70)

Offences decided by the courts to be criminal homicide

(Source: Criminal Statistics, England and Wales, 1978, Table 9.3)

	1968	1969	1970	1971	1972	1973	1974	1975	1976	1977	1978
Murder	73	69	91	86	88	81	153	95	102	108	96
S. 2 Manslaughter	57	65	66	78	95	82	106	83	101	93	85
Other manslaughter	113	117	111	134	135	142	168	180	166	138	144
Infanticide	26	17	15	17	18	9	16	6	6	6	8
Total	269	268	283	315	336	314	443	364	375	345	333*

* Court decisions were still pending in a further 70 cases when the 1978 figure was calculated.

Table IX (see p. 73)

Number of persons dealt with by hospital or guardianship orders under the Mental Health Act 1959 (including hospital and guardianship orders made by Magistrates' Courts without proceeding to a conviction)

(*Source: Criminal Statistics, England and Wales*)

	1968	1969	1970	1971	1972	1973	1974	1975	1976	1977	1978
Hospital Order	1,127	1097	1039	954	832	888	808	861	773	731	682
Hospital Order and Restriction Order	255	254	278	232	212	266	196	156	151	90	127
Guardianship Order	7	7	5	11	4	8	7	4	4	4	8
Total	1389	1358	1322	1197	1048	1162	1011	1021	928	825	817

Table X (see p. 152)

Sentences received by males aged 21 years or over convicted by Higher Courts of breaking and entering offences, 1965–67

(*Source: The Criminal Statistics, England and Wales, Table II*)

	Nominal[a] %	Probation %	Fine %	Imprisonment[b] %	Other %	Total
A. House- and Shop- breaking	3·2	20·3	6·7	68·8	1·0	11,433
B. Entering with intent	5·0	22·6	11·2	60·1	1·0	1,226
C. Attempts	5·5	21·1	15·1	57·3	1·0	584

The difference between distributions A & B, and A & C are too large to be ascribed to chance, but the difference between B & C is not.

Table XI (see p. 152)

Sentences received by males aged 21 years or over convicted by Magistrates' Courts of breaking and entering offences, 1965–67

(*Source: The Criminal Statistics, England and Wales, Table I*)

	Nominal[a] %	Probation %	Fine %	Imprisonment %	Section 29 %	Other %	Total
D Shop- breaking & c.	3·2	11·3	36·9	31·9	16·0	0·7	23,839
E. Entering with Intent	5·8	12·0	40·3	29·6	11·5	0·8	5,103
F. Attempts	6·9	11·8	44·1	27·7	8·9	0·6	2,019

The differences between distributions D & E, E & F and D & F are too large to be ascribed to chance.

a. Includes absolute discharge, conditional discharge and recognizances.
b. Includes imprisonment, corrective training and preventive detention.

Table XII (see p. 163)

Sentences for persons convicted of manslaughter under Homicide Act 1957, section 2

(*Source: Criminal Statistics, England and Wales*)

	1974	1975	1976	1977	1978
Hospital Order	5	7	10	7	7
Hospital Order with Restriction Order	26	20	20	18	20
Probation	10	8	10	8	8
Fixed term prison sentence	15	17	27	27	18
Life imprisonment	19	14	20	21	21
Other	4	0	5	1	5
Total	79	66	92	82	79

Table XIIIA (see p. 172)

Prison sentences for rape

(Source: The Criminal Statistics, England and Wales, Table III)

Year	Length of Imprisonment										Total
	6 mos. and under	Over 6 mos. and up to 1 year	Over 1 year and up to 2 years	Over 2 years and up to 3 years	Over 3 years and up to 4 years	Over 4 years and up to 5 years	Over 5 years and up to 7 years	Over 7 years and up to 10 years	Over 10 years determinate	Life	
1968	2	13	18	40	33	21	21	3	1*	2	154
1969	—	8	15	37	28	21	18*	5	1	3	136
1970	6	12	32	52	30	25*	21	4*	—	6	188
1971	2	10	22	57	36	18	23*	5	1	5	179
1972	2	7	24	55	36	34	19	7	1	3	188
1973	5	8	27	64	44	32	25	8	1	2	216
1968–73	17	58	138	305	207	151	127	32	5	21	1,061
As %	1·6	5·5	13·0	28·7	19·5	14·2	12·0	3·0	0·5	2·0	100·0

* Each of these figures includes one extended sentence

Table XIIIB (see p. 172)

Prison sentences for rape

(*Source: The Criminal Statistics, England and Wales, Table 6*)

Year	Length of Imprisonment										Total
	→6m	6m–1yr	1–2	2–3	3–4	4–5	5–7	7–10	10+	Life	
1974	2	7	28	75	49	28	17	8	2	8	225
1975	4	4	35	58	43	50	34	6	2	5	241
1976	4	8	27	73	41	38	34	8	—	5	238
1977	5	7	17	71	53	47	23	7	2	6	238
1978	8	5	27	71	45	39	26	8	4	6	239
1974–78	23	31	134	353	231	202	134	37	10	30	1,181
as %	1·9	2·6	11·3	29·9	19·6	17·1	11·3	3·1	0·8	2·5	(100·1%)

Table XIV (see p. 179)

Sentences received by males aged 21 years or over sentenced at the Crown Court for blackmail, burglary, theft and handling stolen property, 1976–78

(*Source: The Criminal Statistics, England and Wales, Table 5(e)*)

	Nominal[a]	Probation	Fine	Suspended sentence	Imprisonment[b]	Other[c]	Total
	%	%	%	%	%	%	
Blackmail	2·4	3·1	2·4	23·1	65·5	3·4	290
Burglary[d]	2·0	6·5	4·2	23·5	58·7	5·4	28,399
Theft	4·3	5·1	15·3	24·6	46·0	5·0	28,223
Handling	4·9	2·9	24·9	20·4	33·6	4·2	11,500

a. Includes absolute discharge, conditional discharge and recognizances.
b. Includes a very small number of extended sentences.
c. Includes community service orders.
d. Includes a small number of cases of aggravated burglary.

Table XV (see p. 179)

Sentences received by males aged 21 years or over convicted by Magistrates' Courts of burglary, theft and handling stolen property, 1976–78

(*Source: The Criminal Statistics, England and Wales, Table 1(e)*)

	Nominal[a]	Probation	Fine	Suspended sentence	Imprisonment	Section 29	Other[b]	Total
	%	%	%	%	%	%	%	
Burglary	6·3	8·1	35·4	18·0	18·1	9·0	5·3	35,706
Theft	9·4	4·7	64·9	8·4	7·4	2·7	2·5	218,677
Handling	6·9	2·4	72·6	8·9	4·7	2·6	1·9	25,890

a. Includes absolute discharge, conditional discharge and recognizances.
b. Includes community service orders.

Table XVI (see p. 179)

Male offenders sentenced by the Crown Court to immediate imprisonment after conviction for blackmail, burglary, theft and handling: length of sentence, 1976–78

(*Source: The Criminal Statistics, England and Wales, Table 6*)

	Length of imprisonment									Total
	6 mos. and under	Over 6 mos. and up to 1 year	Over 1 year and up to 2 years	Over 2 years and up to 3 years	Over 3 years and up to 4 years	Over 4 years and up to 5 years	Over 5 years and up to 7 years	Over 7 years and up to 10 years	10 years	
	%	%	%	%	%	%	%	%	%	
Blackmail	4·8	12·6	33·3	24·2	10·6	5·3	3·9	3·9	1·4	207
Burglary[a]	18·9	30·1	36·9	9·9	2·4	1·2	0·4	0·1	0·1	20,280
Theft	39·2	31·7	22·3	4·8	0·9	0·4	0·1	n	n	15,141
Handling	31·1	34·7	24·9	6·3	1·7	1·0	0·2	0·1	n	4,094

a. Includes a small number of convictions for aggravated burglary.
n. Negligible

APPENDIX II

FURTHER READING

A. BOOKS

The principles of sentencing laid down by the Court of Appeal are discussed in the excellent work by D. A. THOMAS, *Principles of Sentencing* (2nd Edn., London 1979); the application of those principles to Magistrates' Courts is discussed by BRIAN HARRIS, *Criminal Jurisdiction of Magistrates* (7th Edn., Chichester 1979). A stimulating book on sentencing policy in general is by NIGEL WALKER, *Sentencing in a Rational Society* (London 1969); and see now NIGEL WALKER, Punishment, Danger and Stigma (1980).

Although somewhat overtaken by events, useful material on sentencing can still be found in:

PAGE, SIR LEO, *The Sentence of the Court*, London 1948.
DEVLIN, K., *Sentencing Offenders in Magistrates' Courts*, London 1971.
HALL WILLIAMS, J. E., *The English Penal System in Transition*, London 1970.
JACKSON, R. M., *Enforcing the Law*, London 1967.
McCLEAN, J. D. and WOOD, J. C., *Criminal Justice and the Treatment of Offenders*, London 1969.
WALKER, N., *Crime and Punishment in Britain* (2nd revised edition reprint) Edinburgh 1970.

Two important special studies are:

HOOD, R., *Sentencing in Magistrates' Courts*, London 1962.
HOOD, R., *Sentencing the Motoring Offender*, London 1972.

Books on theories of punishment are:

Action, H. B. (editor), *The Philosophy of Punishment*, London 1969.

ANDENAES, J., *Punishment and Deterrence*, Ann Arbor 1974.
HONDERICH, T., *Punishment*, London 1969.
HART, H. L. A., *Punishment and Responsibility*, Oxford 1968 (contains some important chapters on punishment).
ROSS, A., *On Guilt and Punishment*, London 1975.

B. ESSAYS AND ARTICLES

BLOM-COOPER, L. (editor), *Progress in Penal Reform*, London 1974: particularly the essays by Louis Blom-Cooper and Sir Arthur James.
BOTTOMS, A. E., and PRESTON, R. H., *The Coming Crisis in Penology*, Edinburgh 1980: particularly the essays by A. E. Bottoms, A. K. Bottomley and R. Plant.
CROSS, SIR RUPERT, *Reflections on the English Sentencing System* (the Child of Co. Lecture 1980).
GIAZEBROOK, P. R. (editor), *Reshaping the Criminal Law*, London 1978: particularly the essays by Sir Rupert Cross, D. A. Thomas, Nigel Walker, Colin Howard, Sir Brian MacKenna, and Michael Tonry and Norval Morris.
HOOD, R. (editor), *Crime, Criminology and Public Policy*, London 1974: particularly the essays by D. A. Thomas and Sir Arthur James.
THOMAS, D. A. (editor), *The Future of Sentencing*, Cambridge 1981: various essays.

Reference is made to a number of other useful articles at appropriate points in the book.

C. OFFICIAL PUBLICATIONS

Home Office, *The Sentence of the Court*, 3rd Edn. 1978.
Home Office, *A Review of Criminal Justice Policy 1976*.
Fifteenth Report from the House of Commons Expenditure Committee, Session 1977–78, The Reduction of Pressure on the Prison System, Vol. 1.
White Paper, The Reduction of Pressure on the Prison System, Cmnd. 7948, 1980.
Report of the Working Party, Judicial Studies and Information, Home Office 1978.
Reports of the Advisory Council on the Penal System:
Non-Custodial and Semi-Custodial Penalties, 1970
Reparation by the Offender, 1970
Young Adult Offenders, 1974
The Length of Prison Sentences, 1977
Sentences of Imprisonment: A Review of Maximum Penalties, 1978.

INDEX